P9-EDZ-189

JEAN MOSS

# SCULPTURED KNITS

XRX BOOKS

48 TIMELY

DESIGNS

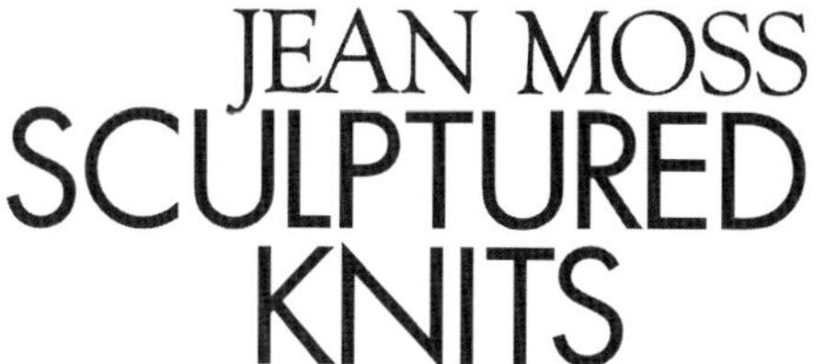


INSPIRED

BY THE

DECORATIVE

ARTS

OF THE

20th CENTURY

ALVIS UPITIS

PUBLISHER
Alexis Yiorgos Xenakis

EDITOR
Elaine Rowley

KNITTING EDITOR
Ann Regis

INSTRUCTION EDITING
Ann Denton
Gitta Schrade

PHOTOGRAPHIC AND FASHION STYLING
Jean Moss

PHOTOGRAPHER
Alexis Yiorgos Xenakis

PUBLISHING DIRECTOR
David Xenakis

GRAPHIC DESIGNER
Bob Natz

BOOK PRODUCTION MANAGER
Lynda Selle

DIGITAL COLOR SPECIALIST
Daren Morgan

PRODUCTION ARTISTS
Kellie Meissner
Jay Reeve
Carol Skallerud

MARKETING DIRECTOR
Tad Anderson

FIRST PUBLISHED IN USA IN 1999 BY XRX, INC.
PO BOX 1525, SIOUX FALLS, SD 57101-1525



ISBN 0-9646391-9-X

Produced in Sioux Falls, South Dakota, by XRX, Inc., 605.338.2450

Printed in Hong Kong

For my mother, Lily, a lifelong knitter,
and for my Grandmother, Annie, who taught me how to knit

This book has been on my mind for more than ten years The designs are all sweaters that I love to wear myself, and even more important, it is the kind of knitting that I enjoy. Not only is textural knitting tremendously exciting and absorbing to do, but often the finished piece, seamlessly fitting into the wardrobe, is infinitely more wearable and versatile than a multi-colored one. Since I have been asked for stylish patterns in one color many times by people who are primarily knitting for relaxation, I decided that the time was right for *Sculptured Knits*.

Fashion is ephemeral, but it has enormous influence on contemporary design. Intarsia knitting with many colors has been dominant in the last decade: bold, colorful patterns which emphasize the knitter's expert craft and make a strong statement for the wearer have been very popular. After all, a sweater takes a large amount of time to knit, so it needs to be noticed. Deceptively simple designs relying on shape, sculptured stitches, or a striking single color for their impact have always been around, but these were often knitted in between or alongside the multi-colored show stoppers. I tend to treat my own intarsia sweaters like treasured old textiles or paintings—I love to have them around my home but have always felt more comfortable wearing single-colored sweaters.

In my own knitting I relish single-color patterns that have texture, color, and knitting interest, but do not entail stranding, weaving, or being driven crazy by many small balls of yarn on the same row. I like to think of my knitting as a close and intimate friend, so naturally I don't like the two of us to quarrel. Although I enjoy fairisle for small projects like socks, gloves, or hats, when knitting a sweater I love to focus on texture and not have to worry about changing colors. With beautiful sculptured stitches and a flattering shape, a sweater in a single, well-chosen shade can be absolutely stunning. I suspect there must be thousands of other knitters who feel the same, and if you are one of them, then this book is for you.

I am a fiber fanatic. I love natural fibers of all types: wool, cotton, cashmere, alpaca, mohair, silk, linen, viscose. The possibilities are endless and I have had such fun choosing the perfect fiber for each design. Some yarns, like cashmere, are beautiful enough in themselves and need only a stylish shape to create a wonderful sweater design. Others with crisp definition, such as cotton and linen, cry out for a sculptured stitch. Painterly random-dyed textured yarns, such as bouclé or slub, at once introduce both exquisite color and texture into a design.

Decorative art is a wonderful source for the knitwear designer: architecture, theater, furniture, ceramics, textiles, jewelry, fashion, and posters all carry the distinctive signatures of their time and creator. While some pieces are firmly rooted in specific examples of decorative art, others in this collection are influenced broadly by the distinctive aesthetic of the period, which also shows up in the way that the piece is styled. Many of the projects are named after particular style icons from the time of their inspiration. There are sweaters for women, men, and children as well as a couple of projects for your home in each section. You will find stylish easy-to-knit pieces as well as the more complex sculptured cables and lacy arans.

There are four sections in the book: Belle Époque, Art Deco, Pop Art, and Into the Millennium. I have found my work has been constantly inspired by the decorative arts movements of this century. I love the extravagant flamboyance of the turn-of-the-century Art Nouveau—the fabulous patterns which developed the ideas of harmony and good design in much the same way as did William Morris' earlier Arts and Crafts movement. I have always been enthralled by the elegant sophistication of Art Deco, influenced by, among other things, the bright colors and bold shapes of Cubism and Fauvism. I still remember, as a teenager, wearing Mary Quant miniskirts and Courrèges boots: Pop Art embodies the spirit of the Swinging Sixties. The fourth section is necessarily more eclectic than the others, as we cannot distance ourselves sufficiently to identify a single coherent style for the period. In true postmodern fashion, I have drawn on a variety of sources, to create contemporary interpretations of traditional designs which will, I hope, have an appeal lasting well into the new millennium.

Knitwear has never been more important in the world of fashion. Luxurious, beautifully crafted, sophisticated pieces which complement, but do not overwhelm, the wearer's personality represent the modern face of handknits. In the twenty-first century I feel that knitted garments should be making the statement, 'I look good, I'm exquisitely made, and I make my wearer feel beautiful as well as comfortable.' *Sculptured Knits* is my celebration of the knitted stitch for the millennium. I hope that you'll get as much enjoyment out of knitting my dreams as I have had from designing them for you.

Here's to a peaceful and happy new knitting millennium.

Jean Moss

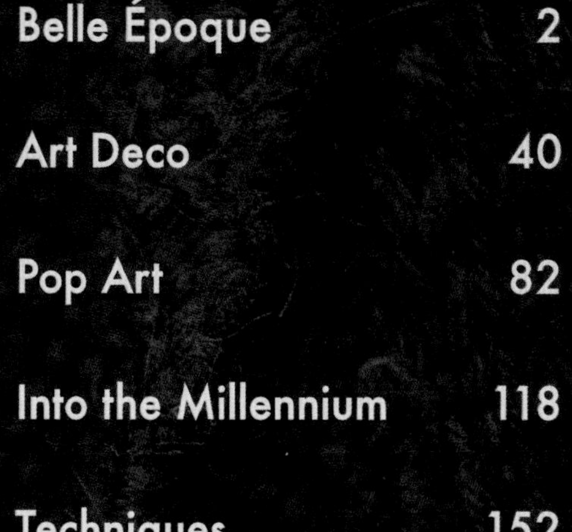

# BELLE ÉPOQUE

Have nothing in your houses that you do not know to be useful, or believe to be beautiful.

William Morris 1882

How wonderfully exciting it must have been after years of Victorian revivalism to witness what was no less than an artistic revolution. This section celebrates that glorious era of gaiety and artistic innovation at the turn of the last century, the Belle Époque. Art Nouveau, which had its roots in William Morris' Arts and Crafts movement in England, captured perfectly the spirit of the period in sinuous lines and undulating arabesques. Looking to the organic energy and life force of plants for its inspiration, Art Nouveau marked the creation of a completely new aesthetic, without reference to contemporary or past styles.

The new art was expressed in all aspects and objects of everyday life, from cutlery to wallpaper and furniture to textiles, giving beauty and unity to the whole environment. As a lifestyle, this is a concept that appeals to me tremendously. I feel certain that the objects around us affect our perception of the world. By surrounding ourselves with beautiful, well-crafted artifacts, we create positive energy in our lives which must in turn generate a sense of well-being. With this in mind, I have tried to capture the mood of the period in Europe and the United States by invoking the vision of my own favorite Art Nouveau artists and designers to inspire this collection.

In England the baroque fantasies of Aubrey Beardsley, particularly his illustrations for the periodical *The Yellow Book* and for Oscar Wilde's *Salome,* carried Art Nouveau to its height. In contrast to Beardsley's dark decadence, though, the fresh innocence of Kate Greenaway's watercolors are a lasting joy among children's book illustrations.

*Fin de siècle* Paris was *the* city for theater and dance. Toulouse Lautrec portrayed the colorful cabaret nightlife of the Folies Bergère and Moulin Rouge and the opulent sets and costumes of Diaghilev's Ballets Russes were a feast to behold. The outrageous American dancer and choreographer, Isadora Duncan, toured Europe and often performed in Paris, scandalizing audiences with her free-form dance and loose, flowing, and revealing robes. At the same time, in Venice Mariano Fortuny was much sought after for his lavishly theatrical textile designs, and Isadora was one of his many famous clients.

Art Nouveau made a great impact on architecture. In Spain the highly idiosyncratic Antoni Gaudi's bold fantastic designs and creations, still to be seen in parks and apartment buildings in Barcelona, give the impression of natural organisms that have sprung from the earth. In sharp contrast, in Scotland the chaste and functional style of Charles Rennie Mackintosh, while unmistakably Art Nouveau, rejected overly decorated Victorian styles in favor of a spare simplicity that featured geometric shapes and unadorned surfaces. This appealed particularly to the avant-garde designers of the Vienna Secession, whose members' style was defined by the geometries of the circle, square, and rectangle. Its famous founder, Gustav Klimt, painted glittering and gorgeous mosaic patterns within patterns, full of erotic symbolism, in his architectural murals.

Since the interplay of light and color has always intrigued me, I love the fantasies of iridescence created by master glassmakers of the period. A lazy tourist, I tend to wander casually around a city, drinking endless cups of coffee and soaking up the street life rather than organizing my time in museums and galleries. Some years ago in Paris I was delighted to come across the past home of René Lalique, whose innovative glass and jewelry designs are so typically Art Nouveau. For me, Lalique's creations, together with the fantastic, shimmering favrile-glass vases and stained-glass lampshades of the American designer, Louis Comfort Tiffany, epitomize the era.

I hope that these designs will take you on an armchair journey through one of my favorite decorative arts periods of the twentieth century, offering a glimpse into the sumptuous opulence and elegant styling which are the hallmarks of the magnificent Belle Époque.

Taking the Moulin Rouge, theater, circus, and brothels for his inspiration, Toulouse-Lautrec depicted exotic Parisian nightlife in portraits and sketches of striking originality and power. In this piece, with its frills and semi-bustle, I wanted to create a sweater which would fit seamlessly into one of his stylish posters, so I've used lustrous alpaca yarn and seductive lacy patterning to create a sensuous garment of the night.

# LAUTREC BOLERO

**Sizes**
S (M, L).
Shown in sizes small (Black #1113) and large (Mochica Teal #1106).
Directions are for smallest size with larger sizes in parentheses.
If there is only 1 set of numbers, it applies to all sizes.

**Finished measurements**
Bust (buttoned) 38 (40, 42)"
Length 18¼ (18½, 18¾)"

**Yarn**
11 (11, 12) skeins Classic Elite Inca Alpaca (each 1¾oz/50g, 115yds/105m, 100% alpaca)

**Needles**
One pair each sizes 3 and 6 (3.25 and 4mm) needles, *or size to obtain gauge.*

**Extras**
Stitch markers and holders.
One ⅞"/22mm button or clasp.

**Gauge**
22 sts and 30 rows to 4"/10cm in St st using size 6 (4mm) needles.

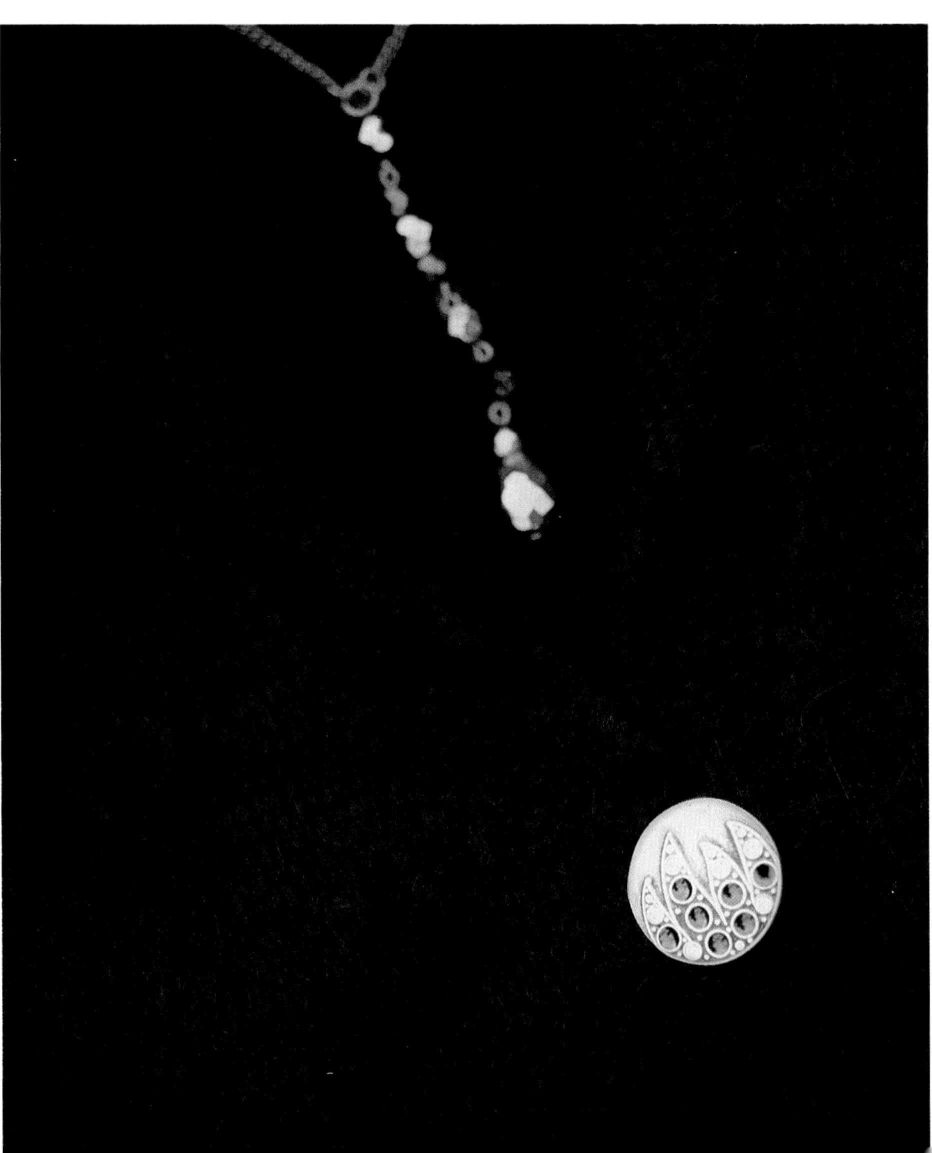

**STITCHES**

*Make Knot (MK)* [K1, p1, k1, p1, k1, p1, k1] in st to make 7 sts from 1, then pass 2nd, 3rd, 4th, 5th, 6th and 7th sts, one at a time, over the first st, then sl first st onto left-hand needle and k into back of it.

**Montmartre pat** (same as used in chart; multiple of 10 sts plus 7)
*Row 1* (RS) Knit.
*Row 2 and all WS rows* Purl.
*Row 3* Knit.
*Row 5* K1, *k2, yo, ssk, k6, rep from* to last 6 sts, k2, yo, ssk, k2.
*Row 7* K1, *k2tog, yo, k1, yo, ssk, k5, rep from* to last 6 sts, k2tog, yo, k1, yo, ssk, k1.
*Row 9* K1, *k2, MK, k7, rep from* to last 6 sts, k2, MK, k3.
*Rows 11 and 13* Knit.
*Row 15* K1, *k7, yo, ssk, k1, rep from* to last 6 sts, k6.
*Row 17* K1, *k5, k2tog, yo, k1, yo, ssk, rep from* to last 6 sts, k6.
*Row 19* K1, *k7, MK, k2, rep from* to last 6 sts, k6.
*Row 20* Purl.
Rep rows 1–20 for Montmartre st.

**BACK AND FRONT** (worked in one piece to armhole)
With larger needles, cast on 16 sts. Working in St st, work 35 rows of Montmartre Chart, casting on every other row as indicated—212 (224, 236) sts. Cont pat as established, maintaining Montmartre pat and taking the pat out to the edges (3 more rosebud motifs) on the next rep. When piece measures 1¾" along vertical edge of center front (A to B on schematic), end with a WS row.

**Shape neckline**
Dec 1 st each side of next row, then every 5th row 2 (6, 10) times more, every 6th row 11 (8, 5) times, AT SAME TIME, when piece measures 9¾ (10, 9¾)" from first cast-on edge, end with a WS row—202 (212, 224) sts on needle.

**Divide for armholes**
*Next row* (RS) Cont pat, work 48 (50, 53) sts (right front), place the foll 106 (112, 118) sts on hold (back), then place rem 48 (50, 53) sts on hold (left front).

**RIGHT FRONT**
Turn work. N*ext row* (WS) Bind off 4 (4, 5) sts (armhole), work to end. Dec 1 st at armhole edge on next 11 (12, 13) rows. Work even until piece measures 13¼ (13½, 13¾)" from A on schematic, end with a WS row.

**Shape shoulders**
At shoulder edge, bind off 8 sts twice. Bind off rem sts.

**BACK**
With RS facing, join yarn and work center 106 (112, 118) sts as foll: Bind off 4 (4, 5) sts at beg of next 2 rows. Dec 1 st each side of next 11 (12, 13) rows—76 (80, 82) sts. Cont in pat as established until piece measures 17¾ (18, 18¼)" from initial cast-on, end with a WS row.

**Shape neck and shoulders**
*Row 1* (RS) Bind off 8 sts, work 17 (18, 18) sts, k2tog (neck), turn. Place rem 49 (52, 54) sts on hold. Work each side of neck separately. *Row 2* Dec 1 st at beg of next row, work to end. *Row 3* Bind off 8 sts at beg of next row, work to last 2 sts, k2tog. *Row 4* Work 1 row. Bind off rem sts. With RS facing, join yarn to rem sts and bind off center 22 (24, 26) sts. Working on rem 27 (28, 28) sts, k2tog (neck), work to end. Complete to correspond to first side, reversing all shaping.

***Montmartre Chart***

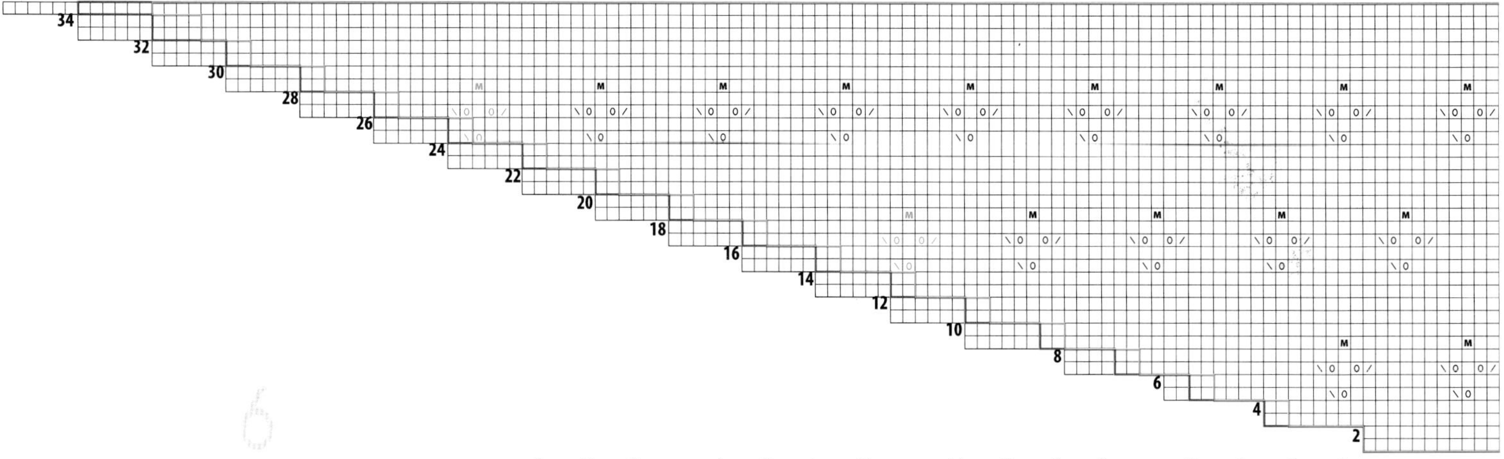

## LEFT FRONT

With RS facing, join yarn to rem 48 (50, 53) sts, bind off 4 (4, 5) sts, work to end. Work to correspond to right front, reversing all shaping.

## SLEEVES

With smaller needles, cast on 47 sts. K every row for ¾". Change to larger needles. Cont in Montmartre pat, AT SAME TIME, inc 1 st each side (working incs into pat) every 7th row 0 (8, 16) times, then every 8th row 14 (7, 0) times—75 (77, 79) sts and 6 (7, 7) rosebud motifs across row. Work even until piece measures 17" from beg, end with a WS row.

### Shape cap

Bind off 4 (4, 5) sts at beg of next 2 rows. Dec 1 st each side of next 14 (18, 16) rows, then every other row 9 (7, 8) times. Work even until piece measures 21¾" from beg, end with a WS row. Bind off 2 sts at beg of next 2 rows, 3 sts at beg of next 2 rows. Bind off rem 11 (9, 11) sts.

## BAND AND COLLAR

### Right front band and collar

(NOTE Sew band to jacket as you work, stretching slightly to fit.)

With smaller needles, cast on 5 sts and work in garter st (k every row) as foll: Work ¾". Work vertical buttonhole: ***Next row*** K3, turn and k 3 rows more on these 3 sts, then place on hold. Join yarn to rem 2 sts and k 4 rows. ***Next row*** K across 5 sts. Cont in garter st across all sts until piece measures 1¾" from beg of vertical edge of right front, end at outside edge of band. ***Beg collar:*** Inc 1 st at end of next row, then every 10th row 6 (6, 7) times—12 (12, 13) sts. Work even until band measures 11¼ (11½, 11¾)" from beg, end at outside edge of band. Place sts on hold.

### Left front band and collar

Work as for right front band, omitting buttonhole and reversing all shaping.

### Neckband

Sew shoulder seams. With RS facing and smaller needles, pick up and k 12 (12, 13) sts on hold at top right front band, 14 sts to shoulder, 24 (26, 28) sts across back, 14 sts along left neck and 12 (12, 13) sts on hold at top left front band—76 (78, 82) sts. Cont in garter st for ¾", then bind off loosely.

## FRILL

With larger needles, cast on 16 sts.

***Rows 1, 3, and 5*** (RS) Knit.

***Rows 2, 4, and 6*** P12, k4.

Shape as foll:

*****Rows 7 and 8*** K2, turn and k2.

***Rows 9 and 10*** K3, turn and k3.

***Rows 11 and 12*** K4, turn and k4.

***Rows 13 and 14*** K5, turn, p1, k4.

***Rows 15 and 16*** K6, turn, p2, k4.

***Rows 17–30*** In same way, cont to work 1 more st every other row, keeping 4 edge sts in garter st.

***Rows 31 and 32*** K14, turn, p10, k4.

***Rows 33 and 34*** K13, turn, p9, k4.

***Rows 35 and 36*** K12, turn, p8, k4.

In same way, cont to work 1 st less every other row until you have worked k2, turn, k2.

***Next row*** Knit. ***Next row*** P12, k4. Rep last 2 rows 3 more times.***

Rep from** to *** 15 (16, 18) times in all. Bind off.

## FINISHING

Set in sleeves, easing in fullness across top of sleeve cap. Sew sleeve seams.

Beg at center front, sew bound-off edge of frill to lower edge of right front band, then cont around hem until cast-on edge of frill is sewn to lower edge of left front band.

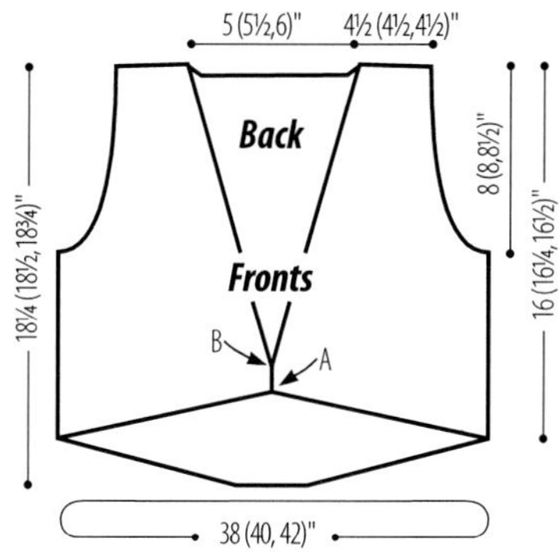

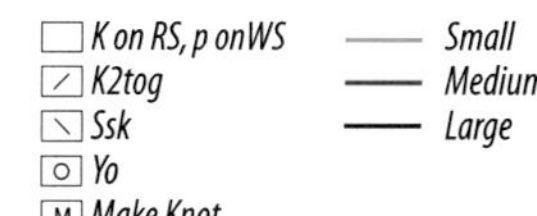


**Note:** For small size, blue symbols are not worked, knit these stitches.

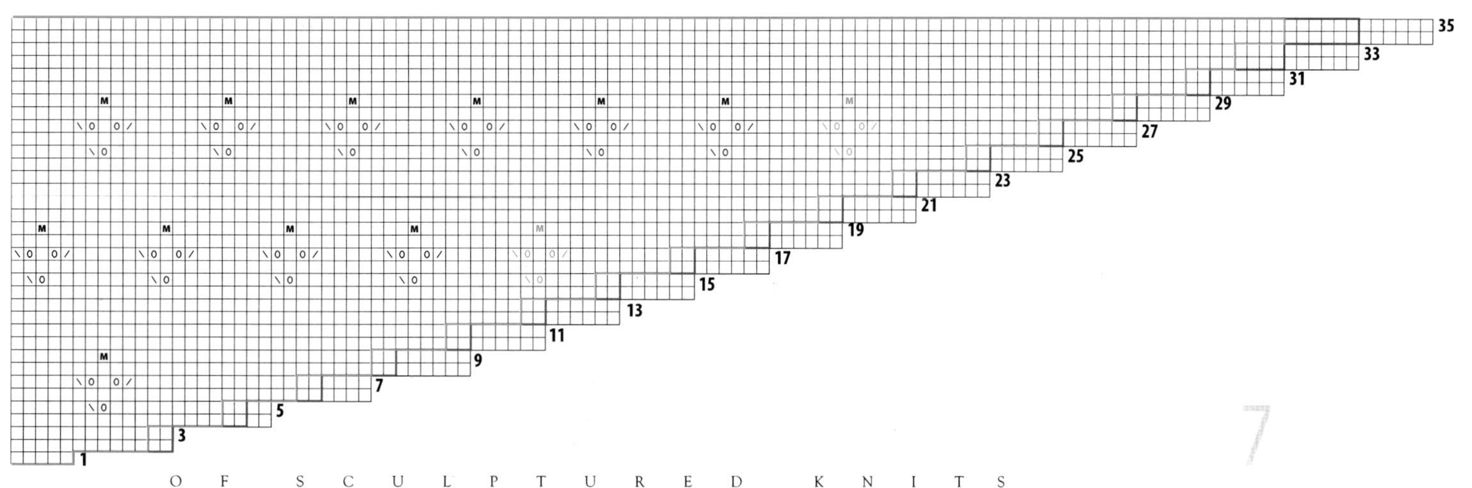

Famous for both his exquisite glass and fabulous jewelry designs, René Lalique worked in Paris and contributed his own unique aesthetic to the Art Nouveau movement. In the luminous gold and blue colors and feminine lacy peplums of this design, I want to capture the stylish combination of baroque fantasy and flawless craftsmanship which epitomized his work.

**Sizes**
S (M, L).
Shown in sizes small (Truffle #2686) and medium (De Nimes Blue #2657).
Directions are for smallest size with larger sizes in parentheses.
If there is only 1 set of numbers, it applies to all sizes.

**Finished measurements**
Bust (buttoned) 38 (42, 46)"
Length 22 (22, 22½)"

**Yarn**
8 (8, 9) skeins Classic Elite Provence (each 3½oz/100g, 256yds/233m, 100% cotton)

**Needles**
One pair each sizes 3 and 5 (3.25 and 3.75mm) needles, *or size to obtain gauge.*
One each sizes 3 and 5 (3.25 and 3.75mm) circular needles, each 29"/72cm long.

**Extras**
Stitch markers and holders. Cable needle. Six ⅜"/10mm pearl buttons.

**Gauge**
28 sts and 32 rows to 4"/10cm in Vitesse pat using size 5 (3.75mm) needles.

# LALIQUE JACKET

**BACK AND FRONTS** (worked in one piece to armholes)

With larger circular needle, cast on 330 (336, 342) sts. Work back and forth in rows as foll: K 2 rows. ***Beg pats: Row 1*** (RS) ***For size M only,*** p3; ***for size L only,*** work 6 sts of Chart A; ***for all sizes,*** work the last 10 sts of Vitesse Chart, then work 40-st rep 8 times; ***for size M only***, end p3; ***for size L only,*** work 6 sts of Chart A. ***Row 2 For size M only,*** p3; ***for size L only,*** work 6 sts of Chart A; ***for all sizes,*** work 40 st-rep of Vitesse Chart 8 times, then work the last 10 sts; ***for size M only,*** p3; ***for size L only***, work 6 sts of Chart A. Cont in chart pats as established, working through row 62 of Vitesse Chart—234 (240, 246) sts. Piece measures approx 7" from beg and is at waistline. There are 9 reps of the 3-twist cable (which correspond to Vendôme Chart) and 8 reps of the 4-twist eyelet cables (Coty Chart) with rev St st in between. With RS facing, mark the 3rd 3-twist cable from right front edge and the 3rd 3-twist cable from the left front edge.

Cont pats as established, AT SAME TIME, inc 1 st each side of 3rd and 7th marked cables (working incs into rev St st) every other row 0 (6, 18) times, every 4th row 0 (8, 2) times, then every 6th row 8 (0, 0) times—266 (296, 326) sts. Work even until piece measures 13½" from beg, end with a WS row.

**Divide for armholes**

*Next row* (RS) Work 63 (71, 80) sts (right front) and place them on hold, bind off 12 (14, 14) sts (underarm), work until there are 116 (126, 138) sts on right-hand needle (back) and place them on hold, bind off 12 (14, 14) sts (underarm), work to end—63 (71, 80) sts (left front). Turn.

**LEFT FRONT**

Cont pats, dec 1 st at armhole edge on next 9 (12, 16) rows, AT SAME TIME, when piece measures 14" from beg, end with a WS row.

**Shape neck**

*Next row* (RS) Work to last 11 (8, 7) sts, work next 2 sts tog, work to end. In same way, dec 1 st at neck edge every row 0 (0, 3) times, every other row 14 (26, 28) times, every 3rd row 9 (1, 0) times—30 (31, 32) sts. Work even until piece measures 22 (22, 22½)" from beg. Bind off all sts. (NOTE Try to make the row before the cast-off row a cabled one so that the shoulders do not stretch.)

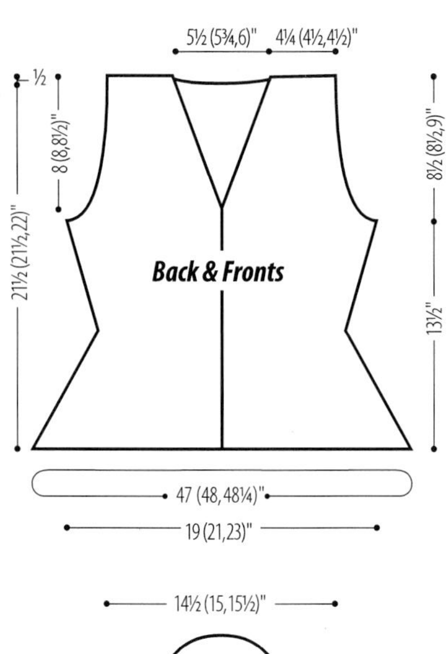


**BACK**

With WS facing, join yarn and work across 116 (126, 138) sts. Dec 1 st each side of next 9 (12, 16) rows —98 (102, 106) sts. Work even until piece measures 21½ (21½, 22)" from beg, end with a WS row.

**Shape neck**

Work 33 (34, 35) sts, turn. Dec 1 st at neck edge every row 3 times. Bind off rem 30 (31, 32) sts. With RS facing, join yarn and bind off next 32 (34, 36) sts, work to end. Work to correspond to first side, reversing shaping.

**RIGHT FRONT**

With WS facing, join yarn and cont pat across 63 (71, 80) sts. Complete as for left front, reversing shaping. At neck edge, work decs after first 9 (6, 5) sts.

**SLEEVES**

With larger needles, cast on 66 (68, 70) sts. K 2 rows. ***Beg pats: Row 1*** (RS) P1 (2, 3), *work 8 sts of Vendôme Chart, p8, 4 sts of Coty Chart, p8; rep from* once, work 8 sts of Vendôme Chart, end p1 (2, 3). Cont chart pats as established, working all other sts in rev St st, AT SAME TIME, inc 1 st each side (working incs into rev St st) every 7th row 0 (4, 0) times, every 8th row 11 (12, 16) times, then every 9th row 4 (0, 0) times—96 (100, 102) sts. Work even until piece measures 16½ (16½, 17)" from beg.

**Shape cap**

Bind off 5 (6, 6) sts at beg of next 2 rows. Dec 1 st each side of next 20 (22, 24) rows. Dec 1 st each side every other row 7 (6, 5) times—32 sts. Bind off 4 sts at beg of next 2 rows, 6 sts at beg of next 2 rows. Bind off rem sts.

**FINISHING**

Block pieces. Sew shoulder seams.

**Front bands** (worked in one piece)

Using photos as guide, place 6 buttonhole markers on right front, the first 7½" from beg, the last at beg of neck shaping, and 4 others spaced evenly between. With RS facing and smaller circu lar needle, beg at lower right front edge and pick up and k a total of 84 sts (including the 2 sts cast on for each buttonhole) evenly to beg of neck shaping, casting on 2 sts at each marker for buttonhole and leaving a corresponding space. Cont to pick up 52 (53, 54) sts to shoulder, 36

(37, 38) sts across back neck, 52 (53, 54) sts down left neck to beg of neck shaping and 84 sts to lower edge of left front—308 (311, 314) sts. K 1 row. ***Work picot bind-off:*** Bind off 2 sts, *sl rem st on right-hand needle onto left-hand needle, cast on 2 sts, bind off 4 sts; rep from* to end. Fasten off.

**Cuff edging**

With RS facing and smaller needles, pick up and k 59 (62, 62) sts across lower edge of sleeve. K 1 row, then work picot bind-off as for neck.

Set in sleeves, easing in any fullness evenly across top of cap. Sew side and sleeve seams.

Sew buttons opposite buttonholes, taking care that the pattern lines up symmetrically across the sweater.

**STITCHES**

***2/1 Right Cross (2/1 RC)*** Sl 1 st to cable needle (cn), hold to back, k2; then k1 from cn.

***2/1 Left Cross (2/1 LC)*** Sl 2 sts to cn, hold to front, k1; then k2 from cn.

***2/2 Right Cross (2/2 RC)*** Sl 2 sts to cn, hold to back, k2; then k2 from cn.

***2/2 Left Cross (2/2 LC)*** Sl 2 sts to cn, hold to front, k2; then k2 from cn.

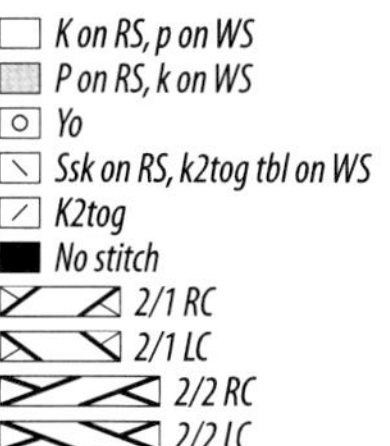


**Vitesse Chart**

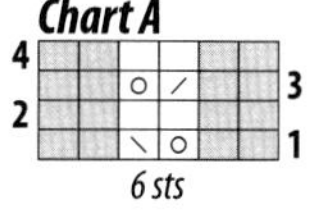


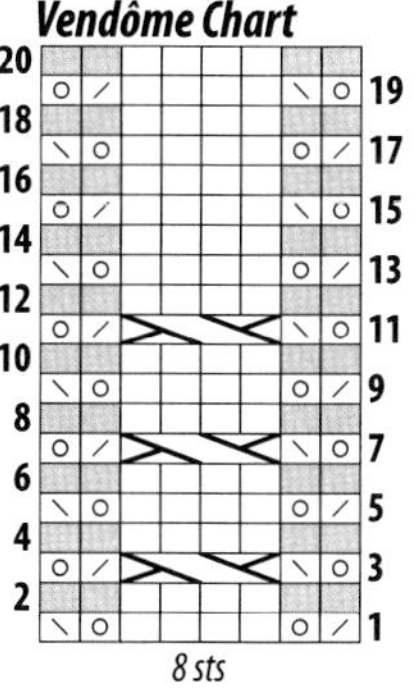


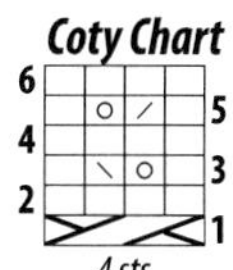

This piece was inspired by the fabulous designs of artist and couturier Mariano Fortuny, who combined color and texture with ingenious cut, taking his inspiration from the velvets and brocades of the Italian fifteenth and sixteenth centuries. Isadora Duncan was among the many famous clients attracted to his Venice studio. His garments emphasized the beauty of the female form in movement, just as I hope this swing tunic in deliciously drapey mercerized cotton will do.

**Sizes**
S (M, L).
Shown in sizes small (French Red #2627) and medium (Cinnamon Spice #2044).
Directions are for smallest size with larger sizes in parentheses.
If there is only 1 set of numbers, it applies to all sizes.

**Finished measurements**
Bust 36 (40, 44)"
Length 30 (31, 32)"

**Yarn**
9 (11, 12) skeins
Classic Elite Provence
(each 3½oz/100g, 256yds/233m, 100% mercerized cotton)

**Needles**
One pair each sizes 3 and 5 (3.25 and 3.75mm) needles, *or size to obtain gauge.*
One each circular needles size 3 (3.25mm), 24"/60cm long and 5 (3.75mm), 36"/90cm long.

**Extras**
Stitch markers and holders.

**Gauge**
24 sts and 32 rows to 4"/10 cm in Delphos pat using size 5 (3.75mm) needles.

# FORTUNY DRESS

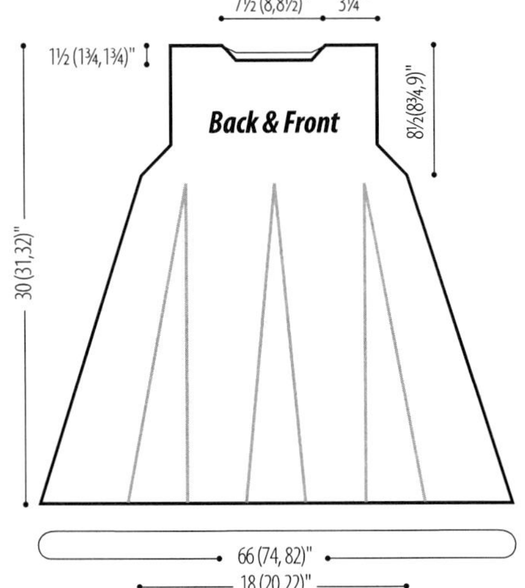


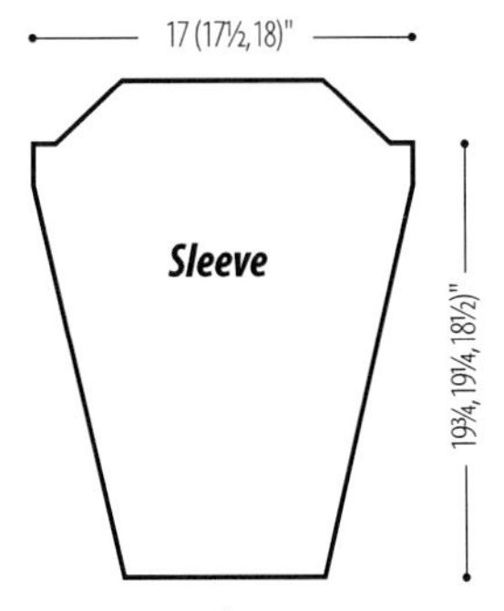


**BACK AND FRONT** (knitted in one piece in the round up to armholes)
With larger circular needle, cast on 396 (444, 492) sts. Being careful not to twist sts, place marker, join and *k31 (35, 39), place marker, k 35 (39, 43) sts; rep from* 6 times.
Work rnds 1–48 of Delphos Chart as foll: Work 66 (74, 82) sts of chart 6 times around, AT SAME TIME, dec as indicated on chart: every 9th rnd 0 (0, 14) times, every 10th rnd 1 (17, 5) times, then every 11th rnd 14 (0, 0) times.
When 48 rnds have been worked, rep chart rnds 37–48, and cont to dec as before (keeping the 6 sets of decs at outer edges of the flower pat godets). When 5 sts rem in each flower pat godet, end at joining marker and cont as foll:
***Rnd 1*** *Work 31 (35, 39) sts of Delphos Chart, work next 5 sts as foll: ssk, yo, k1, yo, k2tog; rep from* 5 times more—216 (240, 264) sts. ***Rnd 2*** *Work 31, (35, 39) sts of Delphos Chart, k5; rep from* 5 times more. Rep Rnds 1–2 until piece measures 21½ (22¼, 23)" from beg.
***Divide for armholes: Next rnd*** Place first 15 (17, 19) sts on hold, rejoin yarn and cont pat over 108 (120, 132) sts. Join another ball of yarn and work across rem 93 (103, 113) sts, then cont pat over first 15 (17, 19) sts on hold.
Work back and forth in rows on back and front separately.

**Back**
(NOTE Work the first 15 (17, 19) sts and the last 16 (18, 20) sts in rev St st.)
Bind off 6 sts at beg of next 2 rows. ***Next row*** (RS) K1, ssk, work in pat to last 3 sts, k2tog, k1.
***Next row*** P2, work in pat to last 2 sts, p2. Rep last 2 rows 5 (9, 14) times more—84 (88, 90) sts.
Work even until piece measures 29½ (30½, 31½)" from beg, end with a WS row.

**Shape neck**
***Next row*** (RS) Work 22 (23, 22) sts, turn and place rem sts on hold. Work each side of neck separately. Dec 1 st at neck edge on next row, then every row twice more. Bind off rem sts.
With RS facing, join yarn to rem sts and bind off center 40 (42, 46) sts, cont pat to end.
Shape other side of neck to correspond to first side, reversing shaping.

**Front**
Work as for back until piece measures 28½ (29¼, 30¼)" from beg, end with a WS row.

**Shape neck**
***Next row*** (RS) Work 25 (27, 27) sts, turn and place rem sts on hold. Work each side of neck separately. Dec 1 st at neck edge on next, then every row 5 (6, 7) times more. Work even until piece measures 30 (31, 32)" from beg. Bind off rem sts.
With RS facing, join yarn to rem sts and bind off center 34 (34, 36) sts, work to end.
Work to correspond to first side, reversing shaping.

**SLEEVES**
With larger needles, cast on 55 sts. K 1 row. Work rows 1–38 of Palazzo Chart, then rep rows 37–40 to top of sleeve, AT SAME TIME, inc 1 st each side (working incs into chart pat) every 5th row 0 (6, 26) times, every 6th row 20 (19, 1) times, every 7th row 4 (0, 0) times—103 (105, 109) sts. Work even until piece measures 19¾ (19¼, 18½)" from beg, end with a WS row.

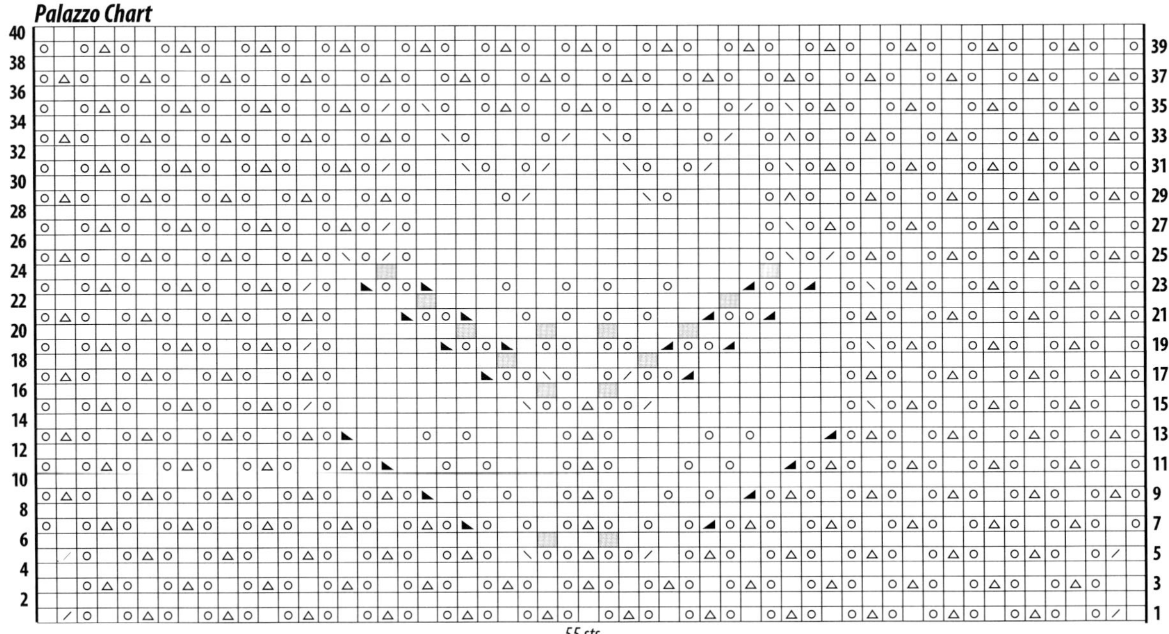

**Shape cap**
Bind off 6 sts at beg of next 2 rows. ***Next row*** (RS) K1, ssk, work to last 3 sts, k2tog, k1. ***Next row*** P2, work to last 2 sts, p2. Rep last 2 rows 5 (9, 14) times more. Bind off 79 (73, 67) sts.

**FINISHING**
Block pieces lightly. Sew shoulder seams.

**Neck edging**
With RS facing and smaller circular needle, beg at left shoulder seam and pick up and k 15 (16, 16) sts down neck edge, 34 (34, 36) sts across center front, 15 (16, 16) sts to shoulder seam and 46 (48, 52) sts across back neck edge—110 (114, 120) sts. Place marker, join and p 1 rnd. ***Work Picot bind-off:*** Bind off 2 sts, *sl st on right-hand needle to left-hand needle, cast on 2 sts, then bind off 4 sts; rep from* to end. Fasten off final st, making sure last st joins invisibly on inside of work behind first st.

**Sleeve edging**
With RS facing and smaller needles, pick up and k 56 sts around lower edge of sleeve. K 1 row. Work Picot bind-off as for neck edging.
Set in sleeves. Sew side and sleeve seams.

- K on RS, p on WS
- P on RS, k on WS
- Yo
- Ssk
- K2tog
- P2tog
- Sl2-k1-p2sso
- K3tog tbl
- K3tog
- No stitch
- Dec for S only
- K for S, yo for M, L
- K for S, dec for M, L
- Dec for M, k for L
- K for M, yo for L
- K for M, dec for L
- Ssk for M, yo for M, L
- K2og for M, yo for M, L
- Large
- Medium
- Small

***Delphos Chart***

L M S — 35 (39, 43) sts — S M L — L M S — 31 (35, 39) sts — S M L

Louis Comfort Tiffany's iridescent glass was my inspiration for this jacket. His favrile glass recreated the glowing colors of paint, varying in texture and hue within each piece. The luminous wool and viscose yarn achieves the same painterly combination of sculptured form and sophisticated gradation of color, perfect for the easy style of this *fin de siècle* smoking jacket.

**Sizes**
S (M, L).
Shown in sizes medium (Raphael #70) and large (Charcoal #25).
Directions are for smallest size with larger sizes in parentheses.
If there is only 1 set of numbers, it applies to all sizes.

**Finished measurements**
Bust 42 (48, 54)"
Length 30 (31, 32)"

**Yarn**
12 (13, 14) hanks Colinette Zanziba (each 3½oz/100g, 102yds/94m, 51% wool, 48% viscose, 1% nylon)

**Needles**
One pair each sizes 9 and 10½ (5.5 and 6.5mm) needles, *or size to obtain gauge.*
Two size 9 (5.5mm) double-pointed needles (dpn).

**Extras**
Stitch marker and holders.

**Gauge**
14 sts and 18 rows to 4" (10 cm) in St st, using size 10½ (6.5mm) needles.

# TIFFANY JACKET

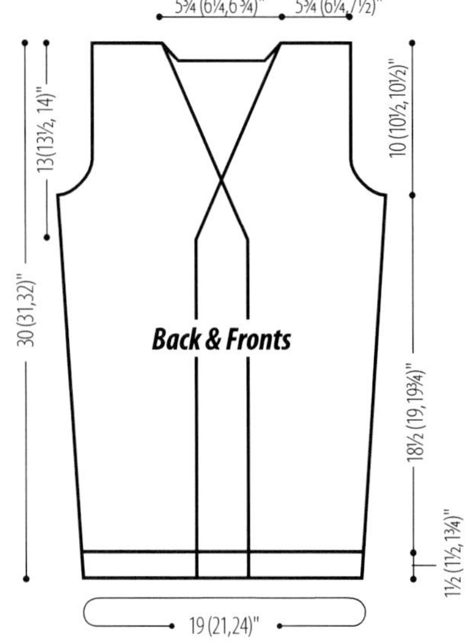


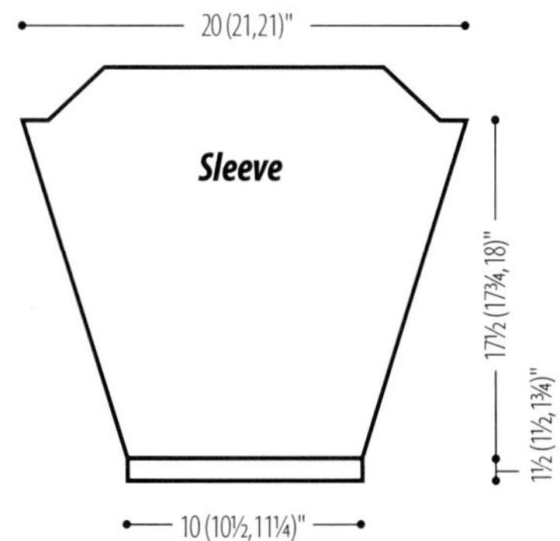


**Double-wrapping a stitch**

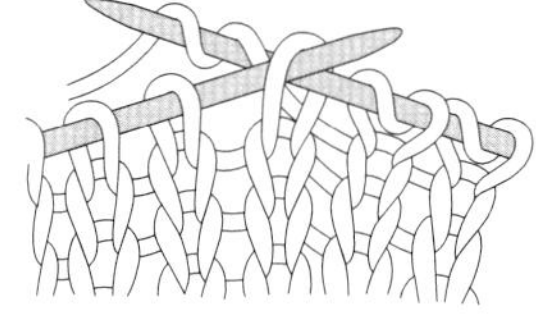

**STITCHES**

**Favrile st**

*Row 1* Knit.
*Row 2* Purl.
*Rows 3, 5, 7, 9, 11* Knit.
*Rows 4, 6, 8, 10, 12* Purl.
*Rows 13 and 15* Knit, wrapping yarn twice around needle for each st.
*Row 14* Knit, dropping 2nd wraps.
*Row 16* Purl, dropping 2nd wraps.
*Rows 17–25* Rep rows 3–11.
*Row 26* Knit.
Rep rows 1–26 for Favrile pat.

**Seed st** (over any number of sts)
*Row 1* *K1, p1; rep from*. *Row 2* K the purl sts and p the knit sts. Rep row 2 for seed st pat.

**BACK**

With smaller needles, cast on 68 (74, 84) sts. K 2 rows. Work 1¼ (1¼, 1½)" in Seed st. Change to larger needles. Beg with row 1, work in Favrile pat, AT SAME TIME, inc 1 st each side every 18th (14th, 12th) rows 4 (5, 6) times—76 (84, 96) sts. Work even until piece measures 20 (20½, 21½)" from beg, end with a WS row.

**Shape armhole**

Bind off 3 sts at beg of next 2 rows. Dec 1 st each side of next 5 (6, 7) rows—60 (66, 76) sts. Cont in pat until piece measures 29¼ (30¼, 31)" from beg, end with a WS row.

**Shape neck**

Work 22 (24, 29) sts, join a 2nd ball of yarn and bind off center 16 (18, 18) sts, work to end. Working both sides at same time, dec 1 st at each neck edge every row 2 (2, 3) times. Bind off rem sts.

**POCKET LININGS** (make 2)

With larger needles, cast on 20 sts. Beg with a p row, work 25 rows in St st. Place sts on hold.

**LEFT FRONT**

With smaller needles, cast on 46 (50, 56) sts. Work as for back to armhole, working incs at side edge (beg of RS rows) every 18th (14th, 12th) rows 4 (5, 6) times, AT SAME TIME, join pocket lining 22 rows from beg as foll: *Next row* (RS) Work 8 (10, 12) sts, place next 20 sts on hold, then with RS facing, work 20 sts of pocket lining, work to end. When piece measures 17 (17½, 18)" from beg, end with a WS row.

**Shape neck**

*Next row* (RS) K to last 3 sts, k2tog, k1. Dec 1 st at neck edge every other row 11 (15, 19) times more, then every 3rd row 10 (8, 6) times, AT SAME TIME, when piece measures same as back to armhole, shape armhole at side edge as for back. When piece measures 30 (31, 32)" from beg, bind off rem sts.

**RIGHT FRONT**

Work as for left front, reversing all shaping and pocket placement.

**SLEEVES**

With smaller needles, cast on 36 (38, 40) sts. K 2 rows. Work 1¼ (1¼, 1½)" in Seed st. Change to larger needles. Work in Favrile pat, AT SAME TIME, inc 1 st each side every 4th row 17 (18, 17) times—70 (74, 74) sts. Work even until piece measures 17½ (17¾, 18)" from beg, end with a WS row.

**Shape cap**

Bind off 3 sts at beg of next 2 rows. Dec 1 st each side of next 6 (7, 8) rows. Bind off rem sts.

**COLLAR**

Block pieces. Sew shoulder seams.

With smaller needles, cast on 2 sts. Work in Seed st and sew edge of collar to sweater, stretching slightly to fit, AT SAME TIME, inc 1 st at neck edge (the inside edge) every row 10 times, then every other row 22 times—34 sts. Mark this position. Work even in seed st until collar is sewn to point opposite marker. Dec 1 st at neck edge every other row 22 times, then every row 10 times, end at beg of neck shaping on left front. Bind off rem 2 sts.

**FRONT BAND**

**I-cord edging**

For ease in handling, pick up 15 to 20 sts at a time. Pick up approx 2 sts for every 3 rows along fronts and 1 st for every row along collar edge. With RS facing and dpn, beg at lower right front edge and insert dpn through suggested 15 to 20 sts along edge. With 2nd dpn and separate ball of yarn, cast on 3 sts, *sl sts to dpn along edge, k2, ssk; rep from* along right front, along outside edge of collar and along left front. Fasten off.

**FINISHING**

**Pocket edgings**

With RS facing and dpn, k 5 rows on 20 pocket sts, binding off firmly on last row. Sew edgings to RS. Sew linings to WS. Set in sleeves. Sew side and sleeve seams. Make belt loops of single crochet and sew in position at waistline on side seams.

**Belt**

With dpn, cast on 7 sts. Work 52 (58, 64)" in Seed st. Bind off.

**SEED ST COLLAR AND BAND OPTION** (shown on Charcoal jacket)

**Right Front Band**

With dpn, cast on 5 sts. Work in Seed st until band, slightly stretched, fits along right front to beg of V-neck shaping. Place sts on hold.

**Collar**

Sew shoulder seams. With RS facing and smaller needles, pick up and k 5 sts on hold and cont seed st, AT SAME TIME, inc 1 st at neck edge on next 10 rows, then every other row 22 times—37 sts. Mark this position. Work even until collar fits to shoulder seam and along back neck opposite marked position. Dec 1 st at neck edge every other row 22 times, then every row 10 times. Collar is at beg of V-neck shaping on left front. Work even on rem 5 sts until piece fits to lower edge of left front. Bind off all sts.

I have always loved the work of Gustav Klimt, and one of his paintings inspired the simple pyramid pattern used in this piece. A Viennese painter and designer of great innovativeness and imagination, he devoted much of his time to architectural decoration in murals such as *The Kiss*. The cotton yarn gives crisp definition to the sculptured stitches, which on closer inspection reveals patterns within patterns in true Klimt style.

# KLIMT VEST

**Sizes**
S (M, L).
Shown in sizes medium (Opaque #112) and large (Vine #103). Directions are for smallest size with larger sizes in parentheses. If there is only 1 set of numbers, it applies to all sizes.

**Finished measurements**
Chest 41 (45, 49)"
Length 25 (26, 27)"

**Yarns**
7 (8, 8) balls Rowan 4-ply cotton (each 1¾oz/50g, 186yds/170m, 100% cotton)

**Needles**
One pair each sizes 1 and 3 (2.25 and 3.25mm) needles, *or size to obtain gauge.*
Circular needle size 1 (2.25mm), 16"/40cm long.

**Extras**
Stitch markers and holders.

**Gauge**
28 sts and 42 rows to 4"/10 cm in Vienna Chart pat using size 3 (3.25mm) needles.

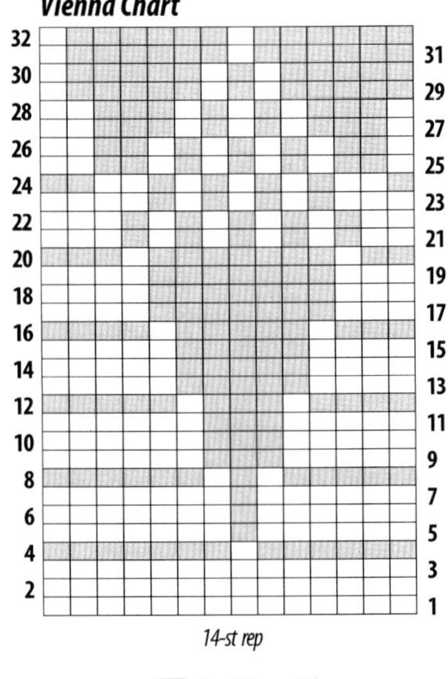


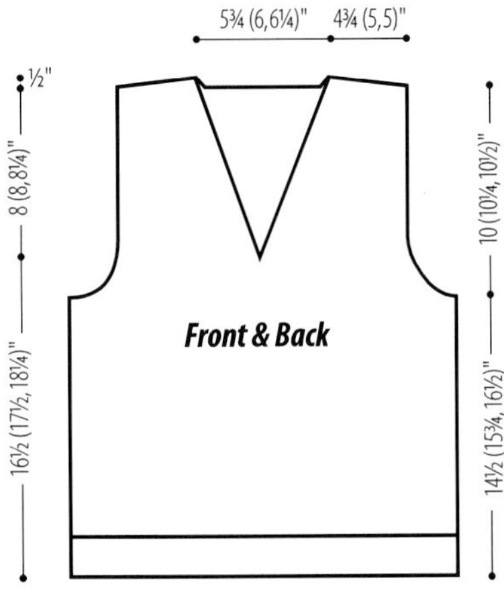


**Mosaic rib pat** (multiple of 4 sts plus 2)
***Row 1*** (RS) *K2, p2; rep from*, end k2.
***Row 2*** *P2, k2; rep from*, end p2.
***Rows 3–4*** Rep rows 1–2.
***Row 5*** *P2, k2; rep from*, end p2.
***Row 6*** *K2, p2; rep from*, end k2.
***Rows 7–8*** Rep rows 5–6.
Rep rows 1–8 for Mosaic rib pat.

**BACK**

With smaller needles, cast on 138 (154, 166) sts. Work 20 rows in Mosaic rib pat, inc 8 (6, 8) sts evenly spaced across last row—146 (160, 174) sts. Change to larger needles. ***Beg Vienna Chart: Row 1*** (RS) Reading chart from right to left, work sts 12–14 of chart, work 14-st rep 10 (11, 12) times, work sts 1–3 of chart. ***Row 2*** (WS) Reading chart from left to right, work sts 3–1 of chart, work 14-st rep 10 (11, 12) times, work sts 14–12. Cont in chart pat as established until piece measures 14½ (15¾, 16)" from beg, end with a WS row.

**Shape armhole**

Bind off 6 (7, 8) sts at beg of next 2 rows. Dec 1 st each side of next row, then every row 0 (4, 8) times more. Dec 1 st each side every other row 13 times—106 (110, 114) sts. Cont pat until piece measures 24½ (25½, 26½)" from beg, end with a WS row.

**Shape neck and shoulder**

***Row 1*** (RS) Work 35 (36, 38) sts, turn and leave rem sts on hold. Work each side of neck separately. ***Rows 2 and 4*** (WS) Dec 1 st, work to end. ***Row 3*** (RS) Bind off 10 (11, 11) sts (shoulder edge), work to last 2 sts, k2tog. ***Row 5*** Bind off 11 sts, work to last 0 (0, 2) sts, k2tog. ***Row 6*** Work across in pat. Bind off rem sts. With RS facing, join yarn and bind off center 36 (38, 38) sts, cont pat to end. Shape neck and shoulders as for first side, binding off for shoulders on WS rows and shaping neck at beg of RS rows.

**FRONT**

Work as for back until piece measures 16½ (17½, 18¼)" from beg, end with a WS row. Place a marker at center of work.

**Shape left side of neck**

***Next row*** (RS) Cont to shape armhole if necessary and work to 1 st before marker, turn and leave rem sts on hold. Work each side separately as foll: Dec 1 st at neck edge on next row, then every 3rd row 2 (6, 8) times, then every 4th row 18 (15, 14) times. Work even until piece measures 24½ (25½, 26½)" from beg, end with a WS row.

**Shape shoulder**

Bind off 10 (11, 11) sts at beg of next row. Work 1 row even. Bind off 11 sts at beg of next row. Work 1 row even. Bind off rem sts.

**Right side of neck**

With RS facing, place center 2 sts on hold, join yarn and cont pat across. Complete to match first side, reversing all shapings.

**FINISHING**

Block pieces. Sew shoulder seams.

**Neckband**

With RS facing and circular needle, beg at left shoulder and pick up and k 60 (64, 64) sts along left front neck, k 2 sts on hold, 60 (64, 64) sts along right front neck to shoulder, 50 sts along back neck—172 (180, 180) sts. Place marker, join and dec 1 st each side of center 2 sts (always k these center 2 sts) as foll: ***Rnds 1–4*** Beg with k2, work k2, p2 rib across 58 (62, 62) sts, work 2 tog, k2, work 2 tog through the back loop (tbl), beg with k2, rib to end. ***Rnds 5–8*** Beg with p2, work rib and dec as in rnds 1–4. Bind off in rib.

**Armbands**

With RS facing and smaller needles, pick up and k 146 (150, 154) sts evenly around armhole. ***Next row*** (WS) Purl. Work rows 1–4 of Mosaic rib pat. Bind off in rib. Sew side seams, including armbands.

The Spanish architect, Antoni Gaudi, inspired this sweater. A master of texture, color, and meandering organic forms, he combined stone, colored mosaics, and ironwork to phantasmagoric effect. I have used the progression of this simple rib into a labyrinthine trellis to suggest a touch of Gaudi genius.

# GAUDI SWEATER

**Sizes**
S (M, L).
Shown in sizes small (Peat #857) and medium (Mallard #860).
Directions are for smallest size with larger sizes in parentheses.
If there is only 1 set of numbers, it applies to all sizes.

**Finished measurements**
Chest 50 (54, 58)"
Length 28 (29, 30)"

**Yarn**
16 (18, 19) skeins Rowan DK Tweed (each 1¾oz/50g, 120yds/110m, 100% wool)

**Needles**
One pair each sizes 3 and 6 (3.25 and 4mm) needles, *or size to obtain gauge.*
Circular needle size 3 (3.25mm), 16"/40cm long.

**Extras**
Stitch markers and holders.
Cable needle.

**Gauge**
24 sts and 28 rows to 4"/10 cm in Güell Chart pat (well blocked) using size 6 (4mm) needles.

**BACK**
With larger needles, cast on 150 (162, 174) sts. ***Beg Güell Chart: Row 1*** Work last 15 (1, 7) sts of chart, work 40-st rep 3 (4, 4) times, work the first 15 (1, 7) sts. Cont in pat as established through chart row 76, then rep rows 75–76 until piece measures 17½ (18, 18½)" from beg, end with a WS row.

**Shape armhole**
Cont pat, bind off 5 (6, 6) sts at beg of next 2 rows. Dec 1 st each side of next 7 (8, 9) rows, then every other row 3 times—120 (128, 138) sts. Work even until piece measures 27 (28, 29)" from beg, end with a WS row.

**Shape neck**
***Next row*** (RS) Work 44 (47, 50) sts, turn and leave rem sts on holder. Work each side of neck separately. Dec 1 st at beg of next row. Bind off 13 (14, 15) sts at beg of next row, work to last 2 sts, k2tog. Dec 1 st at beg of next row. Bind off 14 (15, 16) sts at beg of next row. Work 1 row even, then bind off rem sts.
With RS facing, join yarn to rem sts and bind off center 32 (34, 38) sts, work to end. Work to correspond to first side, reversing shaping.

**FRONT**
Work as for back until piece measures 18½ (19½, 20)" from beg, end with a WS row. Mark the center 24 sts.

**Shape neck**
Work to marker, turn and leave rem sts on holder. Cont armhole shaping and work each side of neck separately. Dec 1 st at neck edge on next row, then every 6th row 0 (0, 9) times, every 7th row 0 (7, 0) times, every 8th row 6 (0, 0) times. Mark the position of last dec. Work even until piece measures 27 (28, 29)" from beg, end with a WS row.

**Shape shoulder**
At shoulder edge, bind off 13 (14, 15) sts once, 14 (15, 16) twice.
With RS facing, place center 24 sts on hold, join yarn to rem sts and work to end. Work to correspond to first side, reversing shaping and marking position of last dec.

**SLEEVES**
(NOTE Scan through instructions to familiarize yourself with shaping and pattern placement.)
With larger needles, cast on 60 (64, 66) sts. ***Beg Güell Chart: Row 1*** Work the last 10 (12, 13) sts of chart, work the 40-st rep once, work the first 10 (12, 13) sts. Work chart pat and shape sleeve simultaneously as foll: Inc 1 st each side (working incs into chart pat, then into 2x2 rib) every 4th row 18 (19, 25) times, then every 5th row 12 (12, 8) times—120 (126, 132) sts. Work through chart row 33, then rep the large diamond (rows 34–73) 3 times over the center 40 sts. Cont the 2x2 rib at each side of the diamond, omitting the garter ridges on rows 28–48. After the 3rd diamond, cont in 2x2 rib until piece measures 20 (20¼, 20½)" from beg, end with a WS row. Bind off 5 (6, 6) sts at beg of next 2 rows. Dec 1 st each side of next 7 (8, 9) rows, then every other row 3 times. Bind off rem sts firmly.

**FINISHING**
Block pieces. Work a firm running stitch along back and front shoulder edges to prevent the ribs from stretching too much—each shoulder should measure approx 6¾ (7¼, 7¾)". Sew shoulder seams.

**Collar**
With RS facing and smaller needles, pick up and work the center 24 sts of front in row 1 of Mosaic collar pat, then cont in pat to end, sewing collar to neckline as you work, stretching slightly to fit, AT SAME TIME, inc 1 st at neck edge (the side closest to left front neckline) every 4th row 14 (16, 16) times—38 (40, 40) sts. Work even until collar fits around back neck and down right neck to marked position of last dec, end with pat row 3. Dec 1 st at neck edge every 4th row 14 (16, 16) times. Bind off rem sts.
With WS of collar facing and smaller circular needle, beg at pick-up row and pick up and k 1 st for every row worked along outside, straight edge of collar. Turn and k 1 row. Bind off all sts. Sew bound-off edge of collar inside neck, behind beg of collar.
Set in sleeves. Sew side and sleeve seams, leaving first 13 rows at lower edge of sweater open.

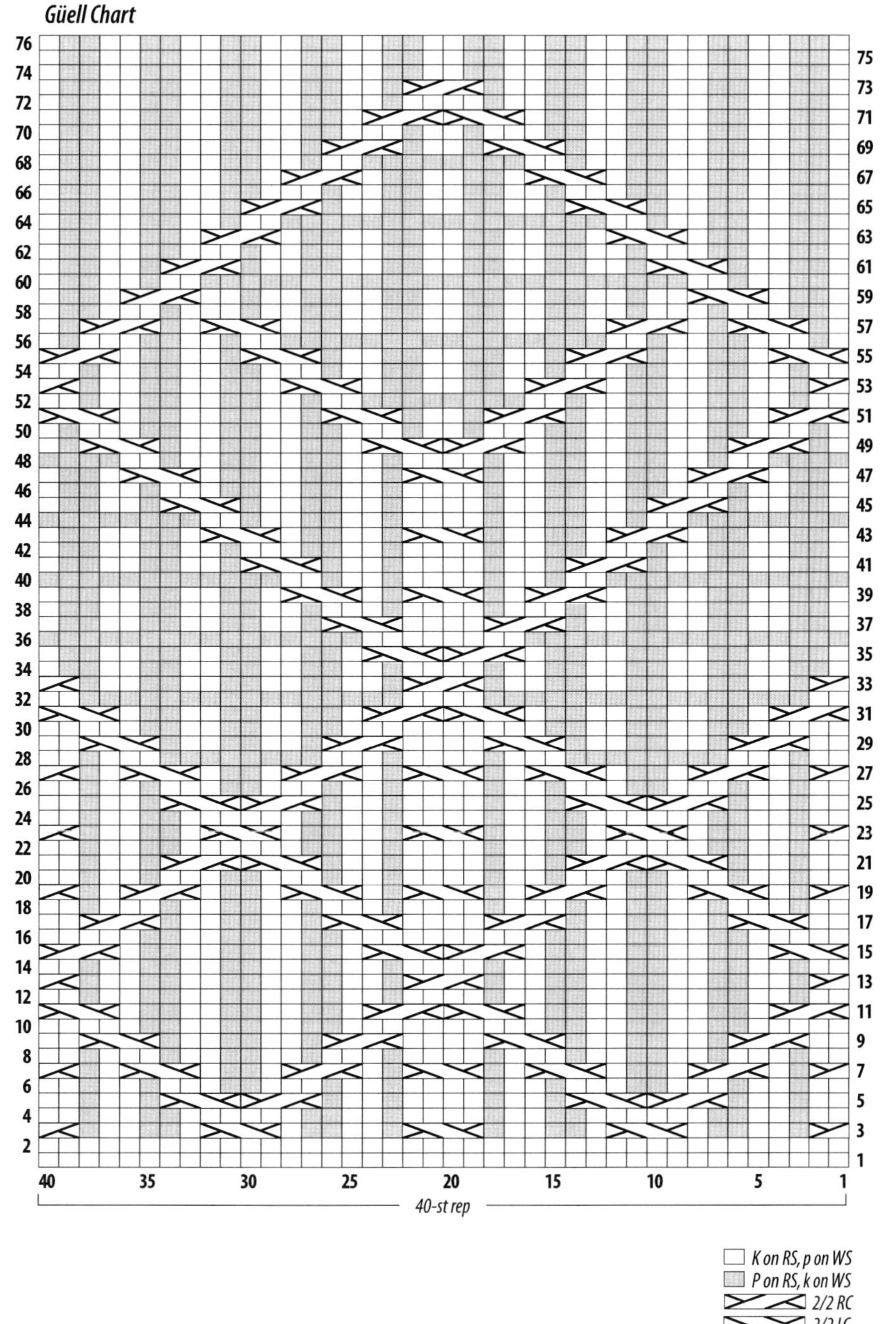


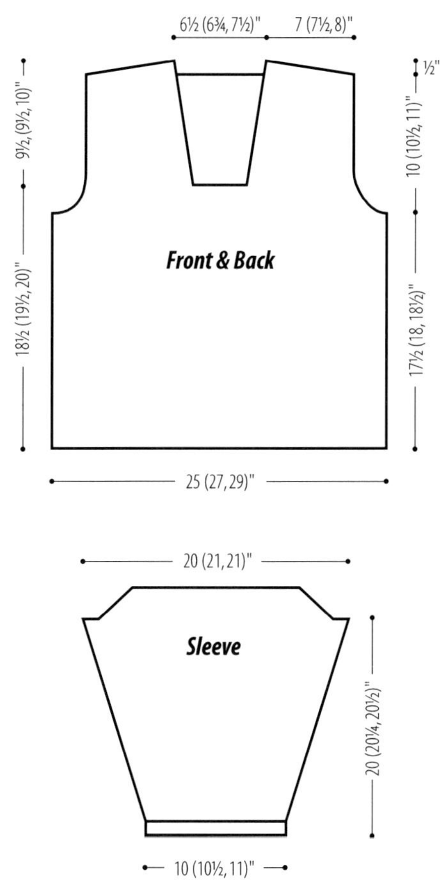


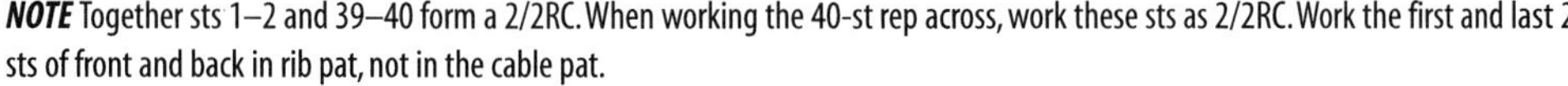

***NOTE*** Together sts 1–2 and 39–40 form a 2/2RC. When working the 40-st rep across, work these sts as 2/2RC. Work the first and last 2 sts of front and back in rib pat, not in the cable pat.

**STITCHES**

***2/2 Right Cross (2/2 RC)*** Sl 2 sts to cable needle and hold in back, k2, then k2 from cable needle.

***2/2 Left Cross (2/2 LC)*** Sl 2 sts to cable needle and hold in front, k2, then k2 from cable needle.

**Mosaic collar pat**

***Row 1*** (WS) K1, *p2, k2; rep from* to last 3 sts, p2, k1. ***Row 2*** Knit. ***Row 3*** Rep row 1. ***Row 4*** Purl. Rep rows 1–4

Kate Greenaway's illustrations in children's books such as *Mother Goose* and *Under the Window* have been longtime favorites. The stylish clothes in her watercolors were widely influential both then and now, and the romantic nostalgia of her empire-line dress with frilled neck and sleeve was my inspiration for this design.

# GREENAWAY DRESS

**Sizes**
S (M, L) to fit 2 (4, 6) yrs.
Shown in sizes medium (Santa Fe #4050) and large (Mother of Pearl #4042).
Directions are for smallest size with larger sizes in parentheses.
If there is only 1 set of numbers, it applies to all sizes.

**Finished measurements**
Chest (buttoned) 26 (28, 30)"
Length 21 (23½, 26)"

**Yarn**
10 (11, 12) skeins Classic Elite Metro (each 1¾oz/50g, 110 yds/100m, 100% rayon)

**Needles**
One pair each sizes 3 and 5 (3.25 and 3.75mm) needles, *or size to obtain gauge.*
Size 3 and 5 (3.25 and 3.75mm) circular needles, 24"/60cm long.

**Extras**
Stitch markers and holders.
Three ⅝"/15mm buttons.

**Gauge**
24 sts and 34 rows to 4"/10 cm in Regency lace pat using size 5 (3.75mm) needles.

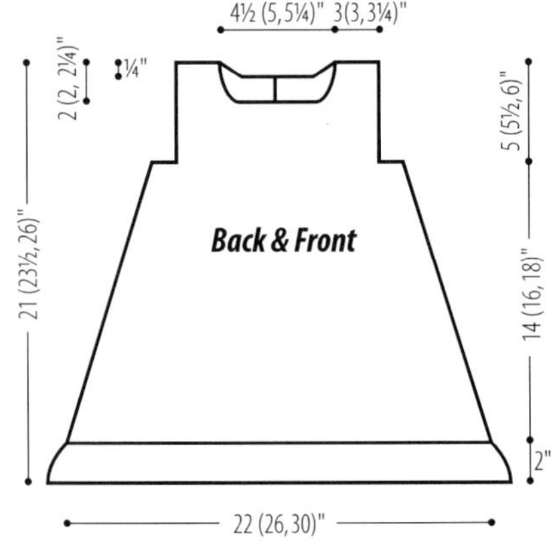

**STITCHES**

**Little Ann Frill** (hem; multiple of 14 sts plus 3)
*Row 1* (RS) P3, *k11, p3; rep from*.
*Row 2* K3, *p11, k3; rep from*.
*Row 3* P3, *ssk, k2, yo, sl 1, k2tog, psso, yo, k2, k2tog, p3; rep from*.
*Row 4* K3, *p9, k3; rep from*.
*Row 5* P3, *ssk, k1, yo, sl 1, k2tog, psso, yo, k1, k2tog, p3; rep from*.
*Row 6* K3, *p7, k3; rep from*.
*Row 7* P3, *ssk, yo, sl 1, k2tog, psso, yo, k2tog, p3; rep from*.
*Row 8* K3, *p5, k3, rep from*.
*Row 9* P3, *ssk, k1, k2tog, p3; rep from*.
*Row 10* K3, *p3, k3; rep from*.
*Row 11* P3, *sl 1, k2tog, psso, p3; rep from*.
*Row 12* K3, *p1, k3; rep from*.

**Regency lace pat** (multiple of 12 sts plus 15)
*Row 1* (RS) K6, *yo, ssk, k10; rep from* to last 9 sts, yo, ssk, k7.
*Row 2* Purl.
*Row 3* K6, *k2tog, yo, k10; rep from* to last 9 sts, k2tog, yo, k7.
*Row 4* Purl.
Rep rows 1–4 for Regency lace pat.

**Lattice pat** (multiple of 2 sts plus 2)
*Row 1* (RS) K1, *yo, ssk; rep from* to last st, k1.
*Row 2* Purl.
*Row 3* K1, *k2tog, yo; rep from* to last st, k1.
*Row 4* Purl.
Rep rows 1–4 for Lattice pat.

**BACK**
With larger circular needle, cast on 465 (549, 633) sts. Working back and forth in rows, turn and k 1 row. Work 12 rows of Little Ann Frill—135 (159, 183) sts. Work pat and shape piece simultaneously as foll: Beg with row 1, work 12 rows in Regency lace pat. ***Next (dec) row*** Cont Regency lace pat, work 27 (27, 39) sts in pat, *ssk, k1, work 2 sts, k1, k2tog, work 28 (40, 40) sts; rep from* once, ssk, k1, work 2 sts, k1, k2tog, work 28 (28, 40) sts in pat. Work 11 (11, 9) rows more in pat. ***Next (dec) row*** Cont pat, work 26 (26, 38) sts, *ssk, k1, work 2 sts, k1, k2tog, work 26 (38, 38) sts; rep from* once, ssk, k1, work 2 sts, k1, k2tog, work 27 (27, 39) sts.
In same way, dec 6 sts every 12th row 7 (2, 0) times more, every 10th row 0 (8, 10) times, every 8th row 0 (0, 3) times, working 1 less st between decs so that lacy zigzag verticals stay correct. Work final 3 dec rows as foll:
***7 (10, 13)th dec*** Work 21 (18, 27) sts, *ssk, k1, work 2, k1, k2tog, work 16 (22, 16), rep from* once, ssk, k1, work 2, k1, k2tog, work 22 (19, 28) sts.
***8 (11, 14)th dec*** Work 21 (18, 27) sts, *ssk, yo, ssk or k2tog (depending whether Row 1 or 3), k2tog, work 16 (22, 16), rep from* once, *ssk, yo, ssk or k2tog (depending whether Row 1 or 3), k2tog, work 22 (19, 28) sts.
***9 (12, 15)th dec*** Ssk, work 19 (16, 25) sts, *k4tog, yo, work 16 (22, 16) sts, rep from* once, k4tog, yo, work 20 (17, 26) sts, k2tog.
Work even on rem 79 (85, 91) sts until piece measures 16 (18, 20)" from beg, end with a WS row.

**Shape armhole**
Bind off 8 (9, 9) sts at beg of next 2 rows. Work even until piece measures 17 (19¼, 21½)" from beg, end with a WS row and ***for sizes S and L only,*** inc 1 st at end of final row and ***for size M,*** dec 1 st at end of final row—64 (66, 74) sts.

**Yoke**
(NOTE Do not work yo without its corresponding dec. Work any extra sts in St st.)
Change to smaller needles. Beg with row 1, work Lattice pat over first 32 (33, 37) sts and leave rem sts on hold. Work even until piece measures 20¾ (23¼, 25¾)" from beg, end with a RS row.

**Shape neck**
Bind off 12 (13, 14) sts at beg of next row. Dec 1 st at neck edge on next 2 rows. Bind off rem sts. Work 2nd side of yoke to correspond to first side, reversing shaping.

**FRONT**
Work as for back to yoke.

**Yoke**
Change to smaller needles. Beg with row 1, work Lattice pat until piece measures 19 (21½, 23¾)" from beg, end with a WS row.

**Shape neck**
Cont pat over 26 (26, 30) sts, turn and leave rem sts on hold.
Work each side of neck separately. Dec 1 st at neck edge 8 (8, 9) times. Work even until piece measures 21 (23½, 26)" from beg, end with a WS row. Bind off rem 18 (18, 21) sts.
With RS facing, join yarn to rem sts, bind off center 12 (14, 14) sts and work to end. Work to correspond to first side, reversing shaping.

**SLEEVES**
Using larger circular needle, cast on 157 (185, 199) sts. K 1 row. Work 12 rows of Little Ann Frill, inc 4 (8, 4) sts evenly across last row—51 (63, 63) sts. Work Regency lace pat, AT SAME TIME, inc 1 st each side (working incs into pat) every 3rd row 5 (0, 0) times, every 4th row 0 (0, 5) times, then every 5th row 0 (2, 0) times—61 (67, 73) sts. Work even in pat as established until piece measures 5 (5½, 6)" from beg. Bind off all sts.

**FINISHING**
Block pieces. Sew shoulder seams.
Using photo as guide, place 3 markers for buttons on left yoke. Work buttonholes on right yoke opposite markers when picking up final 25 (27, 28) sts as foll: cast on 2 sts, leave a 2-st space and cont to pick up.
With RS facing and smaller circular needle, beg at lower edge of left yoke and pick up and k 25 (27, 28) sts to back neck shaping, 16 (16, 17) sts to shoulder seam, 18 sts down neck edge to center front, 12 (14, 14) sts across front, 18 sts to shoulder seam, 16 (16, 17) sts along back neck edge, 25 (27, 28) sts to lower edge of yoke (working buttonholes as explained)—130 (136, 140) sts. K 1 row. ***Work Picot bind-off*** Bind off 2 sts, *sl st on right-hand needle onto left-hand needle, cast on 2 sts, then bind off 4 sts; rep from* across. Fasten off final st.
Sl st the buttonhole band on top of the button band at lower edge of yoke. Sew buttons on. Set in sleeves, placing bind-off edge along the vertical armhole edge. Sew side and sleeve seams. Stabilize neck edge by sewing a tiny running stitch on inside of Picot bind-off.

This piece was inspired by the free spirit of the American dancer and choreographer, Isadora Duncan. Her unorthodox experimental performances, where she appeared wearing only a diaphanous tunic with her long hair unbound, helped popularize a trend towards less restrictive clothing. Lofty cotton yarn and comfortable styling combine to make this sweater definitely one for the dance.

# ISADORA SWEATER

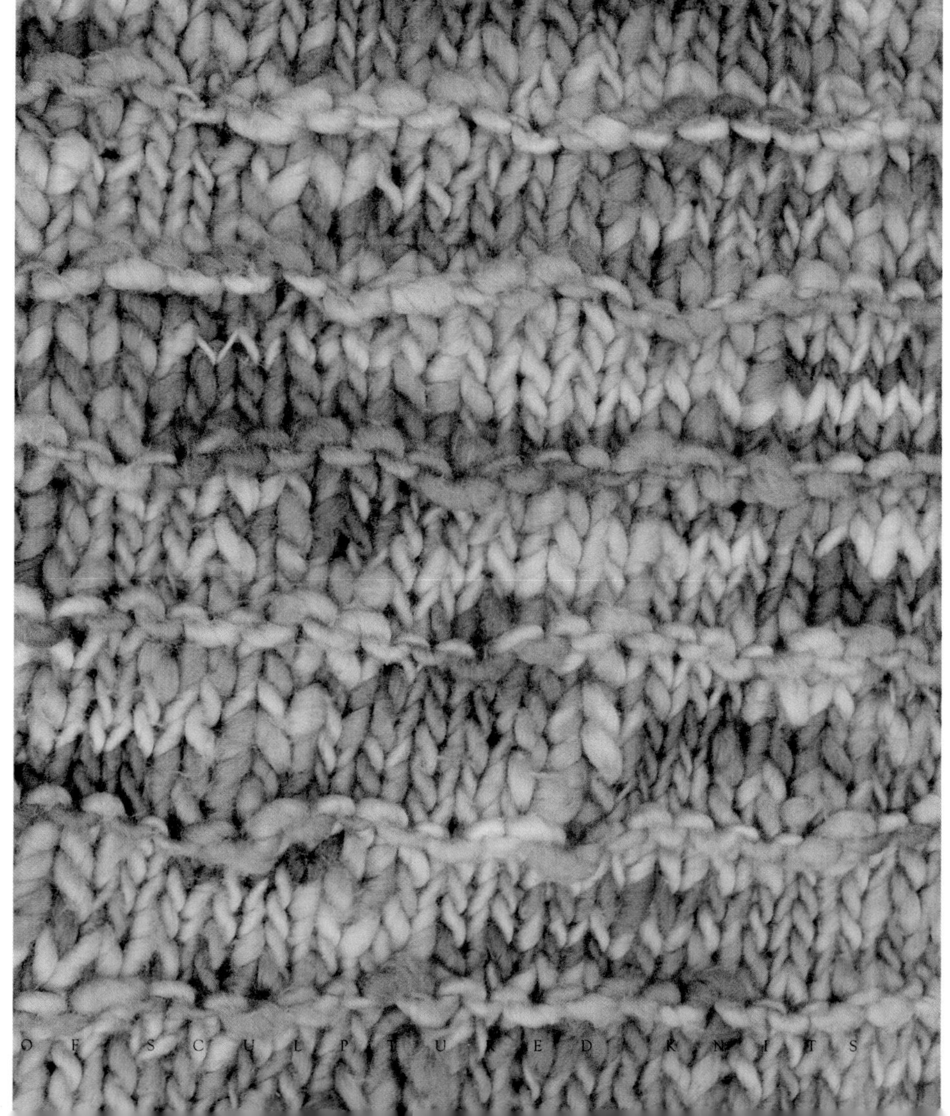

**Sizes**
1–2 (3–4, 5–6, 7–8) yrs.
Shown in sizes 1–2 yrs (Turquoise #21) and 5–6 yrs (Bonnard #104).
Directions are for smallest size with larger sizes in parentheses.
If there is only 1 set of numbers, it applies to all sizes.

**Finished measurements**
Chest 13 (14, 15½, 17)"
Length 14 (15½, 17, 19¼)"

**Yarn**
3 (4, 5) skeins Colinette Salsa (each 3½oz/100g, 109yds/100m, 100% cotton)

**Needles**
One pair each sizes 7 and 8 (4.5 and 5mm) needles, *or size to obtain gauge.*
One each circular needles sizes 7 and 8 (4.5 and 5mm), 16"/40cm long.

**Extras**
Stitch markers and holders.

**Gauge**
15 sts and 22 rows to 4"/10 cm in St st using size 8 (5mm) needles.

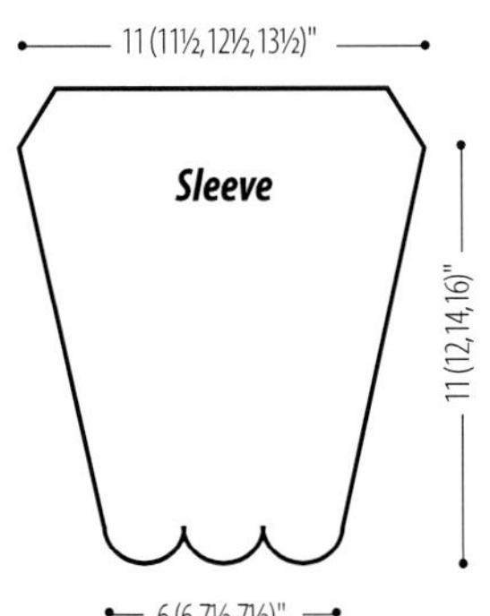


## STITCHES

**Arabesque pat** (multiple of 9 sts plus 3)
***Row 1*** (RS) K2, *yo, k8, yo, k1; rep from* to last st, k1.
***Row 2*** K3, *p8, k3; rep from*.
***Row 3*** K3, *yo, k8, yo, k3; rep from*.
***Row 4*** K4, *p8, k5; rep from* to last 4 sts, k4.
***Row 5*** K4, *yo, k8, yo, k5; rep from* to last 4 sts, k4.
***Row 6*** K5, *p8, k7; rep from* to last 5 sts, k5.
***Row 7*** K5, *k4tog tbl, k4tog, k7; rep from* to last 5 sts, k5.
***Row 8*** Knit.

**Knossos pat**
***Rows 1 and 3*** (RS) Knit.
***Rows 2 and 4*** Purl.
***Rows 5 and 6*** Knit.
Rep rows 1–6 for Knossos pat.

## BACK

With smaller needles, cast on 48 (57, 57, 66) sts. K 2 rows. Work rows 1–8 of Arabesque pat. Change to larger needles. ***Beg Knossos pat: Row 1*** (RS) Knit and dec 0 ( dec 5, inc 1, dec 2) evenly across—48 (52, 58, 64) sts. Work through row 6 of Knossos pat, then rep rows 1–6 until piece measures 8½ (9¾, 10¾, 12½)" from beg, end with a WS row.

**Shape armhole**
Bind off 2 (2, 3, 3) sts at beg of next 2 rows. Dec 1 st each side of next row, then every other row 2 (3, 4, 4) times more—38 (40, 42, 48) sts. Work even until piece measures 13½ (15, 16½, 18¾)" from beg, end with a WS row.

**Shape neck**
*Next row* (RS) Work 11 (12, 12, 15) sts, turn and leave rem sts on hold. Work each side of neck separately. Dec 1 st at beg of next row. Work 1 row even. Bind off rem 10 (11, 11, 14) sts. With RS facing, place center 16 (16, 18, 18) sts on hold. Join yarn to rem sts and work to correspond to first side, reversing shaping.

## *FRONT*

Work as for back until piece measures 11½ (13, 14½, 16¾)" from beg, end with a WS row.

**Shape neck**
*Next row (*RS) Work 16 (17, 17, 20) sts, turn and leave rem sts on hold. Work each side of neck separately. Dec 1 st at beg of next 3 rows, then every other row 3 times more. Work even until piece measures 14 (15½, 17, 19¼)" from beg, end with a WS row. Bind off rem 10 (11, 11, 14) sts. With RS facing, leave center 6 (6, 8, 8) sts on hold. Join yarn to rem sts and work to end. Work to correspond to first side, reversing shaping.

## SLEEVES

With smaller needles, cast on 21 (21, 30, 30) sts and k 2 rows. Work rows 1–8 of Arabesque pat. Change to larger needles. Work Knossos pat, AT SAME TIME, inc 1 st each side (working incs into pat) as foll: ***for first 2 sizes only***, every 4th row 4 (3, 0, 0) times, then every 5th row 6 (8, 0, 0) times; ***for the last 2 sizes only***, every 6th row 0 (0, 1, 0) times, every 7th row 0 (0, 8, 6) times, then every 8th row 0 (0, 0 4) times—41 (43, 48, 50) sts. Work even until piece measures 11 (12, 14, 16)" from beg, end with a WS row.

**Shape cap**
Bind off 2 (2, 3, 3) sts at beg of next 2 rows. Dec 1 st each side every other row 3 (4, 5, 5) times. Bind off the rem 31 (31, 32, 34) sts.

## COLLAR

Sew shoulder seams. With RS facing and smaller circular needle, beg at center of sts on hold in front and pick up and k 3 (3, 4, 4) sts, 12 sts along neck to shoulder, 2 sts down back neck, 16 (16, 18, 18) sts on hold at back neck, 2 sts to shoulder, 12 sts down left neck and 3 (3, 4, 4) sts on hold at front—50 (50, 54, 54) sts. Work 3 (4, 4) rnds of k1, p1 rib. Change to larger circular needle. Working back and forth in rows, k 12 (12, 14, 14) rows. Bind off all sts.

## FINISHING

Block pieces. Set in sleeves. Sew side and sleeve seams.

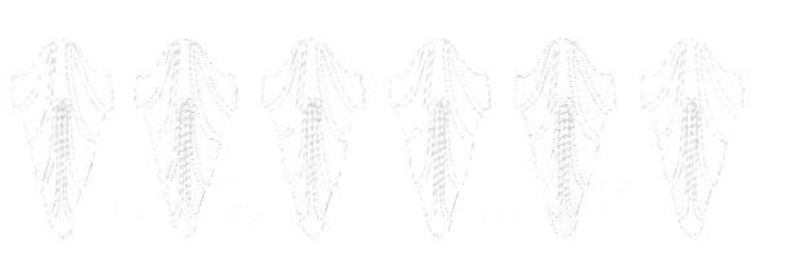

Serge Diaghilev's Ballets Russes revived ballet as a serious art form, unifying dance, drama, music, and painting. Drawing together many of the major talents of the era, Diaghilev was a catalyst for much of the art and music of the period. Knitted in plush chenille, I can easily imagine both these pieces amid the sumptuous settings and brilliant costumes of *Scheherazade*.

# DIAGHILEV BOLSTER AND PILLOW

**Sizes**
One size. Bolster shown in Dark Olive, pillow in Ochre.

**Finished measurements**
**Bolster** width 30", diameter 10"
**Pillow** width 18", length 18"

**Yarn**
Colinette DK Chenille
5 skeins for bolster, 4 skeins for pillow (each 3½oz/100g, 218yds/200m, 100% cotton)

**Needles**
One pair each sizes 3 and 6 (3.25 and 4mm) needles, *or size to obtain gauge.*
**For bolster** Five size 6 (4mm) double-pointed needles (dpn).
Two size 3 (3.25mm) dpn (for I-cord).
**For pillow** Size 6 (4mm) circular needle, 29"/72cm long.

**Extras**
Stitch markers. Cardboard.
**For bolster** Five ⅞"/22mm buttons.
**For pillow** Two ¾"/20mm buttons.

**Gauge**
20 sts and 28 rows to 4"/10 cm in Scheherazade pat using size 6 (4mm) needles.
17 sts and 25 rows to 4"/10 cm in St st using size 6 (4mm) needles.

ELLE EPOQU
CHAMPAGNE
RIER-JOU
EPERNAY-FRANCE
1979

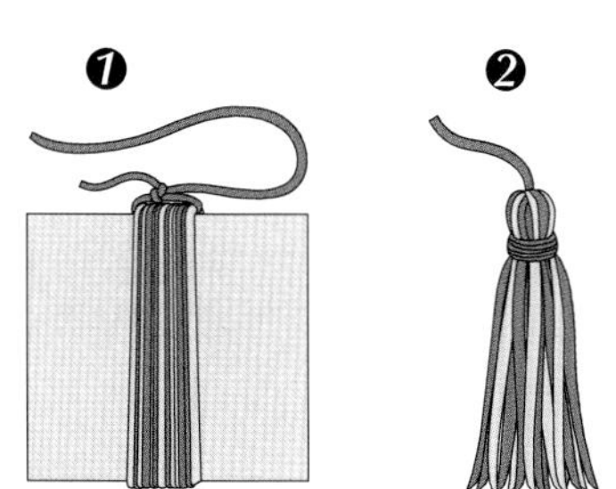

Tassels

**STITCHES**

**Scheherazade pat** (multiple of 6 sts plus 1)

***Rows 1 and 3*** *K4, p2; rep from* to last st, k1.

***Rows 2 and 4*** P1, *k2, p4; rep from*.

***Row 5*** *Insert right-hand needle between 4th and 5th sts on left-hand needle and draw through a loop, k1, p2, k3; rep from* to last st, k1.

***Row 6*** P1, *p3, k2, p2tog; rep from*.

***Rows 7 and 9*** K1, *p2, k4; rep from*.

***Rows 8 and 10*** *P4, k2; rep from* to last st, p1.

***Row 11*** K3, *insert right-hand needle between 4th and 5th sts on left-hand needle and draw through a loop, k1, p2, k3; rep from* to last 4 sts, k1, p2, k1.

***Row 12*** P1, k2, p1, *p3, k2, p2tog; rep from* to last 3 sts, p3.

Rep rows 1–12 for Scheherazade pat.

**Mitsouko frill edging** (multiple of 4 sts)

***Rnds 1 and 2*** (RS) *P3, k1; rep from* around.

***Rnd 3*** *P3, yo, k1, yo; rep from* around.

***Rnd 4*** *P3, k3; rep from* around.

***Rnd 5*** *P3, yo, k3, yo; rep from* around.

***Rnd 6*** *P3, k5; rep from* around.

***Rnd 7*** *P3, yo, k5, yo; rep from* around.

***Rnd 8*** *P3, k7; rep from* around.

***Rnd 9*** *P3, yo, k7, yo; rep from* around.

***Rnd 10*** *P3, k9; rep from* around.

***Rnd 11*** *P3, yo, k9, yo; rep from* around.

***Rnd 12*** *P3, k11; rep from* around.

**BOLSTER**

**Circular side pieces** (make 2)

With larger dpn, cast on 8 sts and divide evenly onto 4 dpn. Place marker, join and work in rnds as foll:

***Rnd 1*** K 8 through the back loop (tbl).

***Rnd 2*** K and inc 1 st in each st—16 sts.

***Rnds 3–5*** Knit.

***Rnd 6*** Rep rnd 2—32 sts.

***Rnds 7–11*** Knit.

***Rnd 12*** Rep rnd 2—64 sts.

***Rnds 13–19*** Knit.

***Rnd 20*** *K1, inc 1 st in next st; rep from* around—96 sts.

***Rnds 21–25*** Knit.

***Rnd 26*** *K2, inc 1 st in next st; rep from* around—128 sts.

***Rnds 27–31*** Knit.

***Rnd 32*** *K3, inc 1 st in next st; rep from* around—160 sts.

***Rnd 33*** Bind off loosely.

Measure circumference of piece.

**Main piece**

With larger needles, cast on 151 sts. Work even in Scheherazade pat until piece measures same as circumference of side pieces, end with a WS row.

**Buttonholes**

Change to smaller needles. Work in k1, p1 rib as foll: ***Next row*** (RS) Work 42 sts, *bind off 3 sts, work 12 sts; rep from*, end last rep with 42 sts. On next row, cast on 3 sts over bound-off sts. Work 4 rows more in rib. Bind off firmly.

**FINISHING**

Overlapping 1¼" with rib on top, sew main piece to circular side pieces. Slipstitch seam along overlap for 6" on each side. Sew buttons opposite buttonholes.

**I-cord edging**

(NOTE For ease in handling, pick up 10–15 sts at a time.)

Work I-cord around each end as foll: With RS facing and smaller dpn, pick up approx 10–15 sts. With 2nd dpn and separate ball of yarn, cast on 3 sts, *sl sts to left-hand needle, k2, ssk; rep from* around seam to beg of work. Fasten off. Sew ends together.

**Tassels** (make 2)

❶ Cut a 7½" wide rectangle of cardboard. Wind yarn around the piece 50 times. Cut yarn, leaving a 36" tail. Using diagram as guide, secure tassel. ❷ Remove cardboard and cut the loops at the opposite end. Wind the tail around all the loops below the fold for approx 3/4" and fasten securely. Draw tail through the top of fold and use to sew in place to centers of side pieces. Trim ends neatly.

**PILLOW**
**FRONT**
With larger needles, cast on 91 sts. Work even in Scheherazade pat until piece measures 18" from beg. Bind off all sts.

**BACK**
With larger needles, cast on 77 sts. Work even in St st until piece measures 10" from beg. Bind off firmly. With smaller needles, cast on 77 sts and work 6 rows in k1, p1 rib. Change to larger needles. ***Next (buttonhole) row*** (RS) *K29, bind off 2 sts, k14, bind off 2 sts, k to end. ***Next row*** (WS) Purl, casting on 2 sts over bound-off sts. Cont in St st until piece measures 9¼" from beg. Bind off firmly.

**FINISHING**
Overlap the back pieces by 1¼" in center of pillow with rib on top. Slipstitch seam in place for 3" on each side. Sew back to front around all 4 sides. Sew buttons on.

**Edging**
With RS facing and circular needle, beg at a corner and pick up and k 90 sts along side seam, *1 st in corner, 90 sts along next side; rep from*, end with 1 st at first corner—364 sts. To join, sl first st onto right-hand needle and pass last st over it onto left-hand needle. Work 12 rounds of Mitsouko frill edging. Bind off loosely.

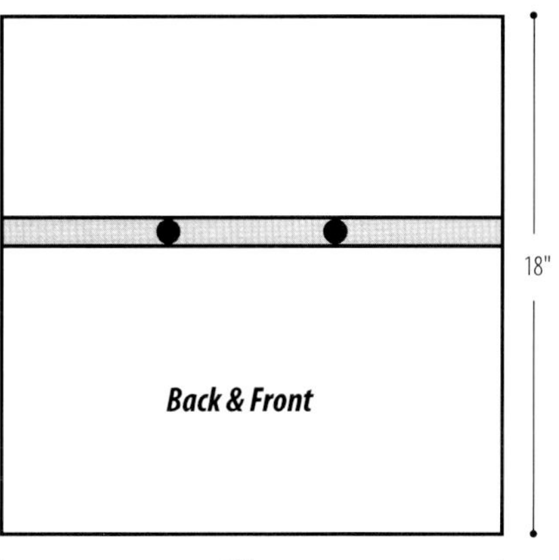

The hedonistic fantasies of Aubrey Beardsley's often macabre illustrations epitomized the decadence of the 1890s. The paisley motif of this design is highly evocative of the Victorian era, but also suggests the overblown exaggeration of form found in Beardsley's work. The beautiful llama and wool mix yarn adds an appropriately sensuous feel to the throw.

# BEARDSLEY SHAWL AND THROW

**Sizes**
30" x 72" including fringe (shawl) and 58" x 72" including fringe (throw). Throw in Ancient Orange (#3868). Shawl in Dyepot Indigo (#3848). The first set of numbers is for shawl; the numbers for throw follow in parentheses. If there is only 1 set of numbers, it applies to both pieces.

**Yarn**
10 (20) skeins Classic Elite Montera (each 3½oz/100g, 127yds/116m; 50% llama, 50% wool)

**Needles**
One pair each circular needles sizes 9 and 10½ (5.5 and 6.5mm), *or size to obtain gauge,* 29"/80cm long.

**Extras**
Stitch markers and holders.

**Gauge**
16 sts and 19 rows to 4"/10 cm in Peacock Chart using size 10½ (6.5mm) needles.

## STITCHES

### Savoy pat

**Make bobble (MB)** K into front, back, front, back, front of stitch—5 sts on right-hand needle. *Turn and k5; turn and p5. Rep from* twice more (6 rows total). Sl the 2nd, 3rd, 4th, and 5th sts, one at a time, over first st on right-hand needle.

*Row 1* Insert needle into first st, *cable cast-on 2 sts, bind off 2 sts, sl rem st to left-hand needle, rep from* 3 times more (4 picot points formed), k and bind off next 5 sts, transfer rem st to left-hand needle, rep from*.

*Rows 2 and 3* *Transfer rem st to left-hand needle, make 4 picot points as in row 1, join to center of first set of 4 picots on row 1 by picking up and knitting a st between the 2 center picot points, bind off 1 st, rep from*.

*Row 4* K1, cast on 1 st using backward lp cast-on, *pick up and k 1 st from between the 2 center picot points from set of 4, cast on 4 sts using backward lp cast-on, rep from* to last 3 sts, pick up and k 1 st as before, cast on 2 sts.

## SHAWL or THROW

### First piece

With larger needles, cast on 121 (236) sts. Work bobble edging: *MB in first st, k4, rep from* to last st, MB and then sl the 2nd st on needle over the first st—120 (235) sts. K 1 row. Change to smaller needles and work rows 1–3 of Savoy pat. Change to larger needles and work row 4 of Savoy pat. Beg with a k row, work 4 rows in St st and ***for throw only,*** inc 1 st at end of first row—120 (236) sts. ***Beg Salome Chart: Row 1*** (RS) K2, beg with st 1, work sts 1–29, work 29-st rep 2 (6) times, work sts 59–87, end k2. ***Row 2*** K2, work sts 87–59, work 29-st rep 2 (6) times, work sts 29–1, end k2. Working first and last 2 sts in garter st, cont chart pat as established through chart row 70. ***Rows 71, 73*** K2, p to last 2 sts, k2. ***Row 72*** Knit. ***Row 74*** K2, inc 1 st (for shawl and throw), k to last 2 sts, and ***for throw only***, inc 1 st, end k2—121 (238) sts. ***Beg Peacock Chart: Row 1*** (RS) K2, beg with st 7 and work sts 7–13, work 13-st rep 8 (17) times, work sts 1–6, end k2. ***Row 2*** K2, work sts 6–1, work 13-st rep 8 (17) times, work sts 13–7, end k2. Work through chart row 32, rep rows 1–32 a total of 3 times more, then work rows 1–16. Place all sts on hold.

### Second piece

Work as for first piece through row 74. Place sts on hold.

## FINISHING

Block pieces lightly. Lay pieces with the 2nd piece on the bottom needle with RS facing you, the first piece on the top needle with WS facing you. Graft the 2 pieces tog in St st. There will be an invisible row of rev St st on RS.

***Peacock Chart***

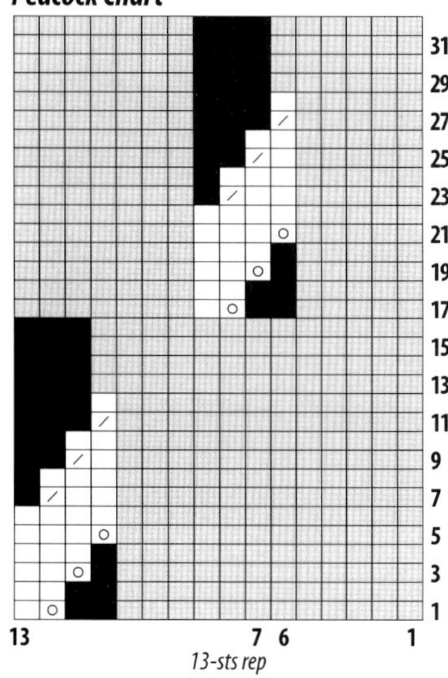


***Salome Chart***

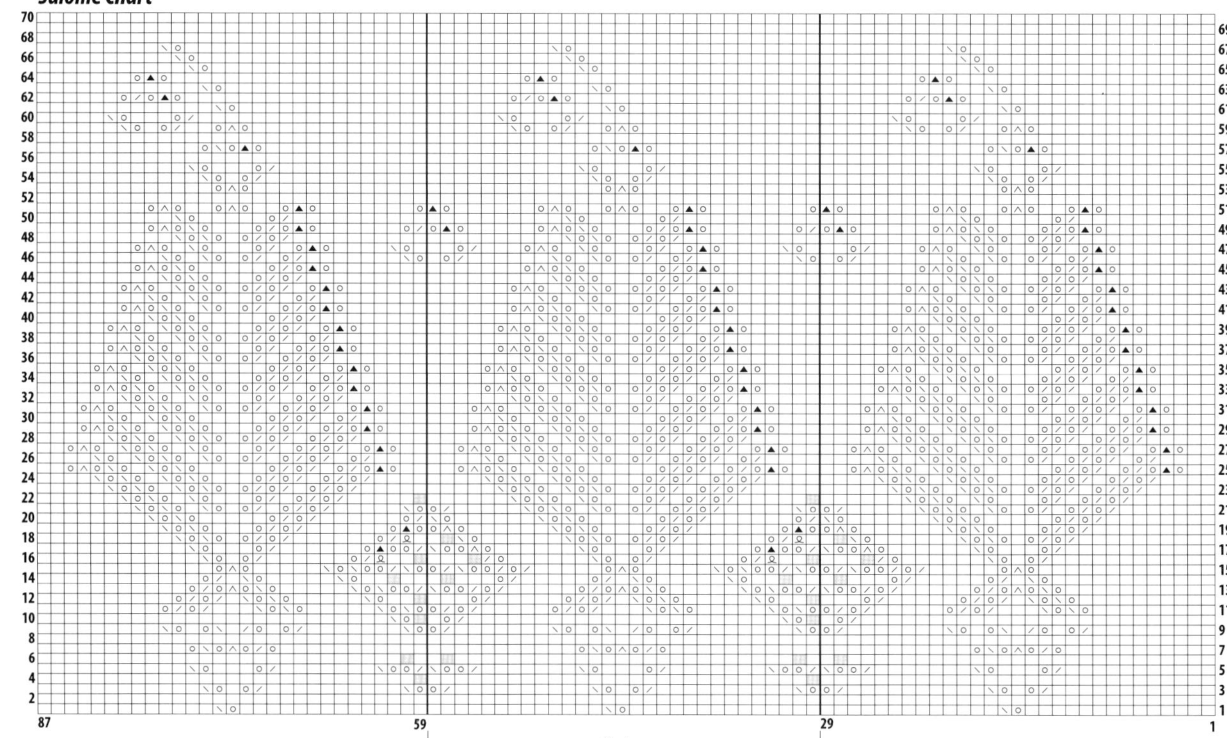


- K on RS, p on WS
- P on RS, k on WS
- Yo
- Ssk on RS, p2tog tbl on WS
- K2tog on RS, p2tog on WS
- Sl1-k2tog-psso
- K3tog on RS, p3tog on WS
- K1 tbl on RS, p1 tbl on WS
- P3tog
- No stitch

# ART DECO

A house is a machine for living in.

Le Corbusier 1923

The sleek, streamlined forms of Art Deco were a stark contrast to the elaborate undulating style of Art Nouveau. While Art Nouveau was essentially a movement which deplored the machine, Art Deco, with its new-age ideals of speed and glamour, used the newest possible machinery to make good design available to the general public. It is an aesthetic which I find very appealing. Its geometric form with bold outlines of fountains, leaping gazelles, sunbursts, and lightning ziggurats used exciting new materials such as Bakelite and chrome. One concept that Art Deco designers shared with those of the previous era was that of total design, every mundane detail—from a keyhole to a radiator grille—was worthy of the designer's attention, with taste and style their prime concern rather than practicality and performance.

Art Deco took its name from the Exposition Internationale des Arts Décoratifs et Industriels Modernes, an exhibition held in Paris in 1925, where artists and designers were given the opportunity to showcase their work. As objects were increasingly mass-produced, Art Deco style became steadily more geometric and linear, and the U.S. supplanted France as the spiritual center of the movement. There it found expression in objects as diverse as locomotives, skyscrapers, roadside diners, radio cabinets, jukeboxes, and advertising displays.

Certain colors like tango (the burnt orange shade named after the popular tea dance), silver, and black were used widely in the jazzy designs of cigarette cases, powder compacts, buckles, and brooches of the period. This bold use of color is also seen in the sensational geometric work of the ceramic designer, Clarice Cliff, who used striking glazes of tangerine, turquoise, cobalt, and yellow in her avant-garde Bizarre pottery.

In the world of fashion, cloche hats, bandeaux worn immediately above the eyebrows, short cropped hair, cupid's bow mouths, and the disappearance of the bust created a revolutionary new look. The Parisian couturier Paul Poiret paved the way for the modern style with his exotic, unconstricted, flowing lines and claimed to have freed women from the shackles of the corset. Coco Chanel, whose name became synonymous with elegance and chic, continued to develop the trend in her classic Chanel look, which consisted of a casual but extremely well-cut wool jersey suit with straight, collarless jacket and short, full-cut skirt, worn with Art Deco costume jewelry and a sailor hat over short hair. At the same time in the United States the exquisitely stylish fashion fantasies of the Russian-born artist and designer, Erté, adorned the covers of *Harper's Bazaar,* which was eagerly awaited each month by women wishing to escape into his glamorous world.

The cinema was gaining in popularity over the theater, and people looked to it for their style icons. With his darkly exotic good looks, Rudolph Valentino won the hearts of a generation of women in the early twenties, while Fred Astaire and Ginger Rogers were the epitome of graceful, sophisticated style in the thirties. But for me the face of the era was Greta Garbo, who embodied the new woman with her cool mannish elegance.

I can remember being intrigued as a child by the stark geometry of the local Odeon cinema in my home town since it was quite different from the earlier Victorian buildings. But after visiting Manhattan, nothing compares to William van Alen's Chrysler Building. With its sleek aluminum-banded facades and arched, pointed spire, it is definitely now my favorite piece of Art Deco architecture.

Finally, no tour of Art Deco would be complete without mentioning two literary figures who epitomize the period: the French writer, Colette, together with her American contemporary F. Scott Fitzgerald. A powerful woman of her time, Colette led an astonishingly full life. A prolific producer of scripts, fiction, and journalism, she also performed on stage, often outraging audiences, and had, predictably, a passionate and complex love life. Meanwhile on the other side of the Atlantic, Fitzgerald was wickedly satirizing the pursuit of the American dream in his novel *The Great Gatsby*—a wonderful exposé of the mores of the Art Deco era.

Paul Poiret was known for loosening the formal silhouette of fashion which had been prevalent in the early 1900s. His designs were exotic, elegant, and softly fitting, made out of boldly colored silks, brocades, and velvets, simply constructed but rich in texture. With this in mind, I designed an asymmetrical V-necked sweater. I think it would look great with his harem pants or his famous hobble skirt, which was denounced by the Pope, satirized by cartoonists, and the subject of fierce public debate at the time.

# POIRET SWEATER

**Sizes**
S (M, L).
Shown in sizes small (Pale Blue #47) and medium (Lavender #127).
Directions are for smallest size with larger sizes in parentheses.
If there is only1 set of numbers, it applies to all sizes.

**Finished measurements**
Bust 39 (43, 47)"
Length 28 (28, 28½)"

**Yarn**
28 (30, 32) skeins Rowan Lightweight DK
(each 1oz/25g, 73 yds/67m, 100% wool)

**Needles**
One pair each sizes 3 and 5 (3.25 and 3.75mm) needles, *or size to obtain gauge.*
Circular needle size 3 (3.25mm), 16"/40cm long.

**Extras**
Stitch markers and holders.
Three ⅜"/10mm buttons.

**Gauge**
30 sts and 36 rows to 4"/10 cm over Rosine pat using size 3 (3.25mm) needles.

**Rosine Pat**

8-st rep

**Harem Pat**

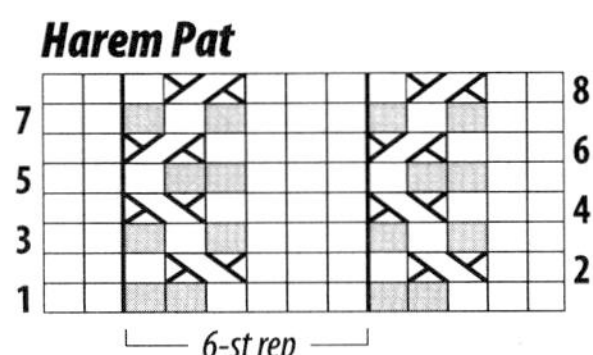


K on RS, p on WS
P on RS, k on WS
RT
LT

**STITCHES**

*Left Twist (LT)* K the 2nd st on left-hand needle through the back loop (tbl), do not sl off needle, k the first and 2nd sts on left-hand needle tog tbl, sl both sts off needle.
*Right Twist (RT)* K the 2nd st on left-hand needle, do not sl off needle, k the first st on left-hand needle, sl both sts off needle.

**Twisted Rib** (multiple of 4 sts plus 2)
*Row 1* (RS) *K2 tbl, p2; rep from* across, end k2 tbl.
*Row 2* *P2, k2 tbl; rep from* across, end p2. Rep rows 1–2 for Twisted Rib pat.

**Seed st** (over an odd number of sts)
*Row 1* (RS) *K1, p1; rep from* across, end k1. Rep row 1 for Seed st.

**Rosine pat** (multiple of 8 sts plus 4)
*Rows 1, 3, and 5* (WS) K1, p3, *k5, p3; rep from* across.
*Row 2* *LT, k1, p5; rep from* across, end LT, k1, p1.
*Row 4* *K1, LT, p5; rep from* across, end k1, LT, p1.
*Row 6* P1, *k2, p4, RT; rep from* across, end k2, p1.
*Row 7* K1, p2, *k1, p1, k4, p2; rep from* across, end k1.
*Row 8* P1, *k2, p3, RT, p1; rep from* across, end k2, p1.
*Row 9* K1, p2, *k2, p1, k3, p2; rep from* across, end k1.
*Row 10* P1, *k2, p2, RT, p2; rep from* across, end k2, p1.
*Row 11* K1, p2, *k3, p1, k2, p2; rep from* across, end k1.
*Row 12* P1, *k2, p1, RT, p3; rep from* across, end k2, p1.
*Row 13* K1, p2, *k4, p1, k1, p2; rep from* across, end k1.
*Row 14* P1, *k2, RT, p4; rep from* across, end k2, p1.
*Rows 15, 17, and 19* P3, *k5, p3; rep from* across, end k1.
*Row 16* P1, *k1, RT, p5; rep from* across, end k1, RT.
*Row 18* P1, *RT, k1, p5; rep from* across, end RT, p1.
*Row 20* P1, *k2, LT, p4; rep from* across, end k2, p1.
*Row 21* Rep row 13.
*Row 22* P1, *k2, p1, LT, p3; rep from* across, end k2, p1.
*Row 23* Rep row 11.
*Row 24* P1, *k2, p2, LT, p2; rep from* across, end k2, p1.
*Row 25* Rep row 9.
*Row 26* P1, *k2, p3, LT, p1; rep from* across, end k2, p1.
*Row 27* Rep row 7.
*Row 28* P1, *k2, p4, LT; rep from* across, end k2, p1. Repeat rows 1–28 for Rosine Pat.

**Harem pat** (multiple of 6 sts plus 1)
*Row 1* (WS) P2, *k2, p4; rep from* across, end last rep p3.
*Row 2* K2, *LT, k4; rep from* across, end last rep LT, k3.
*Row 3* P2, *k1, p1, k1, p3; rep from* across, end last rep p2.
*Row 4* K3, *LT, k4; rep from* across, end last rep LT, k2.
*Row 5* P3, *k2, p4; rep from* across, end last rep k2, p2.
*Row 6* K3, *RT, k4; rep from* across, end last rep RT, k2.
*Row 7* Rep row 3.
*Row 8 K2,* *RT, k4; rep from* across, end last rep RT, k3. Rep rows 1–8 for Harem Pat.

**BACK**

With smaller needles, cast on 146 (162, 174) sts. Work 17 rows in Twisted Rib pat, inc 3 (1,3) sts evenly across last row—149 (163, 177) sts. Change to larger needles. ***Beg pats: Row 1*** (WS) Work 49 (55, 61) sts in Harem Pat, place marker, work 100 (108, 116) sts in Rosine Pat. ***Row 2*** Work 100 (108, 116) sts in Rosine Pat, work 49 (55, 61) sts in Harem Pat. Work even in pats as established until piece measures 18½" from beg, end with a WS row.

**Shape armhole**

Work 12 sts and place them on hold, cont pat across to last 12 sts and place those 12 sts on hold. Turn and cont on rem 125 (139, 153) sts as foll: ***Next row*** (WS) Work 37 (43, 49) sts in Harem Pat, work 84 (92, 100) sts in Rosine Pat, end k4. ***Next row*** (RS) P4, work 84 (92, 100) sts in Rosine Pat, work 37 ( 43, 49) sts in Harem Pat. Cont in pats as established until piece measures measures 27½ (27½, 28)" from beg, end with a RS row.

**Shape right neck and shoulder**
*Next row* (WS) Work 40 (46, 52) sts and place rem sts on hold. Turn. *Next row* (RS) Dec 1 st (neck), work to end. Turn. *Next row* Bind off 12 (14, 16) sts (shoulder), work pat across to last 2 sts, k2tog. *Next row* Dec 1 st, work across. Turn. *Next row* Bind off 12 (14, 16) sts, work across. Turn and work 1 row even. Bind off rem sts.
**Shape left neck and shoulder**
With WS facing, join yarn and bind off center 45 (47, 49) sts, cont pat across. Turn. Reversing shapings, shape shoulder and neck as for right front.

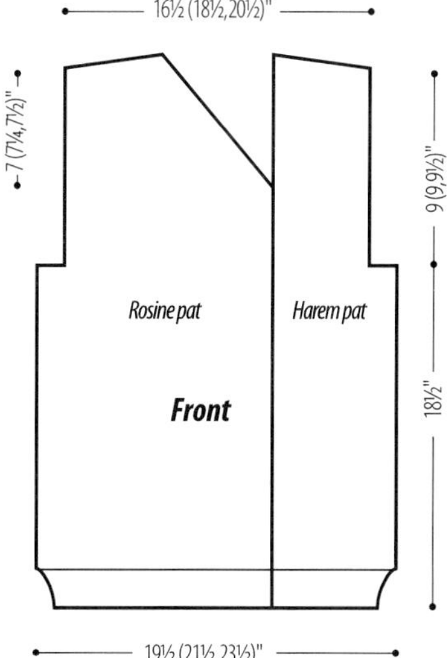


**FRONT**
Cast on and work Twisted Rib as for back. Reverse Rosine and Harem pats as foll: *Row 1* (WS) Work 100 (108, 116) sts in Rosine pat, place marker, work 49 (55, 61) sts in Harem pat. *Row 2* Work 49 (55, 61) sts in Harem pat, work 100 (108, 116) sts in Rosine pat. Work even in pats as established until piece measures 18½" from beg, end with a WS row.
**Shape armhole**
Work 12 sts and place them on hold, cont pat across to last 12 sts and place those 12 sts on hold. Turn and cont on rem 125 (139, 153) sts as foll: *Row 1* (WS) K4, work 84 (92, 100) sts in Rosine Pat, work 37 (43, 49) sts in Harem pat. *Row 2* Work 37 (43, 49) sts in Harem pat, work 84 (92, 100) sts in Rosine pat, p4. Work even in pats as established until piece measures 21 (20¾, 21)" from beg, end with a WS row.
**Work left neck and shoulder**
*Next row* (RS) Work 37 (43, 49) sts and place rem sts on hold. Turn. Cont Harem pat on these 37 (43, 49) sts until piece measures 27½ (27½, 28)" from beg, working shoulder shaping as for back.
**Shape right neck and shoulder**
With RS facing, join yarn to rem 88 (96, 104) sts and work as foll: Cont Rosine pat and dec 1 st at neck edge on next 48 (50, 52) rows, then every other row 3 times—37 (43, 49) sts. Work even until piece measures 27½ (27½, 28)" from beg, end with a RS row. Shape shoulder at beg of WS rows as for back.

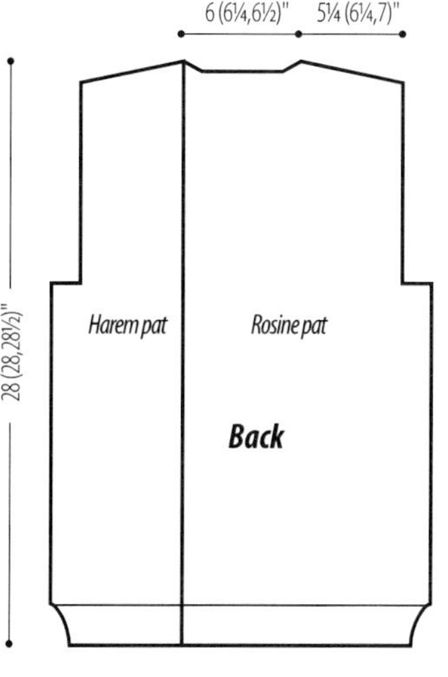


**LEFT SLEEVE**
Stabilize shoulder by working a running st along shoulder edge. Each shoulder seam measures approx 5¼ (6¼, 7)". Sew shoulder seams.
With RS facing and larger needles, pick up and k the 12 sts on hold at front armhole, 66 (66, 70) sts along armhole edge to shoulder seam, 66 (66, 70 ) sts along other side of armhole, 12 sts on hold at back armhole—156 (156, 164) sts. Beg with row 1, work in Rosine pat, AT SAME TIME, dec 1 st each side every 3rd row 10 (6, 16) times, then every 4th row 35 (39, 33) times—66 sts. Piece measures approx 19 (19½, 20)" from armhole. Change to smaller needles. Work 27 rows in Twisted rib pat. Bind off loosely in rib.

**RIGHT SLEEVE**
Pick up sts as for left sleeve, picking up 1 extra st at shoulder seam for sizes S and M, and 1 st less on back armhole edge on size L—157 (157, 163) sts. Beg with row 1, work Harem pat, AT SAME TIME, dec 1 st each side every 3rd row 10 (6, 12) times, then every 4th row 35 (39, 36) times—67sts. Piece measures approx 19 (19½, 20)" from armhole. Change to smaller needles. Dec1 st at beg of of first row and work 27 rows in Twisted rib pat. Bind off loosely in rib.

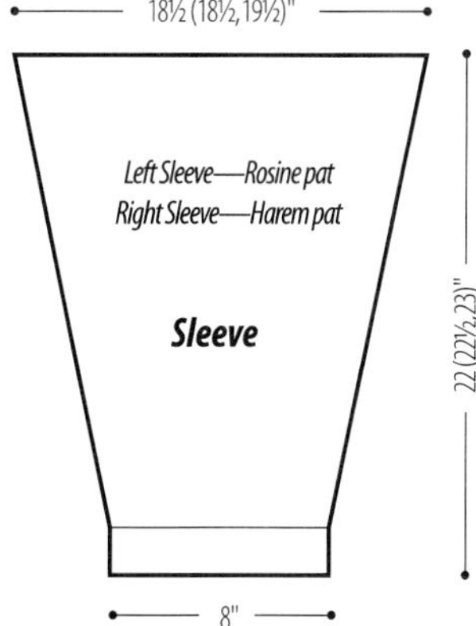


**COLLAR**
Mark sloping edge of front neck into 9 equal parts. Work collar and buttonholes simultaneously as foll: Work 3 buttonholes on RS rows when work measures ¾", 1½" and 2¼" as foll by working 3 sts, binding off 2 sts, working across. On next row, cast on 2 sts over bound-off sts of previous row. *Row 1* (RS) With smaller, circular needle, beg at lower edge of V-neck and pick up and k 7 (7, 8) sts to first marker. Turn. *Row 2* Work seed st over 7 (7, 8) sts. Turn. *Row 3* Work seed st again over these 7 (7, 8) sts, then pick up and k 7 (8, 8) sts to 2nd marker. *Row 4* Work seed st over 14 (15, 16) sts. In same way, work 12 rows more, working in seed st and picking up 7 (7, 8) sts, then 7 (8, 8) sts along neck every other row, until you have picked up 56 (60, 64) sts along neck edge. *Next row* (RS) Work seed st over 56 (60, 64) sts, pick up and k 6 (7, 8) sts to shoulder seam, 42 (44, 46) sts across back neck, 44 (47, 50) sts down vertical edge of front neck—148 (158, 168) sts. Work 15 rows even in seed st. Bind off in seed st.

**FINISHING**
Sew side and sleeve seams.
Sew 3 buttons on left side of neck band.

Colette, one of the great women writers and celebrities of the twentieth century, inspired this jacket. In her life and work, she was always at the heart of Parisian social and cultural life, presenting a liberated sensuality that helped to change the mores of her time. I suspect that she would have enjoyed the delicious contrast in this Norfolk-style jacket between the mannish tailored styling and the exquisite lambswool and silk yarn.

# COLETTE JACKET

**Sizes**

S/M (M/L).
Shown in sizes small/med (Oregano) and med/large (Indigo).
Directions are for smallest size with larger sizes in parentheses.
If there is only1 set of numbers, it applies to all sizes.

**Finished measurements**

Bust (buttoned) 42 (54)"
Length 28 (29)"

**Yarn**

14 (17) balls Jean Moss Lambswool/silk
(each 1¾oz/50g, 120yds/110m, 90% lambswool, 10% silk)

**Needles**

One pair each sizes 5 and 7 (3.75 and 4.5mm) needles,
*or size to obtain gauge.*

**Extras**

Stitch markers and holders.
Five ¾"/20mm buttons.
Two ⅝"/15mm buttons.

**Gauge**

20 sts and 28 rows to 4"/10 cm in St st using size 7 (4.5mm) needles.

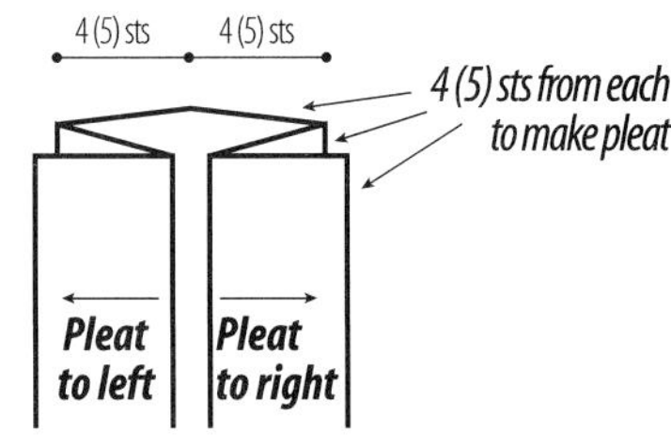


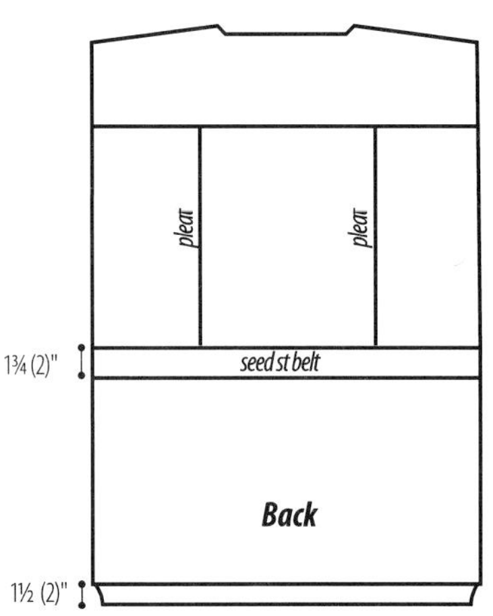


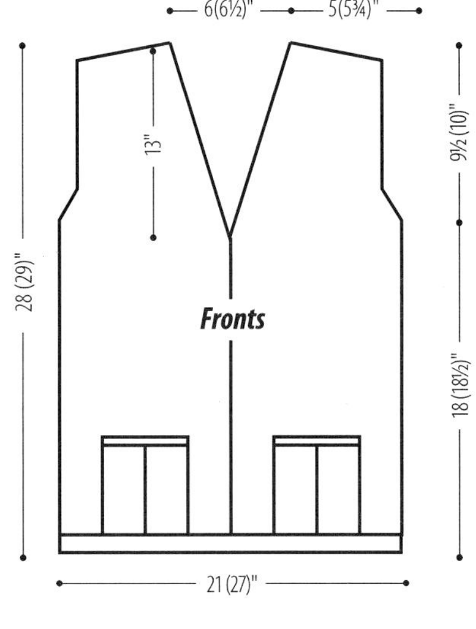


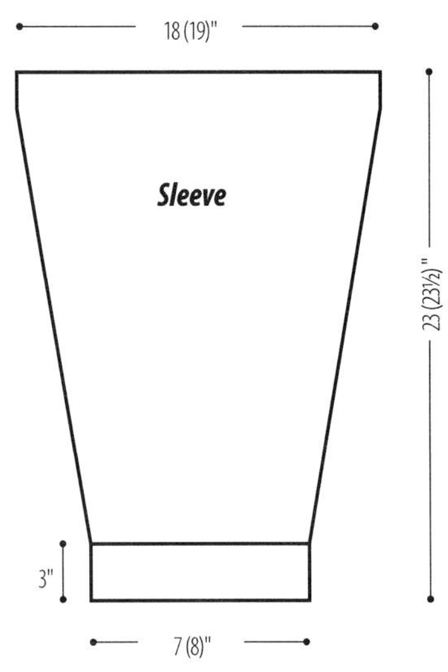


**STITCHES**

**Sido rib** (multiple of 4 plus 2)
***Row 1*** *K2, p2; rep from* to last 2 sts, k2.
***Row 2*** *P2, k2; rep from* to last 2 sts, p2.
Rep rows 1–2 for Sido rib pat.

**Seed st** (over an even number of sts)
***Row 1*** *K1, p1; rep from*.
***Row 2*** *P1, k1; rep from*.
Rep rows 1–2 for Seed st pat.

**BACK**

With smaller needles and 2 strands of yarn held tog, cast on 106 (126) sts. Work 1½ (2)" in Sido rib. Change to larger needles. Work in St st until piece measures 11¾" from beg. Bind off all sts.

**Work seed st belt**

With RS facing and smaller needles, pick up and k 76 (92) sts evenly across bound-off edge. Work 1¾ (2)" in Seed st. Bind off in Seed st. Mark center of belt. Mark 4 (4½)" on each side of center. With RS facing and larger needles, beg at side edge and pick up and k 19 (22) sts along top of belt to first marker, *cast on 16 (20) sts (pleat),* then beg directly after the last st picked up and pick up another 40 (46) sts past center marker to 3rd marker; rep between*'s once, then pick up another 19 (22) sts evenly to end of belt—110 (130) sts. Cont in St st until piece measures 23 (23½)" from beg, end with a WS row. Bind off all sts.

**Shape pleats**

Use diagram as guide to making pleats. Mark center back, then mark 4 (4½)" on each side of center. With RS facing and smaller needles, pick up and k 15 (17) sts, then **pleat next 12 (15) sts to the right as foll: Count 4 (5) sts in and fold back. Count the next 4 (5) sts, then fold again. Count a final 4 (5) sts—3 thicknesses for pleat (see diagram). Insert needle through first st of each layer and k3tog. In same way, work through next 3 (4) sts. Pleat the next 12 (15) sts to the left: *Count 4 (5) sts, fold, rep from*, then count a further 4 (5) sts and then work 4 (5) sts through the 3 thicknesses of pleat as before. Pick up and k 32 (36) sts and then rep the right and left pleat from**. Then pick up and k 15 (17) sts to end of row—78 (90) sts. Cont in Seed st until back measures 27½ (28½)" from beg, end with a WS row.

**Shape neck and shoulders**

Work 28 (32) sts, bind off 22 (26) sts, work to end. Turn and work each side separately. ***Row 1*** (WS) Work to last 2 sts, p2tog. R***ow 2*** K2tog, work to end. ***Row 3*** Bind off 12 (14) sts, work to last 2 sts, p2tog. ***Row 4*** K2tog, work to end. ***Row 5*** Bind off rem sts.
With WS facing, join yarn and work other side to correspond to first side, reversing shaping.

**LEFT FRONT**

With smaller needles, cast on 52 (62) sts and work 1½ (2)" in Sido rib. Change to larger needles. Work in St st until piece measures 15 (15½)" from beg, end with a RS row.

**Shape neck**

Dec 1 st at neck edge on next row, then every 5th row 0 (8) times, every 6th row 14 (8) times—38 (46) sts. AT SAME TIME, when piece measures 18 (18½)" from beg, end with a WS row.

**Shape armhole**

***Next row*** (RS) K2, ssk, work to end. In same way, dec 1 st at armhole edge every other row 14 (18) times. Work even until piece measures 27¾ (28¾)" from beg, end with a WS row.

**Shape shoulder**

Bind off 12 (14) sts at beg of next row. Work 1 row even. Bind off rem 12 (14) sts.

**RIGHT FRONT**

Work to correspond to left front, reversing shaping. Reverse armhole shaping as foll: On a RS row, work to last 4 sts, k2tog, k2.

**SLEEVES**

With smaller needles, cast on 42 (48) sts. Work 3" in Sido rib and inc 14 (16) sts evenly across last row—56 (64) sts. Change to larger needles. Cont in St st, AT SAME TIME, inc 1 st each side every 6th row 10 (0) times, every 7th row 10 (14) times, then every 8th row 0 (4) times—96 (100) sts. Work even until piece measures 23 (23½)" from beg. Bind off all sts.

**POCKETS** (make 2)

With larger needles, cast on 46 sts and work 4½" in St st, end with a WS row.

**Pocket tops**
With smaller needles, k first 8 sts of pocket, then pleat 15 sts to the right: Count 5 sts and fold back. Count the next 5 sts and fold again. Count a final 5 sts—3 thicknesses for pleat. Insert needle through the first st of each layer and k3tog. In same way, work 3 sts tog across rem 4 sts. In same way, pleat the next 15 sts to the left, then k to end of row—26 sts. Work ¾" in Seed st. Bind off all sts.

**LEFT FRONT BAND**
With smaller needles, cast on 7 sts and work in Seed st until band fits along left front to beg of neck shaping. Sew the band to front as you knit, stretching slightly to fit. At neck, leave sts on hold. Place 5 markers for buttons, the first ½" from lower edge, the last ½" from beg of neck shaping, and 3 others spaced evenly between.

**BUTTONHOLE BAND AND LAPEL**
Work as for left front band, working vertical buttonholes on RS rows opposite markers: Work 3 sts, turn, work 2 rows on these 3 sts and then leave on st holder. Cut yarn, join to rem 4 sts and work 3 rows. Cut yarn and work next row across all 7 sts.
When all 5 buttonholes have been worked, end with a WS row.
**Shape lapel**
Working in Seed st, inc 1 st at neck edge on next row, then every 3rd row until there are 27 sts. Work even until piece measures 10½ (11)" from beg of lapel shaping, end with a WS row. Bind off 7 sts at beg of next row. Place rem 20 sts on hold.
Work left lapel in same way, reversing shaping. Both lapels should end 2½" from shoulder when sewn on.

**COLLAR**
With RS facing and smaller needles, pick up and k 28 (32) sts across back neck. Working in Seed st, work 16 short rows, picking up and k (or p depending on whether it is a RS or WS row) 6 sts at end of every row along neck edge for 4 rows (this should bring you to the edge of lapel) and then pick up 4 sts at end of every row from top of lapels for 10 rows, keeping Seed st correct—92 (96) sts. Work another 2". Bind off loosely in Seed st.

**FINISHING**
Sew shoulder seams. On back, fold pleats and sew to top of back belt. Place markers 9½ (10)" down from shoulder on front and back. Sew top of sleeves between markers. Sew side and sleeve seams. Fold pleats on pockets along cast-on edge and sl st in place. Sew pockets 1½ (2)" from front band seam and 1¾ (2)" up from cast-on edge. Using photo as guide, sew larger buttons to band and one smaller button on each pocket.

**Sizes**
S (M, L).
Shown in medium (Boteh Brown #2278) and large (Kani Teal #2260).
Directions are for smallest size with larger sizes in parentheses.
If there is only 1 set of numbers, it applies to all sizes.

**Finished measurements**
**Jacket** Bust (buttoned) 38 (40, 42)", Length 20 (21, 22)"
**Skirt** Hip 36 (38, 40)", Length 18 (19, 20)" or 35 (36, 37)"

**Yarn**
Classic Elite Tapestry
**Jacket** 12 (13, 14) skeins
**Short Skirt** 7 (8, 9) skeins
**Long Skirt** 13 (14, 15) skeins
(each 1¾oz/50g, 95yds/87m, 25% mohair, 75% wool).

**Needles**
**Jacket** One pair each sizes 3 and 6 (3.25 and 4mm) needles, *or size to obtain gauge.* Size 3 (3.25mm) circular needle, 16"/40cm long.
**Skirt** Sizes 3 and 6 (3.25 and 4mm) circular needles, each 24"/60cm long.

**Extras**
**Jacket** Stitch markers and holders. Eight ½"/12mm glass buttons.
**Skirt** 26 (28, 30)" of 1" elastic.

**Gauge**
**Jacket and Skirt** 24 sts and 28 rows to 4"/10 cm in Ninotchka rib pat (slightly stretched) using size 6 (4mm) needles.



Designed with Greta Garbo in mind, I wanted to create a matching skirt and jacket that was glamorous, sexy, and sophisticated just like her. With a choice of long or short skirt length, the shapely jacket is a contemporary take on classic thirties' styling. Knitted in a lustrous mix of mohair and wool, it's just the sort of thing that Garbo might have worn under her trench coat.

# GARBO JACKET AND SKIRT

**STITCHES**

**Seed st** (over any number of sts)
***Row 1*** *K1, p1; rep from* across.
***Row 2*** K the purl sts and p the knit sts.
Rep row 2 for seed st.

**JACKET**

**BACK**

With larger needles, cast on 115 (121, 127) sts. Beg with row 1, work Ninotchka Chart through row 141 (147, 155), shaping armhole from row 83 (87, 91) as foll: bind off 5 sts at beg of next 2 rows. Dec 1 st each side of next row, then every row 12 (16, 14) times more, then every other row 4 (2, 5) times—71 (73, 77) sts. ***Shape neck and shoulder from row 137 (143, 151) as foll:*** Work 19 (20, 22) sts, turn and place next 52 (53, 55) sts on hold. Dec 1 st at beg of next row, work to end. Bind off 8 (9, 10) sts at beg of row, work to last 2 sts, k2tog. Work 1 row even. Bind off rem sts. With RS facing, join yarn to rem sts and bind off 33 sts. Work other side to correspond to first side, reversing shaping.

**LEFT FRONT**

With larger needles, cast on 57 (60, 63) sts. Beg with row 1, work Ninotchka Chart through row 140 (146, 154), working armhole shaping from row 83 (87, 91) as indicated on chart. Shape neck from row 91 (97, 105) as foll: Dec 1 st at neck edge on next row, then every other row 9 times more, then every 3rd row 8 times. Shape shoulder from row 138 (144, 152) as foll: Bind off 8 (9, 10) sts at beg of next row. Work 1 row even. Bind off rem sts.

**RIGHT FRONT**

With larger needles, cast on 57 (60, 63) sts. Beg with row 1, work Ninotchka Chart through row 141 (147, 155), working armhole shaping from row 84 (88, 92) as indicated on chart. Shape neck from row 91 (97, 105) as indicated on chart to correspond to left front. Work shoulder shaping from row 140 (146, 154) as indicated on chart to correspond to left front.

**SLEEVE**

See Camille Chart and directions on p. 54.

**FINISHING**

Block pieces. Sew shoulder seams.

**Band**

With RS facing and circular needle, beg at lower right front edge and pick up and k evenly to beg of neck shaping as foll: Pick up 2 sts, cast on 2 sts and skip a corresponding space on front edge, [pick up 7 (8, 9) sts, cast on 2 sts and leave space as before] twice, pick up 8 (9, 9) sts, cast on 2 sts and leave space, pick up 8 (8, 10) sts, cast on 2 sts and leave space, pick up 8 (9, 9) sts, cast on 2 sts and leave space, [pick up 7 (8, 9) sts, cast on 2 sts and leave space] twice, (space for these last 2 sts should be at point where the V-neck shaping starts). Cont to pick up 46 sts to shoulder seam, 35 (37, 39) sts across back neck, 46 sts along left neck to beg of V-neck shaping and 70 (76, 82) sts down to lower left front edge—267 (281, 295) sts. Work 3 rows in seed st. Bind off all sts.

Set in sleeves, easing any fullness evenly across top of cap. Sew side and sleeve seams. Sew buttons opposite buttonholes, taking care that the pattern is in line across the jacket.

**SKIRT** (knit circularly in one piece)

With larger circular needle, cast on 220 (231, 242) sts. Being careful not to twist sts, place marker, join and work in Ninotchka pat as foll: ***Rnd*** 1 (RS) *K1, p2, k1, yo, k2tog, k1, p2, k1, p1; rep from* around. ***Rnd 2*** *K1, p2, k1, k2tog, yo, k1, p2, k2; rep from* around. Rep rnds 1–2 until piece measures 16¾ (17¾, 18¾)" (short version) or 33¾ (34¾, 35¾)" (long version) from beg, and for size M only, dec 1 st at end of final rnd—220 (230, 242) sts. Change to smaller circular needle and work 1¼" in k1, p1 rib. P 1 rnd for turning ridge. Work 1¼" more in k1, p1 rib. Bind off loosely.

**FINISHING**

Block piece lightly. Fold waistband at turning ridge and sew to WS loosely, leaving an opening for elastic. Cut elastic to fit comfortably around waist. Thread elastic through waistband, making sure it is not twisted. Sew ends tog securely. Sew opening closed, catching lower edge of elastic as you sew. Sew a small stitch at other side, securing lower edge of elastic to waistband to avoid twisting when worn.

**STITCHES**

***Left Twist (LT)*** K the 2nd st on left-hand needle through the back loop (tbl), do not sl off needle, k the first and 2nd sts on left-hand needle tog, sl both sts off needle.

***Right Twist (RT)*** K the 2nd st on left-hand needle, do not sl off needle, k the first st on left-hand needle, sl both sts off needle.

**Seed St** (over an odd number of sts)

***All rows*** *K1, p1; rep from* end k1.

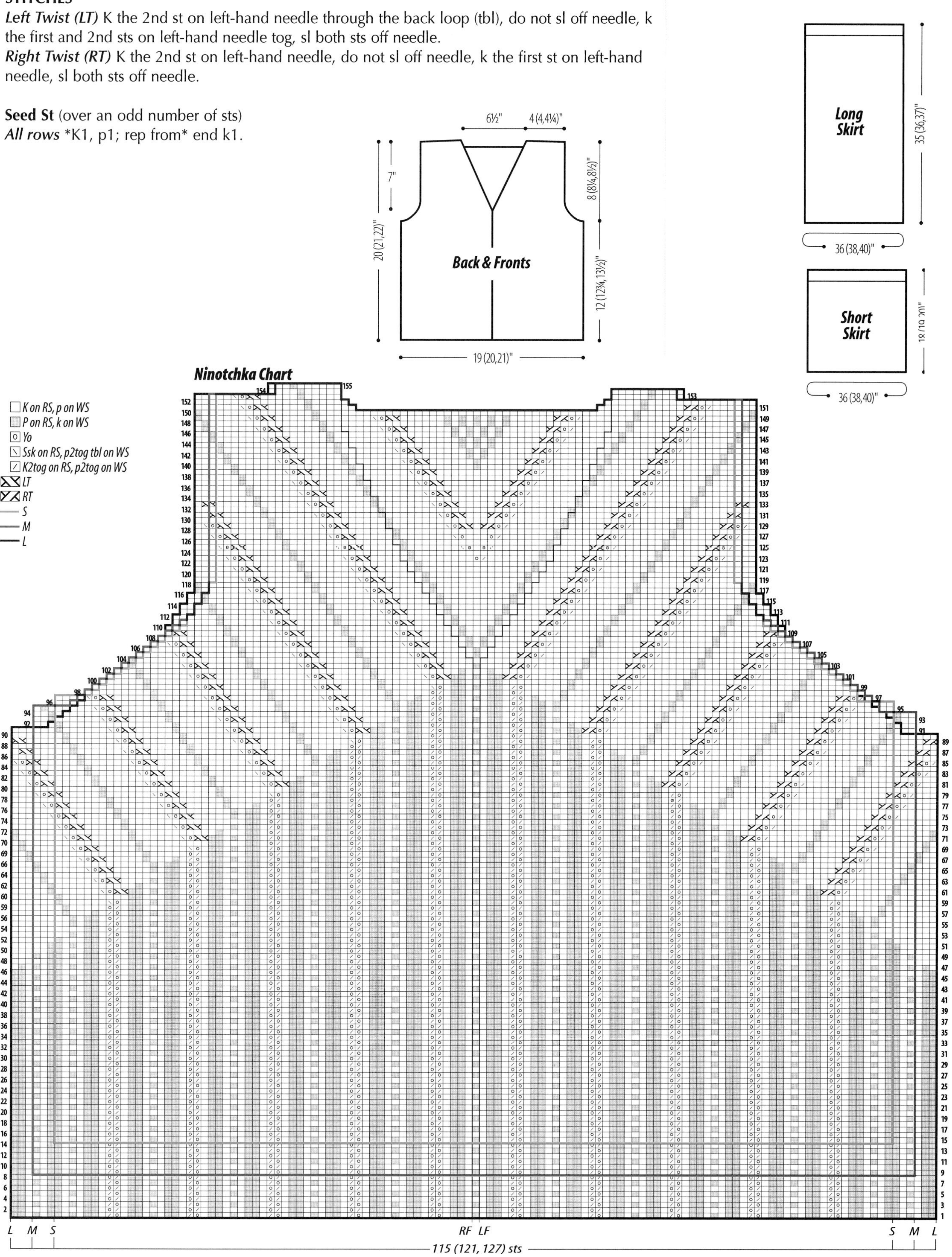

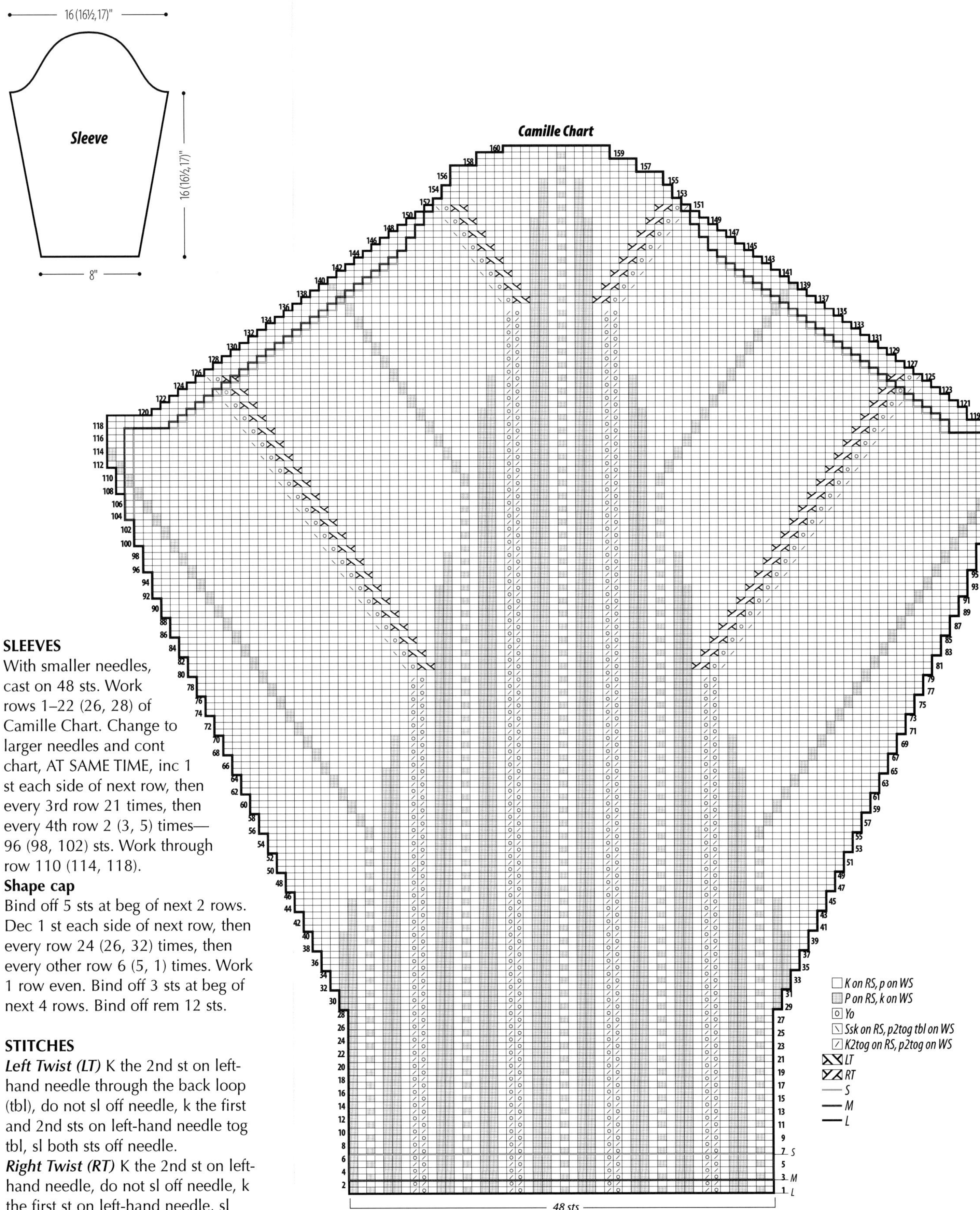


**SLEEVES**

With smaller needles, cast on 48 sts. Work rows 1–22 (26, 28) of Camille Chart. Change to larger needles and cont chart, AT SAME TIME, inc 1 st each side of next row, then every 3rd row 21 times, then every 4th row 2 (3, 5) times—96 (98, 102) sts. Work through row 110 (114, 118).

**Shape cap**

Bind off 5 sts at beg of next 2 rows. Dec 1 st each side of next row, then every row 24 (26, 32) times, then every other row 6 (5, 1) times. Work 1 row even. Bind off 3 sts at beg of next 4 rows. Bind off rem 12 sts.

**STITCHES**

***Left Twist (LT)*** K the 2nd st on left-hand needle through the back loop (tbl), do not sl off needle, k the first and 2nd sts on left-hand needle tog tbl, sl both sts off needle.

***Right Twist (RT)*** K the 2nd st on left-hand needle, do not sl off needle, k the first st on left-hand needle, sl both sts off needle.

The elegant women featured on the covers of *Harper's Bazar* between 1916 and 1926 were in my thoughts when I designed this sweater. The covers were produced by Erté who also designed sets for the Folies Bergère in Paris. I can easily see this sweater in one of his highly stylized drawings, worn with a little velvet bolero and trailing skirt, the whole festooned with scarves and several ropes of jewels. Alpaca yarn in the vibrant Cilantro Green or rich Persimmon Orange typical of the period adds a further touch of luxury.

# ERTÉ SWEATER

**Sizes**

S (M, L).
Shown in sizes small (Cilantro #1172) and medium (Persimmon #1178).
Directions are for smallest size with larger sizes in parentheses.
If there is only 1 set of numbers, it applies to all sizes.

**Finished measurements**

Bust 38 (42, 46)"
Length 22 (23, 24)"

**Yarn**

9 (10, 12) skeins Classic Elite Inca Alpaca (each 1¾oz/50g, 115yds/105m, 100% alpaca)

**Needles**

One pair each sizes 2 and 5 (3 and 3.75mm) needles, *or size to obtain gauge.*

**Extras**

Stitch markers and holders.

**Gauge**

24 sts and 34 rows to 4"/10 cm in Saluki pat using size 5 (3.75mm) needles.

**Harper's Pat**

*6-st rep*

- K on RS, p on WS
- P on RS, K on WS
- Yo
- K2tog
- Ssk
- Sl 1wyif-k2tog-psso

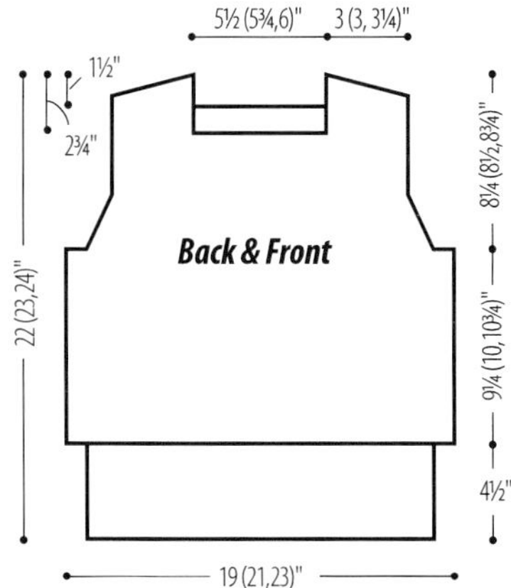


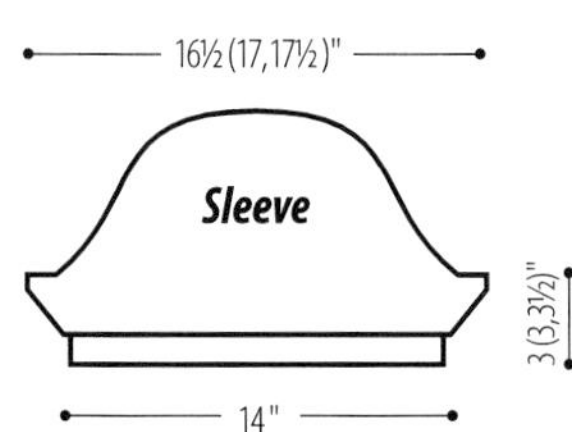


**STITCHES**

**Harper's Rib** (multiple of 10 sts)
*Row 1* (RS) *K1, p2, k1, yo, k2tog, k1, p2, k1; rep from* across.
*Row 2* *P1, k2, p1, yo, p2tog, p1, k2, p1; rep from* across.
Rep rows 1–2 for Harper's rib pat.

**Saluki pat** (multiple of 6 sts plus 1)
*Row 1* (WS) K2, p3, *k3, p3; rep from* across, end k2.
*Row 2* P2, *k3, p3; rep from* across, end k3, p2.
*Row 3* Rep row 1.
*Row 4* K2, *yo, sl 1 wyif, k2tog, psso, yo, k3; rep from* across, end yo, sl 1 wyif, k2tog, psso, yo, k2.
*Rows 5 and 7* P2, k3, *p3, k3; rep from* across, end p2.
*Row 6* K2, *p3, k3; rep from* across, end p3, k2.
*Row 8* K2tog, yo, *k3, yo, sl 1 wyif, k2tog, psso, yo; rep from* across, end k3, yo, ssk.
Rep rows 1–8 for Saluki pat.

**Seed st** (over an odd number of sts)
*Row 1* *K1, p1; rep from* across.
Rep row 1 for seed st pat.

**BACK**

With smaller needles, cast on 110 (120, 130) sts. Work 4½" in Harper's rib pat, end with row 1 and inc 5 (7, 9) sts evenly across last row—115 (127, 139) sts.
Change to larger needles. Beg with row 1, work in Saluki pat until piece measures 13¾ (14½, 15¼)" from beg, end with a WS row.

**Shape armhole**

Cont pat, bind off 6 (6, 7) sts at beg of next 2 rows. Dec 1 st each side every other row 8 (13, 16) times—87 (89, 93) sts. Work even until piece measures 19¼ (20¼, 21¼)" from beg, end with a WS row. *Next row* (RS) Work Saluki pat across 18 (18, 19) sts, place marker, then with smaller needles, work seed st over next 51 (53, 55) sts, place 2nd marker, then with larger needles, work Saluki pat across rem 18 (18, 19) sts. Work even in pats as established until piece measures 20½ (21½, 22½)" from beg, end with a WS row.

**Shape right neck**

With larger needles, work pat across 18 (18, 19) sts, with smaller needles, work seed over 9 sts, turn and place rem sts on hold. Work even on 27 (27, 28) sts until piece measures 21½ (22½, 23½)" from beg, end with a WS row.

**Shape shoulder**

*Bind off 9 sts (shoulder), work to end. Work 1 row even. Rep from* once. Bind off rem sts.

**Shape left neck**

With RS facing and smaller needles, join yarn and bind off 33 (35, 37) sts, work seed st over 9 sts, then with larger needles, work Saluki pat over rem 18 (18, 19) sts. Complete as for right neck and shoulder (binding off at beg of WS rows).

**FRONT**

Work as for back until piece measures 18 (19, 20)" from beg, end with a WS row. *Next row* (RS) Work Saluki pat across 18 (18, 19) sts, place marker, then with smaller needles, work seed st over next 51 (53, 55) sts, place 2nd marker, then with larger needles, work Saluki pat across rem 18 (18, 19) sts. Work even in pats as established until piece measures 19¼ (20¼, 21¼)" from beg, end with a WS row. Shape neck and shoulders as for back.

**SLEEVES**

With smaller needles, cast on 80 sts. Work ¾" in Harper's rib pat, end with row 1 and inc 5 sts evenly across row—85 sts.
Change to larger needles. Beg with row 1, work in Saluki pat, AT SAME TIME, inc 1 st each side (working incs into pat) every other row 7 (8, 10) times—99 (101, 105) sts. Work even until piece measures 3 (3, 3½)" from beg, end with a WS row.

**Shape cap**

Bind off 6 (6, 7) sts at beg of next 2 rows. Dec 1 st each side every row 22 (24, 26) times, then every other row 9 (8, 7) times more. Bind off 3 sts at beg of next 4 rows. Bind off rem sts.

**FINISHING**

Block pieces. Sew shoulder seams. Set in sleeves, easing in any fullness evenly across top of shoulder. Sew side and sleeve seams.

The wonderful films of Fred Astaire and Ginger Rogers are an unforgettable part of my childhood. I can imagine Astaire wearing this vest in *Flying Down to Rio* or *Top Hat,* gracefully twirling Rogers around the set. The herringbone design is an old favorite and I've combined it with light-as-a-feather silken tweed yarn to create a garment which I hope will do justice to Astaire's legendary sartorial elegance.

# ASTAIRE WAISTCOAT

**Sizes**

S (M, L).

Shown in sizes small (Blue Mint #702) and medium (Damson #705).

Directions are for smallest size with larger sizes in parentheses. If there is only 1 set of numbers, it applies to all sizes.

**Finished measurements**

Chest 42 (45, 48)"

Length 21(22, 23)"

**Yarn**

6 (6, 7) balls Rowan Silk Tweed (each 1¾oz/50g, 120yds/110m, 55% wool, 37.5% silk, 7.5% cotton)

**Needles**

One pair each sizes 3 and 6 (3.25 and 4mm) needles. Size 3 (3.25mm) circular needle, 24"/60cm long.

**Extras**

Stitch markers and holders.

Five ⅞"/22mm buttons.

**Gauge**

20 sts and 26 rows to 4"/10cm in Swing st using size 6 (4mm) needles.

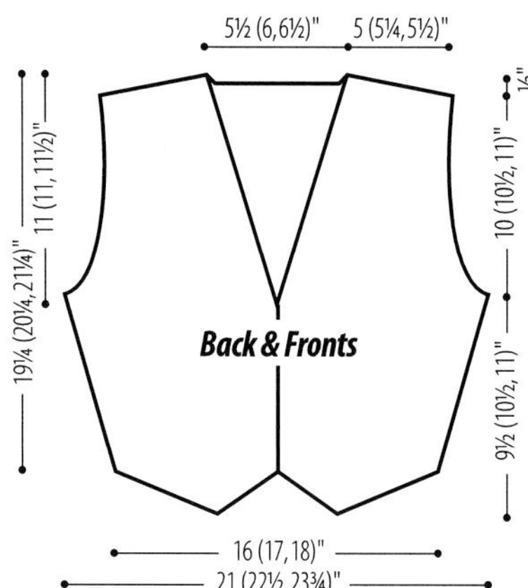


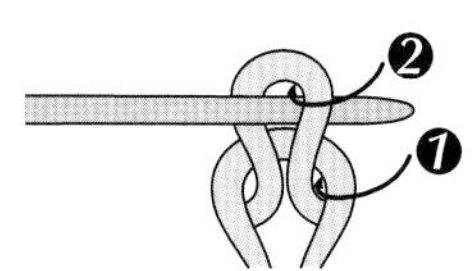


**Lifted Increase**
Knit into next st on left-hand needle in row below as shown in ❶, then knit into next st ❷.

## STITCHES

**Swing stitch** (multiple of 6 sts plus 1)
NOTE Work incs and decs in pairs, working a dec only when you have enough sts to work the corresponding inc.
***Row 1*** (RS) *K2tog, k2, lifted inc, k2; rep from* across, end k1.
***Rows 2 and 4*** Purl.
***Row 3*** (RS) K1, *k2, lifted inc, k2, k2tog; rep from*.
Rep rows 1–4 for Swing st.

## BACK

With smaller needles, cast on 85 (92, 99) sts. K 5 rows. Purl 1 row. Change to larger needles, Beg with row 1, work in Swing st, AT SAME TIME, inc 1 st each side (working incs into Swing st) every 4th row 2 (0, 0) times, every 5th row 8 (8, 4) times, then every 6th row 0 (2, 6) times—105 (112, 119) sts. When piece measures 9¼ (9¾, 10¼)" from beg, end with a WS row.

**Shape armhole**
Bind off 5 sts at beg of next 2 rows. Dec 1 st each side of next 5 rows, then every other row 4 (5, 6) times—77 (82, 87) sts. Work even in pat until armhole measures 9½ (10, 10½)" from beg, end with a WS row.

**Shape neck and shoulder**
Work 25 (27, 28) sts; turn and leave rem 52 (55, 59) sts on hold. Work each side of neck separately. Dec 1 st at beg of next row. Bind off 12 (13, 13) sts at beg of next row. Work 1 row even. Bind off rem sts.
With RS facing, leave center 27 (28, 31) sts on hold and join yarn to rem sts. Work to correspond to first side, reversing shaping.

## LEFT FRONT

**Pocket linings** (make 2)
With larger needles, cast on 21 (24, 25) sts. Beg with a p row, work 2½ (3, 3)" in St st. Leave sts on hold.
With larger needles, cast on 2 sts. Work rows 1–20 of Left Front Chart, using backward loop cast-on on right of chart, and k into front and back of first st for incs on left of chart. When 20 rows are completed, cont in Swing st (rep chart rows 17–20), AT SAME TIME, inc 1 st at beg (side edge) of every 4th row 2 (0, 0) times, then at same edge every 5th row 8 (8, 4) times, every 6th row 0 (2, 6) times—51 (54, 57) sts. When piece measures 5½ (6, 6)" from 2-st cast-on, end with a WS row.
**Place pocket:** ***Next row*** (RS) Pat 13 (13, 15) sts, place next 21 (24, 25) sts on hold, pat 21 (24, 25) sts of first pocket lining, pat 11. Cont pat until piece measures 9½ (10½, 11)" from 2-st cast-on, end with a RS row.

**Shape neck and armhole**
Dec 1 st at beg of next row, then every 5th row 12 (12, 13) times more, AT SAME TIME, when piece measures same as back along side edge, shape armhole at side edge as for back. Work even until armhole measures same as back to shoulder, end with a WS row.

**Shape shoulder**
Bind off 12 (13, 13) sts at beg of next row. Work 1 row even. Bind off rem sts.

## RIGHT FRONT

Work as for left front, referring to Right Front Chart for shaping at lower edge and reversing all other shaping and pocket placement.

## FINISHING

Block pieces. Sew shoulder seams.

**Armbands**
With RS facing and smaller needles, beg at underarm and pick up and k 108 (112, 120) sts evenly around each armhole edge. K 3 rows, binding off on last row.
Beg above the garter st border on the back, sew side seams and armbands.

**Front bands**
With RS facing and circular needle, beg at lower edge of right side seam and pick up and k 33 (36, 38) sts to point of right front, place marker (pm), 1 st at point, pm, 18 sts up sloping edge to center front, pm, 1 st at inside corner, pm, 35 (40, 42) sts along straight edge to beg of V-neck shaping, 58 (58, 60) sts to shoulder seam, 30 (32, 32) sts across back neck, 58 (58, 60) sts down left neck to beg of V-neck shaping, 35 (40, 42) sts down straight edge of left front, pm, 1 st at inside corner, pm, 18 sts along sloping edge to point, pm, 1 st at point, pm and 33 (36, 38) sts to lower side seam of left front—322 (340, 350) sts. ***Row 1*** Knit and inc 1 st before and after each marker. ***Row 2*** K to 2 sts after mitred corner at centerfront, bind off 2 sts, k 5 (7, 7) sts,

bind off 2 sts, k 6 (7, 7) sts, bind off 2 sts, k 6 (7, 8) sts, bind off 2 sts, k 6 (7, 8) sts, bind off 2 sts, k to end. ***Row 3*** Knit and inc 1 st before and after each marker, casting on 2 sts over bound-off sts of previous row. ***Row 4*** Knit. ***Row 5*** Knit and bind off at same time, and inc 1 st before and after markers before binding off, taking care as you go round the mitred edges that you bind off loosely so as not to make them rounded.

**Pocket Edgings**

With RS facing, sl 21 (24, 25) pocket sts onto smaller needles. Join yarn and k 4 rows, binding off on last row.

Sew edgings to fronts. Sew buttons opposite buttonholes.

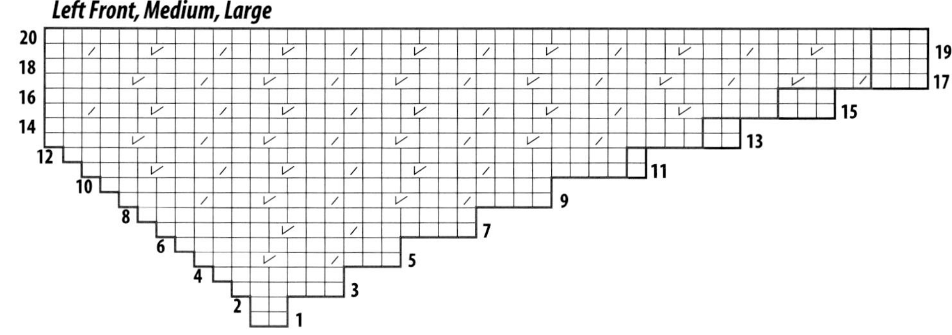


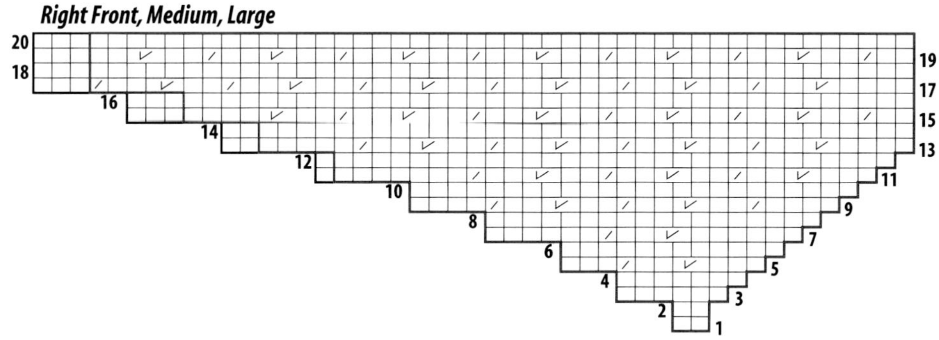


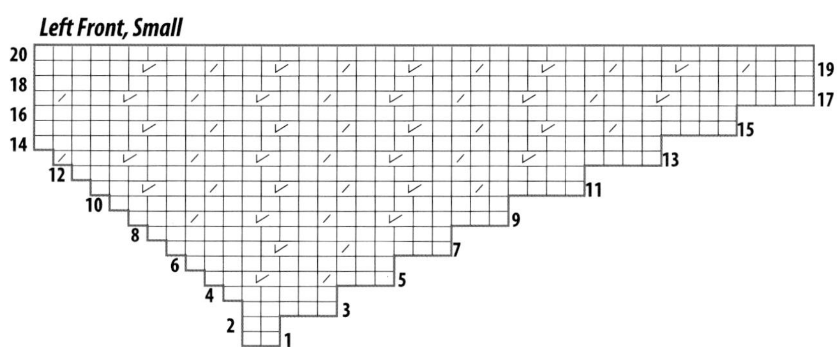


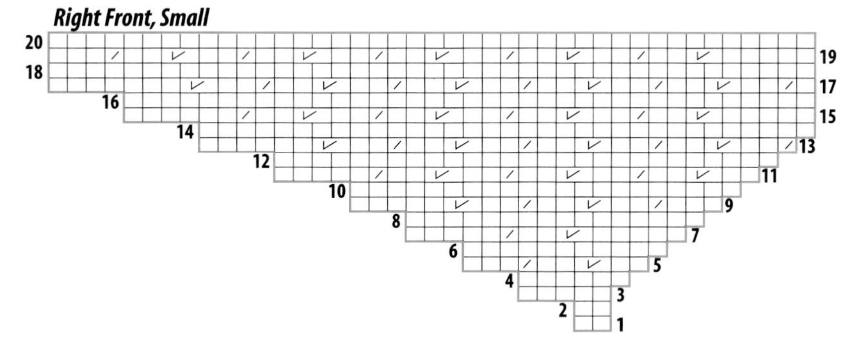


K on RS, p on WS
K2tog
K 2tog on L, k on M
Lifted inc
Lifted inc on L, k2 on M
Small
Medium
Large

I have always loved the clothes worn in the film *The Great Gatsby*. F. Scott Fitzgerald wrote the novel which epitomized the mood and manners of the 1920s and 1930s, the Jazz Age, as he called it. Much of his work was autobiographical. Can't you just see a young Fitzgerald in *Tender is the Night* wearing this sweater?

# FITZGERALD SWEATER

**Sizes**
S (M, L).
Shown in sizes small (Chestnut) and medium (Dark Turquoise).
Directions are for smallest size with larger sizes in parentheses.
If there is only 1 set of numbers, it applies to all sizes.

**Finished measurements**
Chest 49½ (52½, 56)"
Length 28"

**Yarn**
9 (11, 13) skeins Colinette Skye Pure Wool Aran (each 3½oz/100g, 164yds/150m, 100% wool)

**Needles**
One pair each sizes 8 and 10 (5 and 6mm) needles, *or size to obtain gauge.*
Circular needle size 8 (5mm), 16"/40cm long.

**Extras**
Stitch markers and holders.

**Gauge**
17 sts and 24 rows to 4"/10 cm in Gatsby Chart pat using size 10 (6mm) needles.

**Jazz rib pat** (multiple of 10 sts + 2)
***Rows 1 and 3*** *P2, k3, p3, k1, p1; rep from* to last 2 sts, p2.
***Row 2*** K2, *p1, k1, p1, k2, p3, k2; rep from*.
***Row 4*** K2, *p3, k3, p1, k3; rep from*.
***Row 5*** *P2, k1, p1, k1, p2, k3; rep from* to last 2 sts, p2.
***Row 6*** K2, *p3, k3, p1, k3; rep from*.
Rep Rows 1–6 for Jazz rib pat.

**BACK**
With smaller needles, cast on 102 (112, 112) sts. Work 10 rows in Jazz rib pat, inc 4 (0, 8) sts evenly across final row—106 (112, 120) sts. Change to larger needles. ***Beg Gatsby Chart: Row 1*** (RS) Work sts 12–16 (0, 13–16), work 16-st rep 6 (7, 7) times, end by working sts 1–5 (0, 1–4). Cont to work chart pat as established until piece measures 18 (17½, 17½)" from beg, end with a WS row.

**Shape armhole**
Bind off 4 (5, 6) sts at beg of next 2 rows. Dec 1 st each side of next row, then every other row 3 (3, 4) times more—90 (94, 98) sts. Work even in pat until piece measures 27½" from beg, end with a WS row.

**Shape shoulder and neck**
Work 32 (33, 35) sts, place center 26 (28, 28) sts on hold, join a 2nd ball of yarn and work to end. Working both sides at same time, dec 1 st at neck edge once, then bind off from shoulder edge 15 (16, 17) sts once, 16 (16, 17) sts once.

**FRONT**
Work as for back until piece measures 25¼" from beg, end with a WS row.

**Shape neck**
Work 39 (40, 42) sts, place center 12 (14, 14) sts on hold, join a second ball of yarn and work to end. Working both sides at same time, dec 1 st at neck edge every row 4 times, then every other row 4 times. Work even in pat, and when piece measures same as back to shoulder, shape shoulder as for back.

**SLEEVES**
With smaller needles, cast on 42 sts. Work 18 rows in Jazz Rib pat, inc 6 sts evenly across final row—48 sts. Change to larger needles. ***Beg Gatsby Chart: Row 1*** (RS) Work 16-st rep of chart 3 times. Cont to work chart pat as established, AT SAME TIME, inc 1 st each side (working inc sts into chart pat) every 4th row 0 (5, 5) times, every 5th row 6 (14, 14) times, then every 6th row 10 (0, 0) times—80 (86, 86) sts. Work even until piece measures 19¼ (19¼, 19)" from beg, end with a WS row.

**Shape cap**
Bind off 4 (5, 6) sts at beg of next 2 rows. Dec 1 st each side of next row, then every other row 3 (3, 4) times more. Bind off rem sts.

**FINISHING**
Block pieces lightly. Sew shoulder seams.

**Neckband**
With RS facing and circular needle, beg at left shoulder seam, and pick up and k 20 (22, 22) sts along left front neck, 12 (14, 14) sts on hold, 20 (22, 22) sts along right front neck, 3 sts from right back neck, 26 (28, 28) sts on hold, and 3 sts from left back neck—84 (92, 92) sts. Place marker, join and work 2" in rnds of k2, p2 rib. K 5 rnds. Bind off loosely.
Set in sleeves. Sew side and sleeve seams.

6½ (7,7)"
7¼ (7½,8)"
2¾"
9½ (10,10)"
28"
*Front and Back*
16½ (16,16)"
1½"
24¾ (26¼,28)"

19 (20,20)"
*Sleeve*
19¼ (19¼,19)"
3"
9¾"

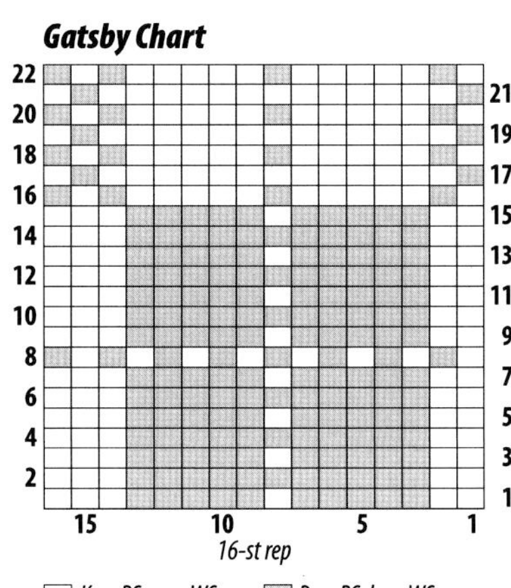

Coco Chanel's wonderfully chic, innovative designs of the twenties and thirties are a constant inspiration. In this infant's jacket I wish to express the pared down simplicity of her style. Never one for dressing my children in traditional baby colors, I love the subtly beautiful painterly tones of the bouclé yarn, which also adds a textured dimension to the piece.

# COCO 1 JACKET

**Sizes**

S (M, L).

Shown in sizes large (Earth #61) and in photo on this page (Toscana #55).

Directions are for smallest size with larger sizes in parentheses. If there is only 1 set of numbers, it applies to all sizes.

**Finished measurements**

Chest (zipped) 26 (29½, 31)"

Length 13 (13¾, 14½)"

**Yarn**

4 (4, 5) skeins Colinette Bouclé (each 3½oz/100g, 98yds/90m, 100% wool).

**Needles**

One pair each sizes 8 and 10 (5 and 6mm) needles, *or size to obtain gauge.*

**Extras**

Stitch holders.

One 10 (11, 12)" zipper.

**Gauge**

14 sts and 21 rows to 4"/10 cm in St st using size 10 (6mm) needles.

### BACK and FRONTS

(NOTE Body is worked in one piece to armhole.)

With smaller needles, cast on 89 (97, 105) sts. Work 2" in k1, p1 rib, inc 1 st at end of last row—90 (98, 106) sts. Change to larger needles. ***Row 1*** (RS) Knit. ***Row 2*** (WS) K2, purl to last 2 sts, k2. Rep rows 1–2 until piece measures 7½ (7¾, 8)" from beg, end with row 2.

**Divide for armholes**

*Next row* (RS) K19 (20, 22) sts and place these sts on hold (right front), bind off 7 (9, 9) sts (underarm), k until there are 38 (40, 44) sts (back), bind off 7 (9, 9) sts (underarm), k to end and place these sts on hold (left front). Do not cut yarn.

### BACK

With larger needles and WS facing, join another ball of yarn and beg with a p row, cont in St st until piece measures 12½ (13¼, 14)" from beg, end with a WS row.

**Shape neck**

*Next row* (RS) K13 (14, 15) sts, place center 12 (12, 14) sts on hold, join a 2nd ball of yarn and k to end. Working both sides at same time, dec 1 st at each neck edge on next row. Bind off rem 12 (13, 14) sts each side.

### LEFT FRONT

With WS facing and larger needles, join yarn and p to last 2 sts, k2. Cont in St st, keeping 2 sts at center front in garter st (k every row). When piece measures 10¾ (11¼, 12)" from beg, end with a WS row.

**Shape neck**

*Next row* (RS) K to last 3 (3, 4) sts and place them on hold. Dec 1 st at neck edge on next row, then every other row 3 times more—12 (13, 14) sts. Work even in St st until piece measures 13 (13¾, 14½)" from beg. Bind off all sts.

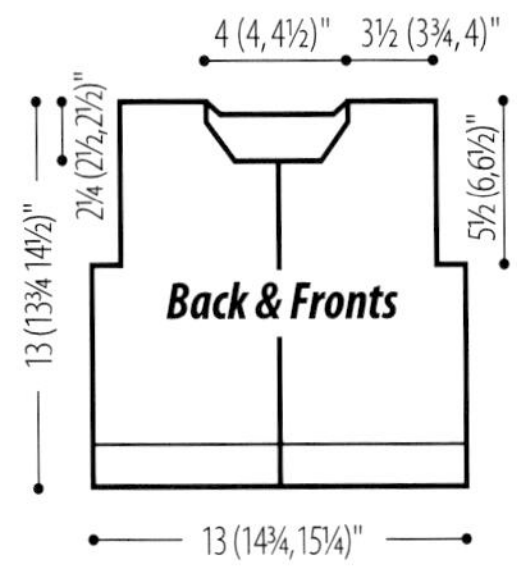


### RIGHT FRONT

With WS facing and larger needles, join yarn and k2, then p across. Complete to correspond to left front, reversing neck shaping and keeping 2 sts at center front in garter st.

### SLEEVES

With smaller needles, cast on 25 (27, 29) sts. Work 2" in k1, p1 rib and inc 1 st at end of last row—26 (28, 30) sts. Change to larger needles. K 1 row and inc 1 st each side. Cont in St st, AT SAME TIME, inc 1 st each side every 6th row 5 (3, 7) times more, then every 7th row 0 (3, 0) times—38 (42, 46) sts. Work even until piece measures 9 (11, 11½)" from beg. Bind off all sts.

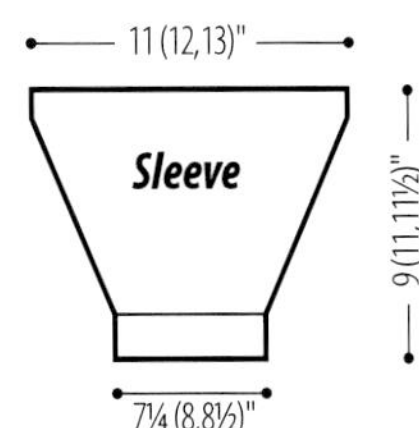


### FINISHING

Block pieces lightly. Sew shoulder seams.

**Hood**

With RS facing and smaller needles, beg at right front neck edge and pick up and k3 (3, 4) sts on hold, 9 (11, 11) sts to shoulder seam, 2 sts along right back neck, [k5 (5, 6), k2tog, k5 (5, 6)] from holder at center back, 2 sts along left back neck, 9 (11, 11) sts to sts on hold and 3 (3, 4) sts on hold at left neck—39 (43, 47) sts. ***Rows 1 and 3*** (WS) K2, *k1, p1; rep from* to last 3 sts, end k3. ***Rows 2 and 4*** K2, *p1, k1; rep from* to last 3 sts, end p1, k2. Change to larger needles. ***Row 5*** K2, p4 (4, 6), *p2, M1; rep from* to last 7 (7, 9) sts, end p5 (5, 7), k2—52 (58, 62) sts, 13 (15, 15) incs in all. Cont in St st, keeping 2 sts at center front in garter st as established, until hood measures 5¾ (6, 6½)" from beg, end with a WS row.

**Shape hood**

***Row 1*** K25 (28, 30), k2tog, k25 (28, 30). ***Row 2*** K2, p23 (26, 28), p2tog, p22 (25, 27), k2. ***Row 3*** K24 (27, 29), k2tog, k24 (27, 29). ***Row 4*** K2, p22 (25, 27), p2tog, p21 (24, 26), k2. ***Row 5*** K23 (26, 28), k2tog, k23 (26, 28). ***Row 6*** K2, p21 (24, 26), p2tog, p20 (23, 25), k2. ***Row 7*** K22 (25, 27), k2tog, k22 (25, 27). ***Row 8*** K2, p20 (23, 25), p2tog, p19 (22, 24), k2—44 (50, 54) sts. With RS facing, k22 (25, 27) sts, then fold hood with RS tog, placing needles parallel. With a 3rd needle, work 3 needle bind-off in purl.

Set in sleeves. Sew sleeve seams. Sew zipper evenly along front opening.

The simple elegance in the work of Coco Chanel inspired this cozy all-in-one. Easy and quick to knit in cuddly and colorful bouclé yarn, it's guaranteed to keep your baby snug through the worst winter weather.

**Sizes**
S (M, L).
Shown in sizes small (Toscana #55) and in photo on this page (Earth #61).
Directions are for smallest size with larger sizes in parentheses. If there is only 1 set of numbers, it applies to all sizes.

**Finished measurements**
Chest 26 (29½, 31)"
Length 24 (27¾, 30½)"

**Yarn**
5 (5, 6) skeins Colinette Bouclé (each 3½oz/100g, 98yds/90m, 100% wool)

**Needles**
One pair each sizes 8 and 10 (5 and 6mm) needles, *or size to obtain gauge.*

**Extras**
Stitch holders.
One 10 (11, 12)" zipper.

**Optional**
6 snaps.

**Gauge**
14 sts and 21 rows to 4"/10 cm in St st using size 10 (6mm) needles.

# COCO 2 ALL-IN-ONE

4 (4, 4½)" 3½ (3¾, 4)"

Back & Fronts

24 (27¾, 30½)"

5½ (6, 6½)"

7½ (7¾, 8)"

11 (14, 16)"

13 (14¾, 15¼)"

11 (12, 13)"

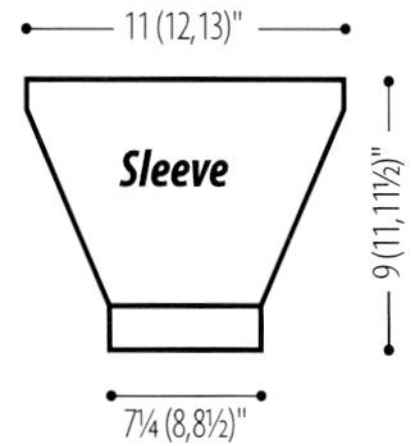


9 (11, 11½)"

7¼ (8, 8½)"

**LEGS**

With smaller needles, cast on 25 (27, 29) sts. Work 2" in k1, p1 rib. Change to larger needles and St st. ***Next (inc) row*** (RS) K2, M1, work to last 2 sts, M1, k2—27 (29, 31) sts. Cont in St st, AT SAME TIME, inc 1 st each side every 5th row 8 (5, 3) times, then every 6th row 0 (4, 7) times—43 (47, 51) sts. When piece measures 11 (14, 16)" from beg, end with a RS row. *Next row* (WS) Inc 1 st each side and p across—45 (49, 53) sts. Place sts on hold. In same way, make 2nd leg.

**Join legs and work body**

*Next row* (RS) K across both legs—90 (98, 106) sts. *Next row* (WS) K2, p 86 (94, 102), k2. Cont in St st, keeping first and last 2 sts each row in garter st (k every row), and when piece measures 18½ (21¾, 24)" from beg, end with a WS row.

**Divide for armholes**

*Next row* (RS) K19 (20, 22) sts and place on hold (right front), bind off 7 (9, 9) sts (underarm), k until there are 38 (40, 44) sts more on right-hand needle (back), bind off 7 (9, 9) sts (underarm), k to end and place on hold (left front). Do not cut yarn.

**BACK**

With larger needles and WS facing, join another ball of yarn and cont in St st until piece measures 23½ (27¼, 30)" from beg, end with a WS row.

**Shape neck**

*Next row* (RS) K13 (14, 15), place center 12 (12, 14) sts on hold, join a 2nd ball of yarn and k to end. Working both sides at same time, dec 1 st at neck edge on next row, then bind off rem sts.

**LEFT FRONT**

With larger needles and WS facing, join yarn and k2, then p to end. Cont in St st, keeping 2 sts at center front in garter st, until piece measures 21¾ (25¼, 28)" from beg, end with a WS row.

**Shape neck**

*Next row* (RS) Work to last 3 (3, 4) sts and place them on hold. Dec 1 st at neck edge on next row, then every other row 3 times more. Work even on rem sts in St st until piece measures 24 (27¾, 30½)" from beg. Bind off all sts.

**RIGHT FRONT**

With larger needles and WS facing, join yarn and p to last 2 sts, k2. Cont in St st and complete to correspond to left front, keeping 2 sts at center front in garter st and reversing shaping.

**SLEEVES**

With smaller needles, cast on 25 (27, 29) sts. Work 2" in k1, p1 rib and inc 1 st at end of last row—26 (28, 30) sts. Change to larger needles. K 1 row and inc 1 st each side—27 (29, 31) sts. Cont in St st, AT SAME TIME, inc 1 st each side (working incs into St st) every 6th row 6 (4, 8) times, then every 7th row 0 (3, 0) times—38 (42, 46) sts. Work even until piece measures 9 (11, 11½)" from beg. Bind off all sts.

**FINISHING**

Block pieces lightly. Sew shoulder seams.

**Hood**

With RS facing and smaller needles, beg at right front neck and pick up and k3 (3, 4) sts on hold, 9 (11, 11) sts to shoulder seam, 2 sts along right back neck, [k5 (5, 6), k2tog, k5 (5, 6)] from holder at center back, 2 sts along left back neck, 9 (11, 11) sts to sts on hold, and 3 (3, 4) sts on hold at center front—39 (43, 47) sts. ***Next row: Rows 1 and 3*** (WS) K2, *k1, p1; rep from* to last 3 sts, end k3. ***Rows 2 and 4*** K2, *p1, k1; rep from* to last 3 sts, end p1, k2. Change to larger needles. ***Row 5*** K2, p4 (4, 6), *p2, M1; rep from* to last 7 (7, 9) sts, end p5 (5, 7), k2—52 (58, 62) sts and 13 (15, 15) incs in all. Work even in St st, working 2 sts each side at center front in garter st, until hood measures 5¾ (6, 6½)" from beg, end with a WS row.

**Shape hood**

***Row 1*** K25 (28, 30), k2tog, k25 (28, 30). ***Row 2*** K2, p23 (25, 27), p2tog, p22 (25, 27), k2. ***Row 3*** K24 (27, 29), k2tog, k24 (27, 29). ***Row 4*** K2, p22 (25, 27), p2tog, p21 (24, 26), k2. ***Row 5*** K23 (26, 28), k2tog, k23 (26, 28). ***Row 6*** K2, p21 (24, 26), p2tog, p20 (23, 25), k2. ***Row 7*** K22 (25, 27), k2tog, k22 (25, 27). ***Row 8*** K2, p20 (23, 25), p2tog, p19 (22, 24), k2—44 (50, 54) sts. With RS facing, k22 (25, 27) sts, then fold hood with RS tog and needles parallel to each other. With a 3rd needle, work 3-needle bind-off in purl.

Set in sleeves. Sew sleeve seams. Sew zipper along fronts. Sew rest of center front seam to crotch. Sew leg seams OR sew ribs and attach 6 snaps along inseam if preferred.

The joyous combinations of bold color and offbeat geometric design found in the work of ceramic designer Clarice Cliff inspired this boxy jacket. The diamond sculptured pattern, highlighted also in the ribs and collar, is colored with the vibrant orange and jazzy royal blue so often found in her work.

# CLARICE JACKET

**Sizes**

1–2 (3–4, 5–6) yrs. Shown in sizes 3–4 yrs (Regent's Park Orange) and 5–6 yrs (Victoria Royal). Directions are for smallest size with larger sizes in parentheses. If there is only 1 set of numbers, it applies to all sizes.

**Finished measurements**

Chest (buttoned) 30 (32½, 35)"

Length 14 (15½, 17)"

**Yarn**

4 (4, 5) skein Classic Elite London Tweed (each 3½oz/100g, 196yds/180m, 100% wool)

**Needles**

One pair each sizes 8 and 10 (5 and 6mm) needles, *or size to obtain gauge.*

**Extras**

Stitch markers and holders. Five ¾"/18mm buttons.

**Gauge**

22 sts and 22 rows to 4"/10 cm in Bizarre pat using size 10 (6mm) needles.

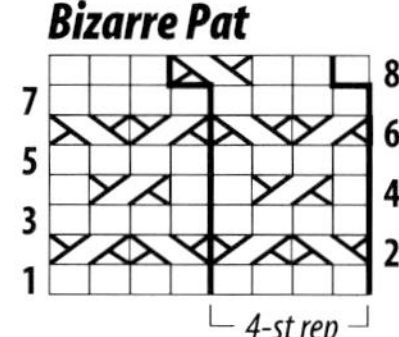


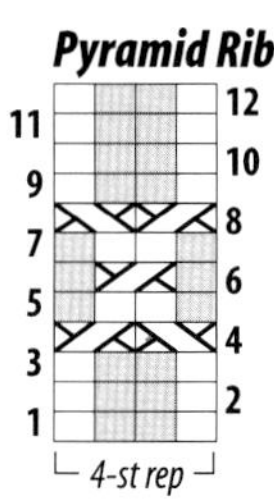


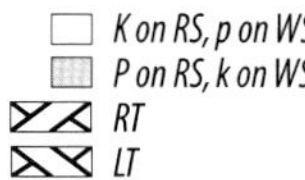


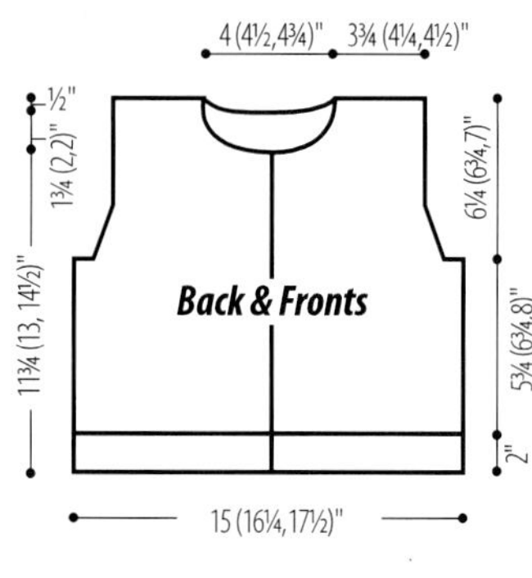


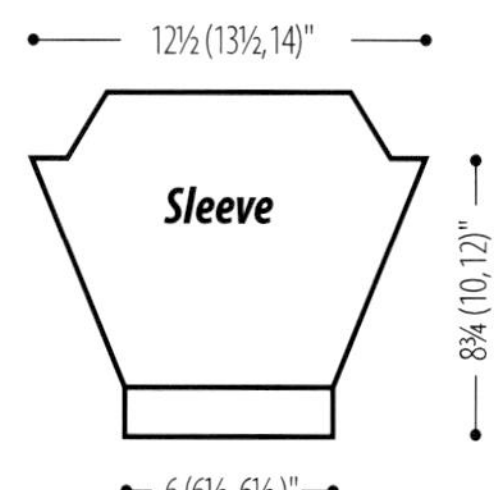


**STITCHES**

***Left Twist (LT)*** K the 2nd st on left-hand needle through the back loop (tbl), do not sl off needle, k the first and 2nd sts tog tbl, sl both sts off needle.
***Right Twist (RT)*** K the 2nd st on left-hand needle, do not sl off needle, then k first st, sl both sts off needle.

**Bizarre pat** (multiple of 4 sts)
***Row 1 and all WS rows*** (WS) Purl.
***Row 2*** *LT, RT; rep from*.
***Row 4*** *K1, RT, k1; rep from*.
***Row 6*** *RT, LT; rep from*.
***Row 8*** K1, *k2, LT; rep from* to last 3 sts, k3.
Rep rows 1–8 for Bizarre pat.

**Pyramid rib** (multiple of 4 sts)
***Rows 1 and 3*** (WS) *P1, k2, p1; rep from*.
***Row 2*** *K1, p2, k1; rep from*.
***Row 4*** *LT, RT; rep from*.
***Rows 5 and 7*** *K1, p2, k1; rep from*.
***Row 6*** *P1, RT, p1; rep from*.
***Row 8*** *RT, LT; rep from*.
***Rows 9 and 11*** *P1, k2, p1; rep from*.
***Rows 10 and 12*** *K1, p2, k1; rep from*.

**BACK**

With smaller needles, cast on 84 (92, 96) sts and work rows 1–12 of Pyramid rib pat. Change to larger needles. Beg with row 1, work in Bizarre pat until piece measures 7¾ (8¾, 10)" from beg, end with a WS row.

**Shape armhole**

Bind off 5 sts at beg of next 2 rows. Dec 1 st each side of next row, then every other row 4 times more—64 (72, 76) sts. Work even until piece measures13½ (15, 16½)" from beg, end with a WS row.

**Shape neck**

Work 23 (26, 27) sts, turn and leave rem 41 (46, 49) sts on hold. Work each side of neck separately. Dec 1 st at beg of next row. Dec 1 st at end of next row. Bind off rem 21 (24, 25) sts. With RS facing, leave center 18 (20, 22) sts on hold, join yarn to rem sts and work to end. Reverse shaping and work to correspond to first side.

**Pocket linings** (make 2)
With larger needles, cast on 16 (16, 18) sts. Work 2 (2½, 2½)" in St st. Leave sts on hold.

**LEFT FRONT**

With smaller needles, cast on 45 (49, 53) sts. Work Pyramid rib and work odd st as foll: ***Row 1*** (WS) P1, *p1, k2, p1; rep from* to end. ***Row 2*** *K1, p2, k1; rep from* to last st, k1. Cont to p first st on WS rows and k the last st on RS rows, AT SAME TIME, work buttonhole (for boys) starting on Row 3 as foll: ***Row 3*** P1, *p1, k2, turn, and work 2 more rows on these 4 sts, keeping pat correct. With WS facing join yarn to rem sts and work 3 rows in pat, then work across all sts on row 4. Work through row 12 of rib pat.
Change to larger needles. Place first 6 sts on hold. Work row 1 of Bizarre pat on rem 39 (43, 47) sts and inc 1 st at beg of row—40 (44, 48) sts. Cont in Bizarre pat until piece measures 4 (4¼, 4½)" from beg, end with a RS row. ***Place pocket: Next row*** (WS) P12 (14, 15), place next 16 (16, 18) sts on hold, with WS facing, p across 16 (16, 18) sts of pocket lining, p to end. Cont pat until piece measures 7¾ (8¾, 10)" from beg, end with a WS row.

**Shape armhole**

*Next row* (RS) Bind off 5 sts, work to end. Cont pat and dec 1 st at beg of next 5 RS rows—30 (34, 38) sts. Work even until piece measures 11¾ (13, 14½)" from beg, end with a RS row.

**Shape neck**

*Next row* (WS) Bind off 3 (3, 4) sts, work to end. Dec 1 st at neck edge on next row, then every other row 5 (6, 8) times more. Work even until piece measures 14 (15½, 17)" from beg. Bind off rem sts.

**RIGHT FRONT**

Work to correspond to left front. Work Pyramid rib as foll: ***Row 1*** (WS) *P1, k2, p1; rep from* to last st, p1. ***Row 2*** K1, *k1, p2, k1; rep from* to end. Cont to p last st on WS rows and k first st on RS rows through row 12. Work buttonhole (for girls) starting on row 3. Change to larger needles. Work in Bizarre pat, working row 1 as foll: ***Row 1*** (WS) P38 (42, 46), inc 1 st in next st, place rem 6 sts on hold. Cont on 39 (43, 47) sts, reversing pocket placement, armhole, and neck shaping.

**SLEEVES**

With smaller needles, cast on 36 (40, 40) sts. Work rows 1–12 of Pyramid rib and for last 2 sizes only, rep rows 11–12 once. Change to larger needles. Work in Bizarre pat, AT SAME TIME, inc 1 st each side (working incs into Bizarre pat) every other row 13 (12, 8) times, then every 3rd row 3 (5, 11) times—68 (74, 78) sts. Work even until piece measures 8¾ (10, 12)" from beg, end with a WS row.

**Shape cap**

Bind off 5 sts at beg of next 2 rows. Dec 1 st each side of next row, then every other row 4 times more. Bind off rem sts.

**FINISHING**

Block pieces lightly.

Place 5 markers for buttons on right (for girls) or left (for boys) front, the first opposite buttonhole in bottom rib, the last ¼" from beg of neck shaping and 3 others spaced evenly between.

**Left band**

Sew band to front as you knit, stretching slightly to fit. With WS facing, sl 6 sts on hold to smaller needles and cont rib as foll: ***Row 1*** (WS) P2, k2, p2. ***Row 2*** K2, p2, k2. Rep rows 1–2, working 4 vertical buttonholes (for boys) to correspond to button markers. Bind off all sts.

**Right band**

Work as for left band, working buttonholes (for girls) if necessary.

**Collar**

Sew shoulder seams. With RS facing and smaller needles, beg 3 sts in from center front edge of band and pick up and k 6 (6, 7) sts along horizontal neck edge, 17 (19, 19) sts to shoulder, 28 (28, 30) sts across back, 17 (19, 19) sts down left neck and 6 (6, 7) sts along neck edge, end 3 sts in from edge of band—74 (78, 82) sts. ***Row 1*** (WS) K2, *p2, k2; rep from*. ***Row 2*** P2, *k2, p2; rep from*. ***Rows 3-10*** Rep rows 1–2. ***Row 11*** K1, *LT, RT; rep from* to last st, k1. ***Row 12*** P1 *k1, p2, k1; rep from* to last st, p1. ***Row 13*** K1, *p1, RT, p1; rep from* to last st, k1. ***Row 14*** Rep row 12. ***Row 15*** K1, *RT, LT; rep from* to last st, k1. Change to larger needles. ***Row 16*** Rep row 2. ***Row 17*** Rep row 1. Bind off loosely.

**Pocket edgings**

Sl 16 (16, 18) pocket sts to smaller needles, ready to work a RS row. ***Row 1*** K1 (1, 2), *p2, k2; rep from* to last 3 (3, 0) sts, p2 (2, 0), k1 (1, 0). Work 1 (1, 2) rows more in rib pat as established. Bind off all sts.

Set in sleeves. Sew side and sleeve seams. Sew pocket linings to WS. Sew pocket edgings to RS. Sew buttons opposite buttonholes.

The New York City skyline would not be the same without the Chrysler Building. Built by the American car maker Walter Percy Chrysler in 1929, it is a perfect example of its period. Its stylish contours and elegant design are reflected in the cable fan pattern of this throw, the gorgeously luminous mercerized cotton shimmering like its namesake.

# CHRYSLER THROW

**Size**

Approx 48" wide by 62" long (without fringe).

Shown in Mediterranean Olive (#2081) and Hydrangea (#2088).

**Yarn**

34 balls Classic Elite Newport (each 1¾oz/50g, 70yds/64m, 100% cotton)

**Needles**

Size 9 (5.5mm) circular needle, 36"/90cm long, *or size to obtain gauge.*

Size K/10½ (7mm) crochet hook.

**Extras**

Cable needle.

**Gauge**

20 sts and 22 rows to 4"/10 cm in Van Alen pat using size 9 (5.5mm) needles.

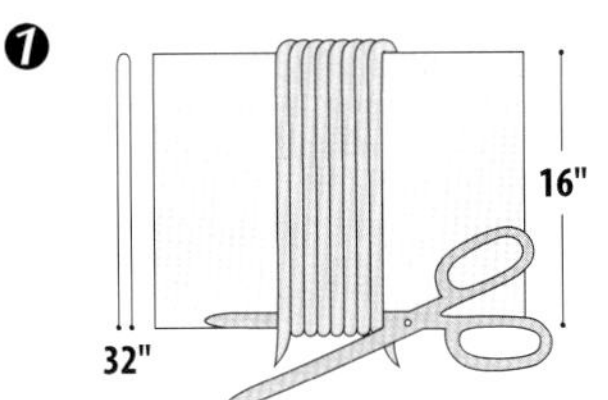


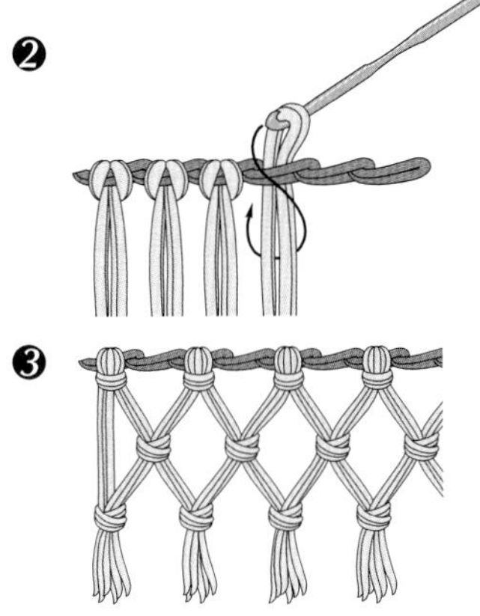

## STITCHES

**Seed st** (over an odd number of sts)
*Row 1* *K1, p1, rep from* to last st, k1. Rep row 1 for Seed st.

**3/4 Right Cross (3/4RC)**
Sl 4 sts to cable needle, hold to back of work, k3, then k4 from cable needle.

## THROW

Cast on 217 sts. Work back and forth in rows as foll: ***Beg Van Alen Chart: Row 1*** (WS) Work 7 sts in Seed st, reading chart from left to right, work sts 38–6, then work 30-st rep 5 times across, rep sts 35–16, end by working 7 sts in Seed st. ***Row 2*** (RS) Work 7 sts in Seed st, reading chart from right to left, work chart sts 16–35, work 30-st rep 5 times across, rep sts 6–38, end by working 7 sts in Seed st. Omitting the start of another fan at side edge on rows 20–31, work chart rows 1–32 a total of 9 times more, then rep rows 1–19—339 rows. Bind off all sts.

## FINISHING

Make a tasseled edging along the cast-on and bound-off edges. Attach tassels evenly along width of throw, beg at side edge and placing one tassel at end of each row of fan cables and one tassel in between.
❶ Cut 32" long strands of yarn. ❷ Fold 6 strands of yarn held tog in half. With crochet hook, pull the 6 folded strands through throw edge, then draw ends through and tighten. There should be an even number of fringe when attached. ❸ Make 4 rows of knots by taking 6 strands from one fringe and tying them to 6 strands in the next fringe across the row (leave the first and last 6 strands loose on the first row of knots). Rep this process, starting and ending with the 6 loose strands. Rep the first row of knots as in diagram.

***Van Alen Chart***

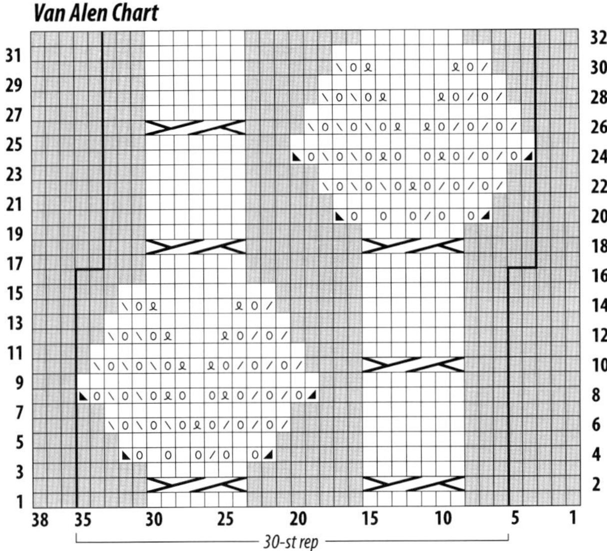


- K on RS, p on WS
- P on RS, k on WS
- Yo
- K2tog
- Ssk
- K3tog
- K3tog tbl
- K1 tbl
- 3/4 RC

In Rudolph Valentino the Art Deco period saw the emergence of the world's first great screen lover. Exotic and romantic, he was idolized by millions of women, many of whom deeply mourned his untimely death. This asymmetrical design, using lustrous mercerized cotton, is the perfect pillow for sweet dreams.

# VALENTINO PILLOW

**Size**

Small 18" x 18"; large 28" x 28". Shown in small (Natural #2016) and large (Periwinkle #2092). Directions are for smaller size with larger size in parentheses. If there is only 1 set of numbers, it applies to both sizes.

**Yarn**

9 (20) balls Classic Elite Newport (each 1¾oz/50g, 70yds/64m, 100% cotton)

**Needles**

One pair each sizes 7 and 9 (4.5 and 5.5mm) needles, *or size to obtain gauge.* Size 7 (4.5mm) double-pointed needles (dpn).

**Extras**

Stitch markers and holders. Two (three) ¾"/18mm buttons.

**Gauge**

21 sts and 21 rows to 4"/10 cm in Sheik pat using size 9 (5.5mm) needles.

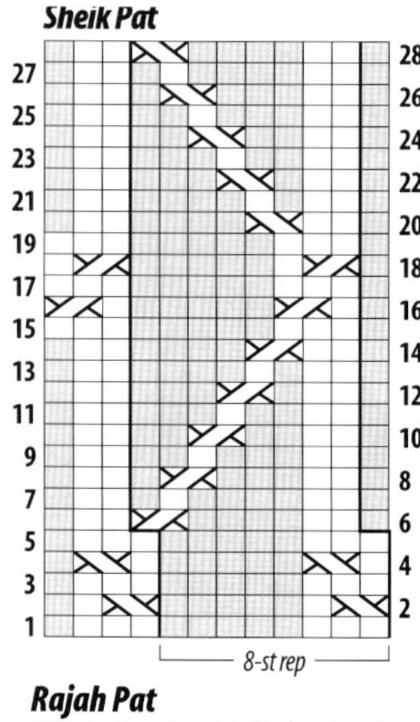


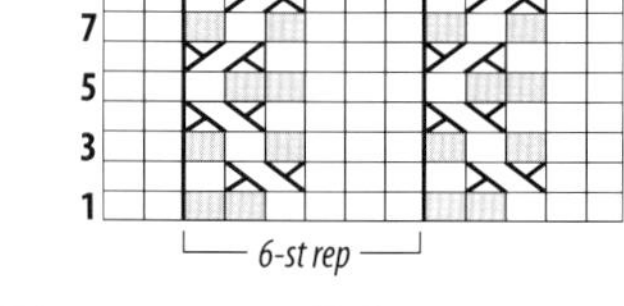


K on RS, p on WS — LT
P on RS, k on WS — RT

## STITCHES

**Left Twist** (LT) K the 2nd st on left-hand needle through the back loop (tbl), do not sl off needle, then k first and 2nd sts tog tbl and sl both sts off needle.

**Right Twist** (RT) K 2nd st on left-hand needle, do not sl off needle, k first st and sl both sts off needle.

**Seed st** (over an odd number of sts)
*Row 1* *K1, p1; rep from* to last st, k1.
Rep row 1 for Seed st.

**Twisted Rib** (multiple of 2 sts plus 1)
*Row 1* (RS) *K1 tbl, p1; rep from* to last st, k1 tbl.
*Row 2* *P1, k1 tbl; rep from* to last st, p1.
Rep rows 1–2 for Twisted Rib.

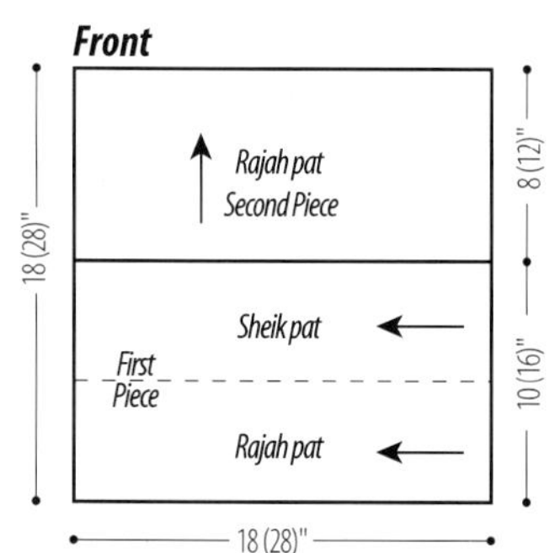


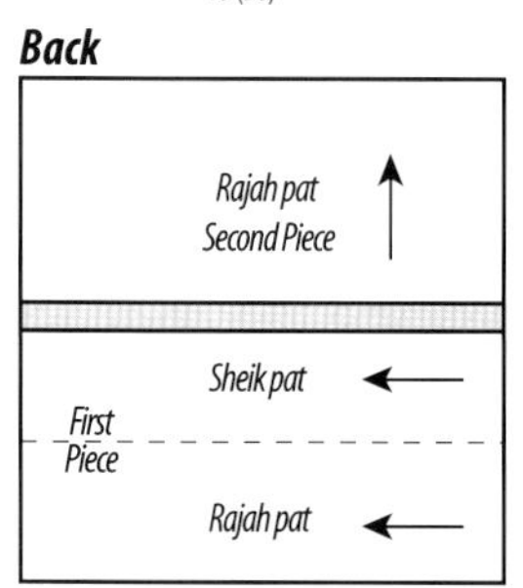


Arrows indicate direction of work.

**Sheik Pat** (multiple of 8 sts plus 4)
***Rows 1, 3, and 5*** (WS) K1, p3, *k5, p3; rep from* to end.
***Row 2*** *LT, k1, p5; rep from*, end LT, k1, p1.
***Row 4*** *K1, LT, p5; rep from*, end k1, LT, p1.
***Row 6*** P1, *k2, p4, RT; rep from*, end k2, p1.
***Row 7*** K1, p2, *k1, p1, k4, p2; rep from*, end k1.
***Row 8*** P1, *k2, p3, RT, p1; rep from*, end k2, p1.
***Row 9*** K1, p2, *k2, p1, k3, p2; rep from*, end k1.
***Row 10*** P1, *k2, p2, RT, p2; rep from*, end k2, p1.
***Row 11*** K1, p2, *k3, p1, k2, p2; rep from*, end k1.
***Row 12*** P1, *k2, p1, RT, p3; rep from*, end k2, p1.
***Row 13*** K1, p2, *k4, p1, k1, p2; rep from*, end k1.
***Row 14*** P1, *k2, RT, p4; rep from*, end k2, p1.
***Rows 15, 17, and 19*** P3, *k5, p3; rep from*, end k1.
***Row 16*** P1, *k1, RT, p5; rep from*, end k1, RT.
***Row 18*** P1, *RT, k1, p5; rep from*, end RT, p1.
***Row 20*** P1, *k2, LT, p4; rep from*, end k2, p1.
***Row 21*** Rep row 13.
***Row 22*** P1, *k2, p1, LT, p3; rep from*, end k2, p1.
***Row 23*** Rep row 11.
***Row 24*** P1, *k2, p2, LT, p2; rep from*, end k2, p1.
***Row 25*** Rep Row 9.
***Row 26*** P1, *k2, p3, LT, p1; rep from*, end k2, p1.
***Row 27*** Rep row 7.
***Row 28*** P1, *k2, p4, LT; rep from*, end k2, p1.
Rep rows 1–28 for Sheik pat.

**Rajah Pat** (multiple of 6 sts plus 1)
***Row 1*** (WS) P2, *k2, p4; rep from*, end last rep, p3.
***Row 2*** K2, LT, k1, *k3, LT, k1; rep from*, end k2.
***Row 3*** P2, *k1, p1, k1, p3; rep from*, end last rep p2.
***Row 4*** K3, LT, *k4, LT; rep from*, end k2.
***Row 5*** P2, *p1, k2, p3; rep from*, end last rep p2.
***Row 6*** K3, RT, *k4, RT; rep from*, end k2.
***Row 7*** Rep row 3.
***Row 8*** K2, RT, k1, *k3, RT, k1; rep from*, end k2.
Rep rows 1–8 for Rajah pat.

## PILLOW

### Front: first piece

With larger needles, cast on 53 (87) sts. ***Beg pats: Row 1*** (WS) Work 25 (43) sts in Rajah pat, 28 (44) sts in Sheik pat. ***Row 2*** Work 28 (44) sts in Sheik pat, 25 (43) sts in Rajah pattern. Work 8-row rep of Rajah pat and 28-row rep of Sheik pat until a total of 94 (148) rows have been worked. Piece measures approx 18 (28)" from beg. Bind off all sts.

### Front: 2nd piece

With RS of first piece facing and smaller needles, pick up and k 97 (151) sts evenly along side edge. Beg with row 1, work Rajah pat for a total of 42 (64) rows, or until piece measures 18 (28)" from lower edge. Bind off.

### Back: first piece

With larger needles, cast on 56 (92) sts. ***Beg pats: Row 1*** (WS) Work 25 (43) sts in Rajah pat, 28 (44) sts in Sheik pat, 3 (5) sts in Seed st. ***Row 2*** Work 3 (5) sts in Seed st, 28 (44) sts in Sheik pat, 25 (43) sts in Rajah pat. Work 8-row rep of Rajah pat and 28-row rep of Sheik pat until a total of 94 (148) rows have been worked. Piece measures approx 18 (28)" from beg. Bind off all sts.

### Back: 2nd piece

With smaller needles, cast on 97 (151) sts and work 1" in twisted rib, making buttonholes on final row as foll: Work 30 (52) sts, bind off 3 sts, work 30 (18) sts, bind off 3 sts, work 29 (18) sts, bind off 0 (3) sts, work to end. On next row, cast on 3 sts over bound-off sts of previous row. Work the cast-on sts tbl on foll row. Change to smaller needles and work 42 (64) rows in Rajah pat, or until piece measures 9 (13)" from end. Bind off.

## FINISHING

Block pieces lightly. Overlap the rib on top of seed st edge by 1" at center back of pillow and sew 4 sides of back and front tog. For size L, sew down 6" along opening at each side. Sew the 2 (3) buttons directly beneath buttonholes, where seed st meets Sheik pat.

### I-cord edging

With dpn, cast on 3 sts. *K3; do not turn work. With RS of pillow facing, pick up 1 st from side edge and pass the last st on dpn over the picked up st. Slide 3 sts to other end of dpn. Rep from* evenly around pillow. Bind off neatly and dovetail into beg of I-cord.

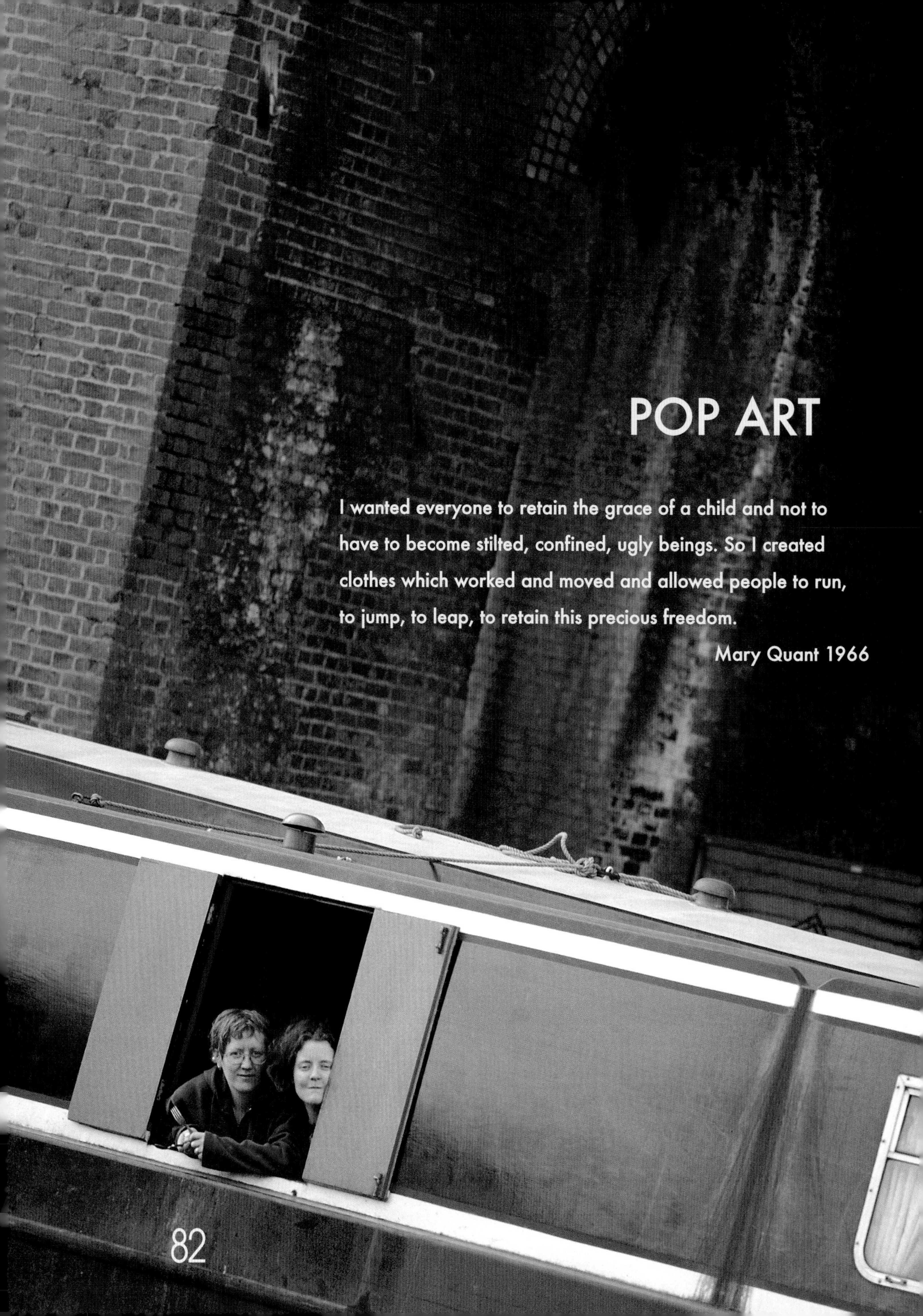

# POP ART

I wanted everyone to retain the grace of a child and not to have to become stilted, confined, ugly beings. So I created clothes which worked and moved and allowed people to run, to jump, to leap, to retain this precious freedom.

Mary Quant 1966

In May1968, during the general strike in France, I was hitchhiking out of Paris, and there standing beside me by the roadside, amid the piles of uncollected refuse, was a life-size cut-out model of President De Gaulle—also hitching a lift out of town. This is one of my lasting Pop Art images from a dynamic period when it almost seemed as if all aspects of life could be art in the making.

Pop Art, the visual arts movement of the fifties and sixties, aimed to close the gap between real life and art. Its images were taken from mass culture, artists duplicating beer bottles, soup cans, comic strips, road signs, and similar objects in paintings, collages, and sculptures. Others incorporated the objects themselves into their paintings or sculptures, which often used the materials of modern technology, such as plastic, polyurethane foam, and acrylic paint. The movement had a significant impact on commercial, graphic, and fashion design since many of its originators were commercial artists.

London was humming in the 'swinging sixties.' I remember busking with my guitar in the Portobello Road street market, where the atmosphere was electric, a cosmopolitan circus of exotic foods, weird curios, and friendly people wearing beads, bells, and amazing clothes, the whole belting out the message that anything goes. With its cheap imports and ubiquitous scent of patchouli, Carnaby Street also encouraged individual expression and became the epicenter of the new youth culture. Youth was empowered! The Beatles and other Liverpool bands revolutionized popular music with the Mersey beat. In the States Bob Dylan rallied a generation with his protest songs, and the wild, inventive guitar playing of Jimi Hendrix made him a style icon of the time. Pop festivals mushroomed, and Woodstock defined a generation of flower-powered, pot-smoking peace-lovers, who read Aldous Huxley's *Doors of Perception* and J.R. Tolkien's *Lord of the Rings*.

Many of the younger generation shunned western religion, and the Buddhist search for nirvana had a wide appeal. In London it was not unusual to see the saffron robes usually worn by Tibetan monks, even if the wearer hailed from no further east than Stepney. One of my favorite cookery books was *The Tassajara Bread Book*, a collection of deliciously scrumptious breads, biscuits, and cakes edited by one of the monks at the Californian Zen Buddhist monastery at Tassajara. My family has feasted regularly ever since on their heavenly banana bread.

Food played a big part in Pop Art. In England David Hockney produced *Typhoo Tea*, one of the earliest paintings to portray a brand-name commercial product. In the US Rauschenberg painted cast bronzes of Ballantine beer cans, Claes Oldenburg constructed garish, humorous plastic sculptures of hamburgers and other fast-food items, while Andy Warhol immortalized the Campbell's soup can.

However, it was the powerfully graphic images of Op Artists like Victor Vasarely and Bridget Riley that intrigued me. Op Art got its name from the optical tricks used to create the illusion of movement through spirals, circles, stripes, and squares. Some years ago I was delighted to come across many of Vasarely's magical paintings and shimmering tapestries in a gallery which was once his home in Gordes, Provence. In Britain, Bridget Riley's dynamic and dazzling canvases focused attention on Op Art and influenced many aspects of decorative art and fashion. Black and white zebra stripes popped up everywhere. Mary Quant invented the mini-skirt which, when worn with white Courègges boots, created a striking space-age image every fashion-conscious young woman craved—from Twiggy even to Germaine Greer.

I was thinking of the atmosphere of the famous London antiques street market when I designed this sweater. Situated in the traditionally bohemian and relaxed area of Notting Hill, Portobello Road was always a hive of creative energy in the swinging sixties, frequented by a mixture of local people and fashion-conscious celebrities. I can well imagine this piece being worn there with matching Courrèges boots and mini skirt, its decorative rib pattern in exquisitely lightweight silk tweed yarn capturing the mood of the time.

# PORTOBELLO TUNIC

**Sizes**

S (M, L).
Shown in sizes small (Rosy #701) and medium (Grape #703).
Directions are for smallest size with larger sizes in parentheses.
If there is only 1 set of numbers, it applies to all sizes.

**Finished measurements**

Bust 40 (43, 46)"
Length 27 (27½, 28)"

**Yarn**

10 (11, 12) balls Rowan Silken Tweed (each 1¾oz/50g, 120yds/110m; 55% wool, 37.5% silk, 7.5% cotton)

**Needles**

One pair each sizes 5 and 7 (3.75 and 4.5mm) needles, *or size to obtain gauge.*
Size 5 (3.75mm) circular needle, 16"/40cm long and double-pointed needles (dpn).

**Extras**

Stitch markers and holders.

**Gauge**

19 sts and 28 rows to 4"/10 cm over Notting Hill Chart using size 7 (4.5mm) needles.

**BACK**
Work lower edge in 3 pieces as foll:
**First piece** (right side)
With larger needles, cast on 20 (24, 28) sts. K 2 rows. ***Beg Notting Hill Chart: Row 1*** (RS) Reading chart from right to left, work sts 25–44 (25–48, 25–52). ***Row 2*** Reading chart from left to right, work sts 44–25 (48–25, 52–25). Work 41 rows more in chart pat as established. Place sts on hold.
**2nd piece** (left side)
With larger needles, cast on 20 (24, 28) sts. K 2 rows. ***Beg Notting Hill Chart: Row 1*** (RS) Work sts 13–32 (9–32, 5–32). ***Row 2*** Work sts 32–13 (32–9, 32–5). Work 41 rows more in chart pat as established. Place sts on hold.
**3rd piece** (center)
With larger needles, cast on 56 sts. K 2 rows. ***Beg Notting Hill Chart: Row 1*** (RS) Work sts 1-56. **Row 2** Work sts 56–1. Work 41 rows more in chart pat as established. Place sts on hold.
**Join pieces: Row 22** (WS) With WS facing, work sts 32–13 (32–9, 32–5) from first piece, work sts 56-1 across 3rd piece, then work sts 44–25 (48–25, 52–25) across 2nd piece—96 (104, 112) sts. Cont chart pats as established until piece measures 17½ (17½, 18)" from beg, end with a WS row.
**Shape armhole**
Bind off 8 sts at beg of next 2 rows—80 (88, 96) sts. Work even until piece measures 26½ (27, 27½)" from beg, end with a WS row.
**Shape neck and shoulder**
Work 28 (31, 34) sts, turn and place rem sts on hold. Work each side separately: ***Rows 1, 3 and 5*** (WS) Work pat across. ***Row 2*** Bind off 8 (9, 10) sts, work to last 3 sts, k2tog, k1. ***Row 4*** Bind off 9 (10, 11) sts, work to last 3 sts, k2tog, k1. Bind off rem sts. With RS facing, leave center 24 (26, 28) sts on hold, join yarn and work across 28 (31, 34) sts. Work to correspond to first side, reversing shaping.

**FRONT**
Work as for back until piece measures 19½ (20, 20½)" from beg, end with a WS row.
**Divide for keyhole opening**
Work 40 (44, 48) sts, join a 2nd ball of yarn and work to end. Working both sides at same time, cont in pat until piece measures 24½ (25, 25½)" from beg, end with a WS row.
**Shape neck**
Work 32 (35, 38) sts, place 8 (9, 10) sts on each side of center front on hold. Rejoin yarn and work rem 32 (35, 38) sts. Working both sides at same time, dec 1 st at neck edge every other row 6 times, AT SAME TIME, when piece measures same as back to shoulder, shape shoulder as for back.

**SLEEVES**
With larger needles, cast on 48 sts. K 2 rows.
**Divide for slit**
***Beg Notting Hill chart: Row 1*** (RS) Work sts 13–36 of chart, join a 2nd ball of yarn and work sts 37–44, then work sts 13–28. Working both sides at same time, cont in pats as established until one 22-row rep of chart is complete.
**Join slit**
***Row 1*** (RS) Cont in pat across all sts. Work 1 row even. Inc 1 st (working incs into 32-st sleeve rep) each side of next row, then every 4th row 5 (11, 7) times, then every 5th row 14 (10, 14) times—86 (90, 90) sts. Work even until piece measures 18 (18½, 19)" from beg. Bind off all sts.

**FINISHING**
Block pieces lightly. Sew shoulder seams.
**Neck slit**
With RS facing and smaller needles, beg at top left neck edge and pick up and k 25 sts from left side of slit, 1 st at base of slit and 25 sts from right side of slit—51 sts. K 2 rows, binding off 50 sts on 2nd row—1 st rem. Pick up and k the first bound-off st. Sl the 51st st over the first st and leave this rem st on hold.
**Neckband**

With RS facing and circular needle, beg at left shoulder and pick up and k 16 sts from left front neck, 8 (9, 10) sts on hold, 1 st on hold at center front, k 6 (7, 8) sts on hold, then k2tog, 16 sts from right front neck, 2 sts from right back neck, 24 (26, 28) sts on hold at back, and 2 sts from left back neck—76 (80, 84) sts. Place marker, join and work in rnds as foll: ***Rnds 1–3*** *K2, p2; rep from*. ***Rnd 4*** P. Rep rnds 1–4 until neckband measures 2¼" from beg. Bind off all sts knitwise.

**Body slits**

With RS facing and smaller needles, beg at lower edge of slit and pick up and k 30 sts to top of slit, then 30 sts to lower edge—60 sts. K 2 rows, binding off on 2nd row.

**Sleeve slits**

With RS facing and dpn, beg at lower edge of slit and pick up and k 15 sts to top of slit, 1 st at center, then 15 sts to lower edge—31 sts. Purl 1 rnd, then bind off knitwise.

Set in sleeves. Sew side and sleeve seams.

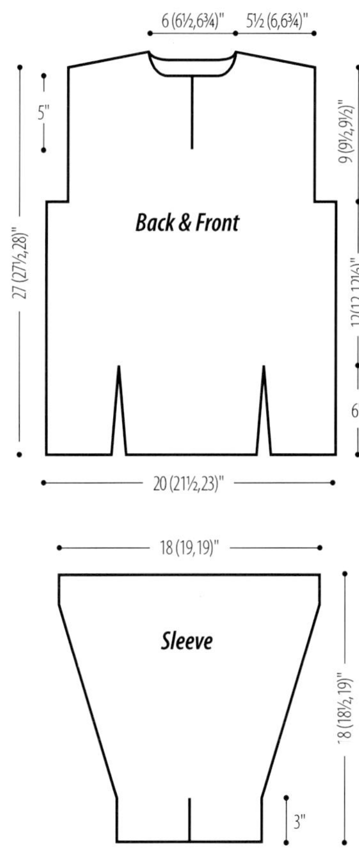

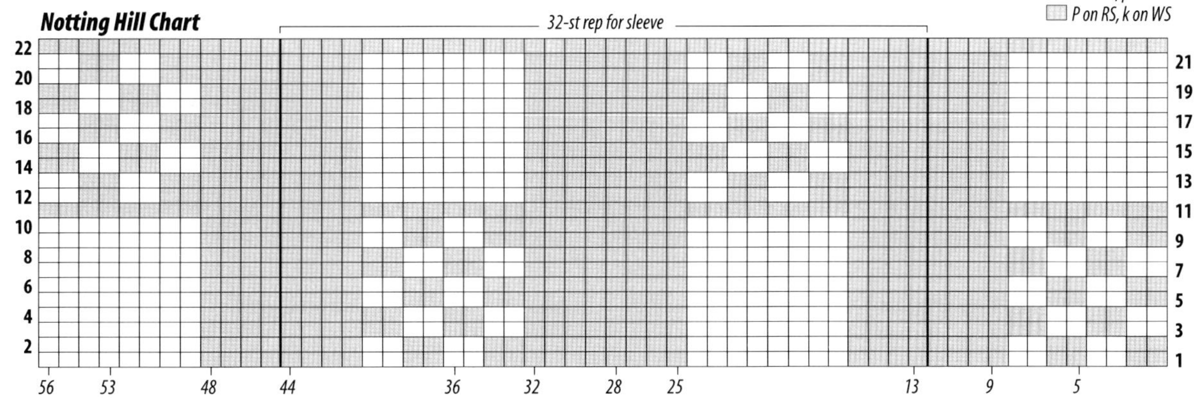

This piece is named after the Hungarian painter Victor Vasarely, who believed in the artist as a workman who could make prototypes reproducible at will. His large Op Art canvases and tapestries, often painted in contrasting psychedelic colors, depicted clean-cut geometric abstractions. In the elegant simplicity of this skinny rib sweater, with its graphic rib stitch pattern, I have tried to capture the purity of form which characterised Vasarely's work.

# VASARELY VEST

**Sizes**
XS (S, M, L).
Shown in sizes extra small (Cream #373) and medium (Bamboo #378).
Directions are for smallest size with larger sizes in parentheses.
If there is only 1 set of numbers, it applies to all sizes.

**Finished measurements**
Chest 32 (34, 36, 38)"
Length 19 (19¾, 20½, 21¼)"

**Yarn**
6 (7, 7, 8) balls Jaeger Java (each 1¾oz/50g, 141yds/129m, 55% rayon, 25% acrylic, 20% silk)

**Needles**
One pair each sizes 2 and 3 (2.75 and 3.25 mm) needles, *or size to obtain gauge.*
Size 2 and 3 (2.75 and 3.25 mm) circular needles, each 16"/40cm long.

**Extras**
Stitch markers and holders.

**Gauge**
28 sts and 32 rows to 4"/10 cm in Gordes pat using size 3 (3.25mm) needles.

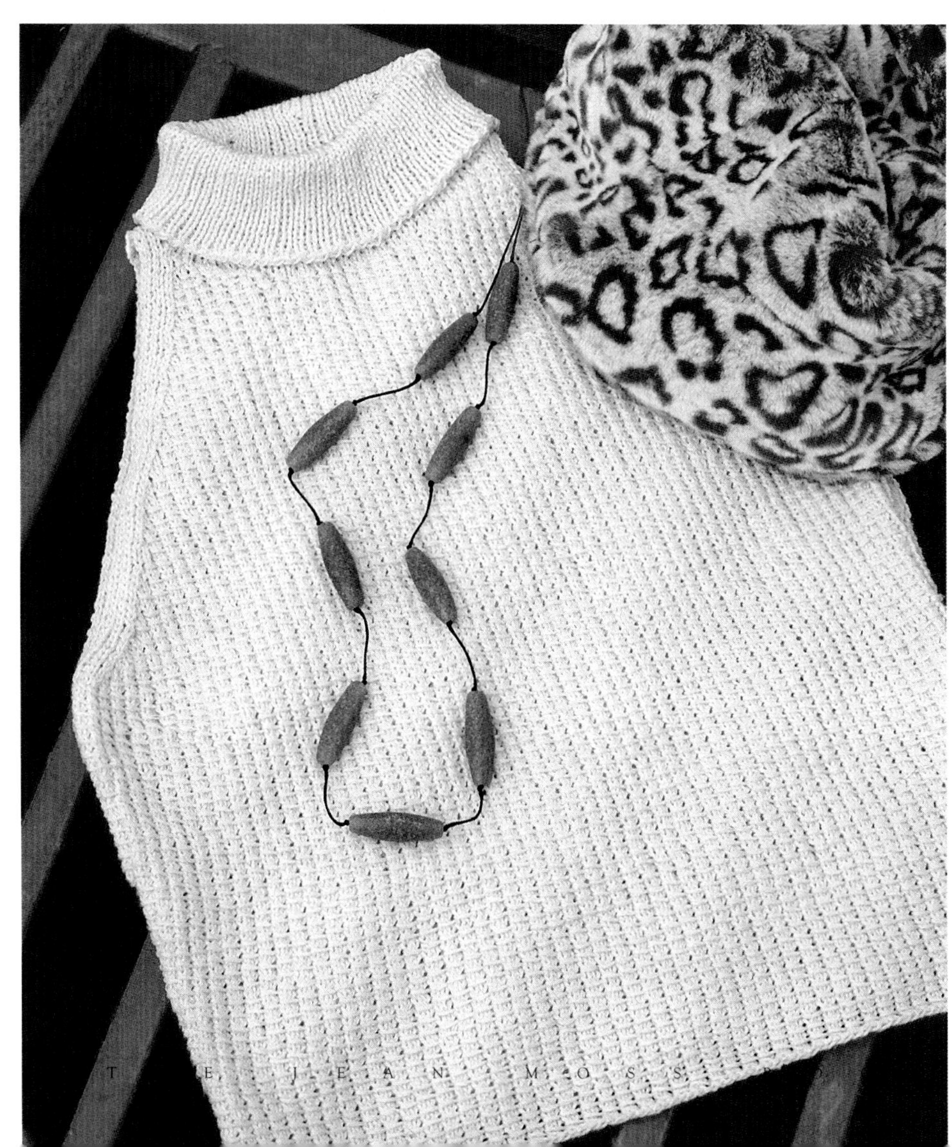

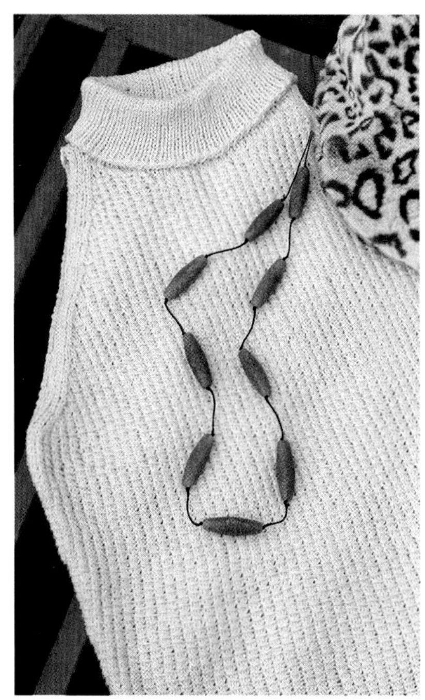

**GORDES PATTERN** (multiple of 2 sts)
(NOTE When shaping, work single edge sts in St st.)
***Row 1*** *Yo, k2, pass yo over k2; rep from*.
***Row 2*** Purl.
Rep rows 1–2 for Gordes pat.

**BACK**
With smaller needles, cast on 98 (106, 112, 118) sts. Beg with row 1, work in Gordes pat for 2¾ (3¼, 3½, 4)".
Change to larger needles. Cont in pat, AT SAME TIME, inc 1 st each side of next row, then every 6th row 0 (0, 0, 5) times, every 7th row 0 (0, 5, 3) times, then every 8th row 6 (6, 2, 0) times—112 (120, 128, 136) sts.
Work even until piece measures 10½ (11, 11½, 12)" from beg, end with a WS row.
**Shape armhole**
***Next (dec) row*** (RS) K3tog tbl, cont pat to last 3 sts, k3tog. Work dec row every other row 3 (3, 4, 4) times more. Dec 1 st each side every other row 9 (16, 16, 20) times, then every 3rd row 14 (10, 10, 8) times—50 (52, 56, 60) sts, AT SAME TIME, when piece measures 18½ (19¼, 20, 20¾)" from beg, end with row before next to final armhole dec. Mark 2 center sts.
**Shape neck**
***Next row*** Work armhole dec, work to center marked sts and place them on hold, join a 2nd ball of yarn and work to last 2 sts, work armhole dec. Working both sides at same time, dec 1 st at neck edge on next 2 rows, then work final armhole dec. Bind off rem sts.

**FRONT**
Work as for back until piece measures 16½ (17¼, 18, 18¾)" from beg, end with a WS row before an armhole dec row—64 (66, 70, 74) sts rem. Mark center 2 sts.
**Shape neck**
***Next row*** Work armhole dec, work to center marked sts and place them on hold, join a 2nd ball of yarn and work to last 2 sts, work armhole dec. Working both sides at same time, dec 1 st at each neck edge every row 12 times, AT SAME TIME, work armhole decs as for back. When piece measures same as back to shoulder, bind off rem sts.

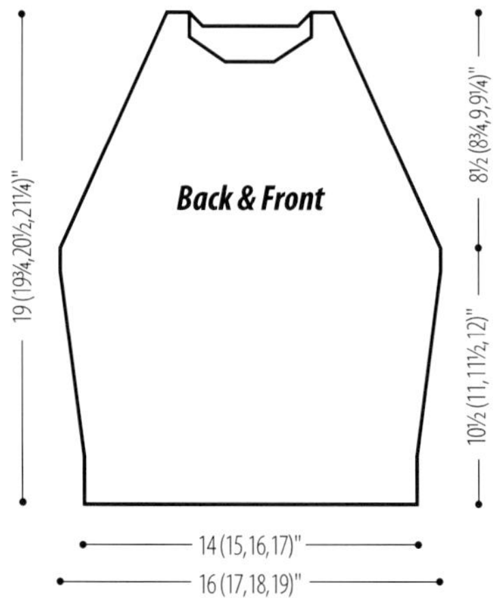


**FINISHING**
Block pieces lightly. Sew shoulder seams.
**Collar**
With RS facing and smaller circular needle, beg at left shoulder, pick up and k 22 sts from left front neck, 18 (20, 22, 24) sts on hold at center front, 22 sts from right front neck, 3 sts from right back neck, 38 (40, 42, 44) sts on hold at center back, and 3 sts from left back neck—106 (110, 114, 118) sts. Place marker and join. Work in rnds of k1, p1 rib for 1½". ***Next (inc) rnd*** Work 2 sts, *working inc sts into k1, p1 rib, inc 2 sts in next st, work 10 (13, 17, 17) sts; rep from* 7 (7, 5, 5) times more, work to end—124 (128, 128, 132) sts. Cont in rib until collar measures 3¼", then change to larger circular needle and cont rib until collar measures 5". Bind off very loosely in rib.
**Armbands**
With RS facing and smaller needles, pick up and k 109 (111, 115, 119) sts evenly spaced around armhole. Work 3 rows in k1, p1 rib. Bind off loosely in rib.
Sew side seams, including armbands.

Carnaby Street in London's bohemian Soho is famous for its fashionable inexpensive boutiques, and was at the cutting edge of street fashion in the 1960s. One of my most memorable images of that time was the pinafore dress worn with polo neck and tights in a contrasting color and knee-high boots. In this dress I'm trying to recreate this look. If the cut-out squares reveal a little too much for you, it would look just as good without them.

# CARNABY DRESS

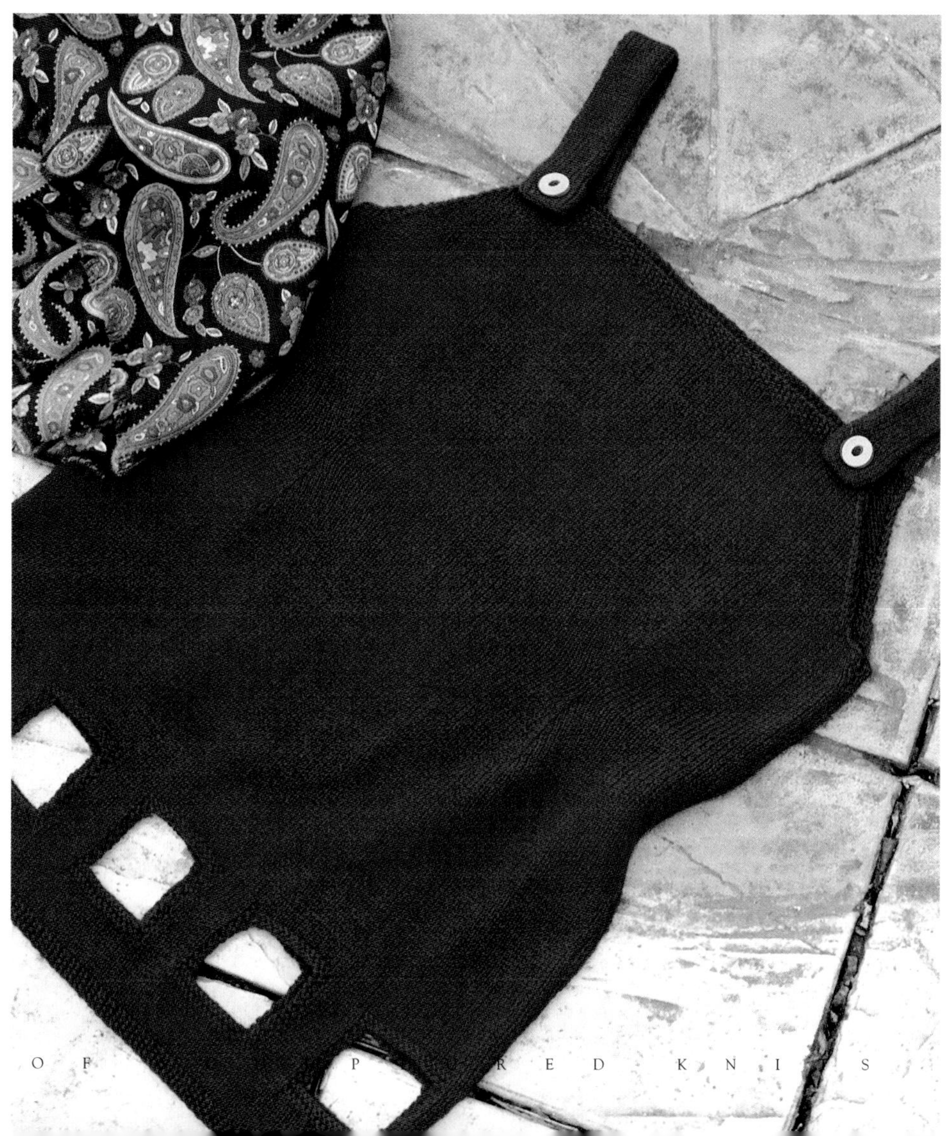

**Sizes**
S (M, L).
Shown in sizes small (Aubergine #659) and medium (Slate #65).
Directions are for smallest size with larger sizes in parentheses. If there is only 1 set of numbers, it applies to all sizes.

**Finished measurements**
Bust 38 (42, 46)"
Length (including straps) 30 (32, 34)"

**Yarn**
14 (16, 18) balls Rowan Lightweight DK (each 1oz/25g, 73yds/67m, 100% wool)

**Needles**
One pair each sizes 2 and 5 (2.75 and 3.75mm) needles, *or size to obtain gauge.*

**Extras**
Stitch markers and holders.
Two ⅞" (22mm) buttons.

**Gauge**
24 sts and 32 rows to 4"/10 cm in St st using size 5 (3.75mm) needles.

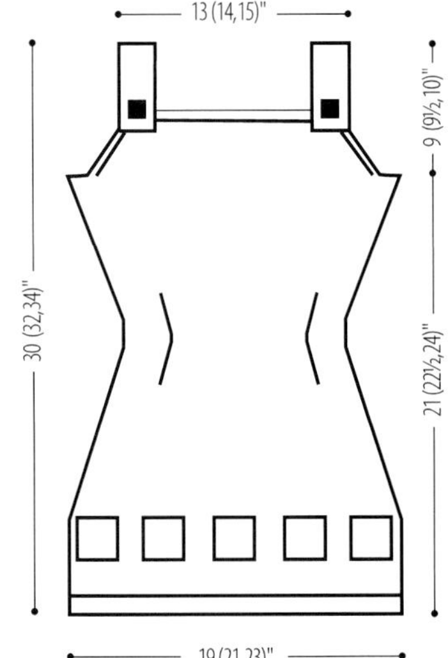


**1**

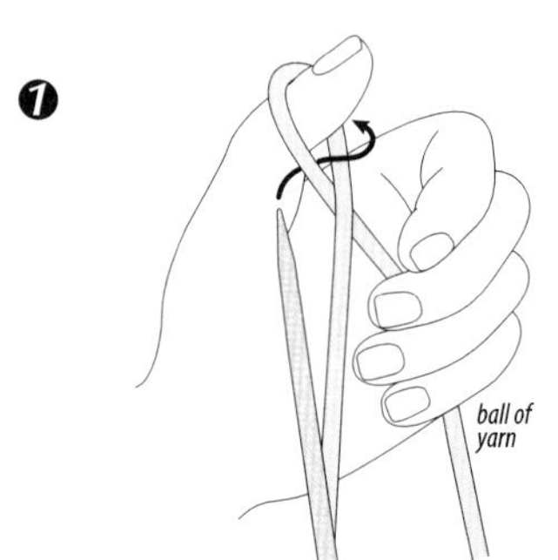


**2**

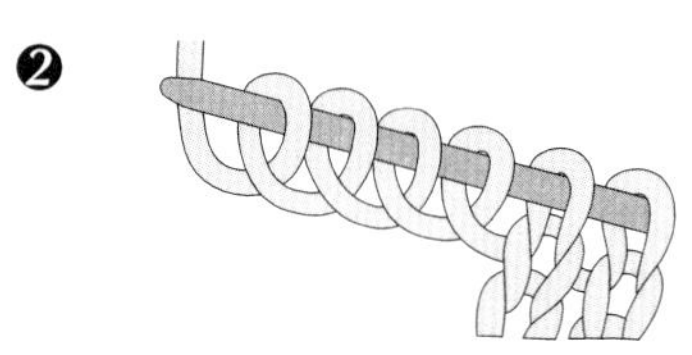

**Backward loop cast-on (for cut-outs)**
**1** Loop the yarn over your left thumb. Insert the needle into the loop.
**2** Slip loop off thumb and tighten: one stitch cast on.

**STITCHES**

**Sl2, k1, p2sso**
Sl the next 2 sts tog knitwise, k1, then pass both sl sts over.

**Make one (M1)**
Inc 1 st by working into the loop directly below next st (st from previous row).

**Seed st**
*Row 1* *K1, p1; rep from*. *Row 2* K the purl sts and p the knit sts. Rep row 2 for Seed st.

**BACK and FRONT**
With smaller needles, cast on 118 (129, 141) sts. Work 6 rows in Seed st. Change to larger needles. Cont in St st until piece measures 2" from beg, end with a WS row. ***Beg cut-outs. Frame row*** (RS) K5 (6, 5), *p16 (17, 16), k7 (8, 7); rep from* 4 (4, 5) times more, end last rep k5 (6, 5). *Next row* Purl. *Next row* K5 (6, 5), *p2, bind off 12 (13, 12) sts purlwise, p2, k7 (8, 7); rep from* 4 (4, 5) times more, end last rep k5 (6, 5). Work each of the rem groups of stitches separately for 17 rows as foll: P all WS rows. On RS rows, p the 2 sts before and after each cut-out and k. *Next (joining) row* (RS) K5 (6, 5), p2, *cast on 12 (13, 12) sts using backward loop method, p2, k7 (8, 7), p2; rep from* 4 (4, 5) times more, end last rep k5 (6, 5)—118 (129, 141) sts. P 1 row across all sts. Rep Frame row. Beg with a p row, cont in St st until piece measures 12½ (13¾, 15½)" from beg, end with a WS row.

**Shape waist**
*Next row* (RS) K28 (31, 34), sl2, k1, p2sso, k56 (61, 67), sl2, k1, p2sso, k28 (31, 34). Work 5 rows even in St st. *Next row* K27 (30, 33), sl2, k1, p2sso, k54 (59, 65), sl2, k1, p2sso, k27 (30, 33). Work 3 rows even. *Next row* K26 (29, 32), sl2, k1, p2sso, k52 (57, 63), sl2, k1, p2sso, k26 (29, 32). Work 3 rows even. *Next row* K25 (28, 31), sl2, k1, p2sso, k50 (55, 61), sl2, k1, p2sso, k25 (28, 31). Work 1 row even. *Next row* K24 (27, 30), sl2, k1, p2sso, k48 (53, 59), sl2, k1, p2sso, k24 (27, 30).
**For sizes M and L only** Work 1 row even. *Next row* K26 (29), sl2, k1, p2sso, k51 (57), sl2, k1, p2sso, k26 (29).
**For size L only** Work 1 row even. *Next row* K28, sl2, k1, p2sso, k55, sl2, k1, p2sso, k28.
**For all sizes** Work 5 rows even. *Next row* K24 (26, 28), M1, k1, M1, k48 (51, 55), M1, k1, M1, k24 (26, 28). Work 1 row even.
**For sizes M and L only** *Next row* K27 (29), M1, k1, M1, k53 (57), M1, k1, M1, k27 (29). Work 1 row even.
**For size L only** *Next row* K30, M1, k1, M1, k59, M1, k1, M1, k30. Work 1 row even.
**For all sizes** *Next row* K25 (28, 31), M1, k1, M1, k50 (55, 61), M1, k1, M1, k 25 (28, 31). Work 3 rows even. *Next row* K26 (29, 32), M1, k1, M1, k52 (57, 63), M1, k1, M1, k26 (29, 32). Work 3 rows even. *Next row* K27 (30, 33), M1, k1, M1, k54 (59, 65), M1, k1, M1, k27 (30, 33). Work 5 rows even. *Next row* K28 (31, 34), M1, k1, M1, k56 (61, 67), M1, k1, M1, k28 (31, 34)—118 (129, 141) sts. Work even in St st until piece measures 21 (22½, 24)" from beg, end with a WS row.

**Shape armhole**
Bind off 6 (6, 7) sts at beg of next 2 rows. *Next (dec) row* (RS) K2, ssk, k to last 4 sts, k2tog, k2. *Next row* K2, purl to last 2 sts, k2. Rep these two rows 13 (15, 17) times more—78 (85, 91) sts. Change to smaller needles and work 6 rows in Seed st, working 2 sts at beg and end of each row in k2. Bind off in pat.

**LEFT STRAP**
On back, place 2 markers on top of bound-off edge, 1¾" in from each side. With RS facing and larger needles, beg at left marker and pick up and k 10 sts from bound-off edge, end at side edge. Cast on 10 sts—20 sts. Work in St st until strap measures 10¾" from beg, end with a WS row.

**Buttonhole**
*Next row* (RS) K5, turn, place rem sts on holder. Work 3 more rows, then place sts on hold. With RS facing, work 4 rows on center 10 sts. Place on hold. In same way, rep for rem 5 sts.
*Next (joining) row* (RS) Work across 20 sts. Cont in St st until strap measures 12" from beg, end with a WS row.
*Next row* (RS) K10, then fold strap lengthwise with WS tog. Working with a spare needle, work 3-needle bind-off.

**RIGHT STRAP**
Cast on 10 sts. With RS facing, beg at side edge and pick up and k 10 sts from bound-off edge to marker—20 sts. Complete to correspond to left strap.

**FINISHING**
Block pieces lightly. Sew side seams. Sew long edges of straps. Sew cast-on sts of strap to inside of dress. Sewing through both thicknesses, neaten buttonholes. Sew buttons on front to correspond to buttonholes on straps.

RÇA
PUSH

The three days of love and peace at the Woodstock Festival in 1969 heralded the birth of a new age and was the rallying cry for a generation. At the time my favorite sweater was a Missoni design of multi-colored horizontal zigzags, copied endlessly in the high street. Using a similar shape, I have made the pattern into monotone sculptured stitches and given the design a contemporary look by continuing the zigzag at hem and cuffs. Knitted in mercerized cotton, it's perfect for today's summer festivities.

# WOODSTOCK SWEATER

**Sizes**

S (M, L).
Shown in sizes small (Black) and medium (Jade Green).
Directions are for smallest size with larger sizes in parentheses.
If there is only 1 set of numbers, it applies to all sizes.

**Finished measurements**

Bust 38 (42, 46)"
Length 17 (18, 19)" to tip of points

**Yarn**

6 (6, 7) balls Jean Moss 4-ply Mercerized Cotton (each 1¾oz/50g, 172yds/157m, 100% cotton)

**Needles**

One pair each sizes 2 and 3 (2.75 and 3.25mm) needles, *or size to obtain gauge.*
Size 2 (2.75mm) circular needle, 16"/40cm long.

**Extras**

Stitch markers and holders.

**Gauge**

30 sts and 40 rows to 4"/10 cm in Yasgur pat using size 3 (3.25mm) needles.

## BACK

With larger needles, cast on 120 (140, 160) sts. ***Beg Yasgur Chart: Row 1*** (RS) Work 20-st rep 6 (7, 8) times. Work through chart row 52 once, then rep rows 19–52, AT SAME TIME, inc 1 st (working inc sts into chart pat) each side of first row 19, then on every foll 5th (7th, 10th) row 11 (8, 6) times more, —144 (158, 174) sts. Work even in pat until piece measures 8¼ (9, 9¾)" from beg, end with a WS row.

**Shape armhole**

Bind off 7 sts at beg of next 2 rows. Dec 1 st each side of next row, then every other row 8 (7, 8) times more—112 (128, 142) sts. Work even in pat until piece measures 14 (15, 16)" from beg, end with a WS row.

**Shape neck**

Work 41 (48, 54) sts, place center 30 (32, 34) sts on holder, join a 2nd ball of yarn and work to end. Working both sides at same time, dec 1 st at each neck edge every row 20 times. Work even in pat until piece measures 16½ (17½, 18½)" from beg, end with a WS row.

**Shape shoulder**

Bind off at shoulder edge 7 (9, 11) sts twice. Bind off rem sts.

## FRONT

Work as for back until piece measures 13 (14, 15)" from beg, end with a WS row.

**Shape neck**

Work 41 (48, 54) sts, place center 30 (32, 34) sts on hold, join a 2nd ball of yarn and work to end. Working both sides at same time, dec 1 st at each neck edge every row 10 times, then every other row 10 times. Work even in pat, and when piece measures same as back to shoulder, shape shoulder as for back.

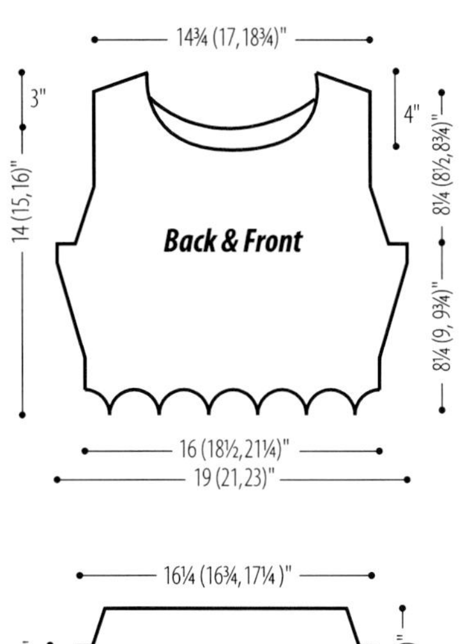


## SLEEVES

With larger needles, cast on 100 sts. ***Beg Yasgur Chart: Row 1*** (RS) Work 20-st rep 5 times. Work through chart row 52 once, then work in St st to end of sleeve, AT SAME TIME, inc 8 sts evenly across row 19, then inc 1 st (working incs into chart pat) each side every other row 7 (9, 11) times, working inc sts into chart pat—122 (126, 130) sts. (NOTE At row 24, there will be 112 sts on needles. Pat placement for this row is as foll: (WS) Working chart from left to right, work sts 6–1, work 20-st rep 5 times, then work sts 20–15.) Cont in pat as established until piece measures 4¾ (5¼, 5¼)" from beg.

**Shape cap**

Bind off 7 sts at beg of next 2 rows. Dec 1 st each side of next row, then every other row 8 (7, 8) times more. Bind off rem sts.

## FINISHING

Block pieces lightly. Sew shoulder seams.

**Neckband**

With RS facing and circular needle, beg at left shoulder, pick up and k 39 sts from left front neck, 30 (32, 34) sts on hold at center front, 39 from right front neck, 33 from right back neck, 30 (32, 34) from holder at center back, and 33 from left back neck—204 (208, 212) sts. Place marker, join and work 5 rnds in k1, p1 rib. Bind off in rib.

Set in sleeves. Sew side and sleeve seams.

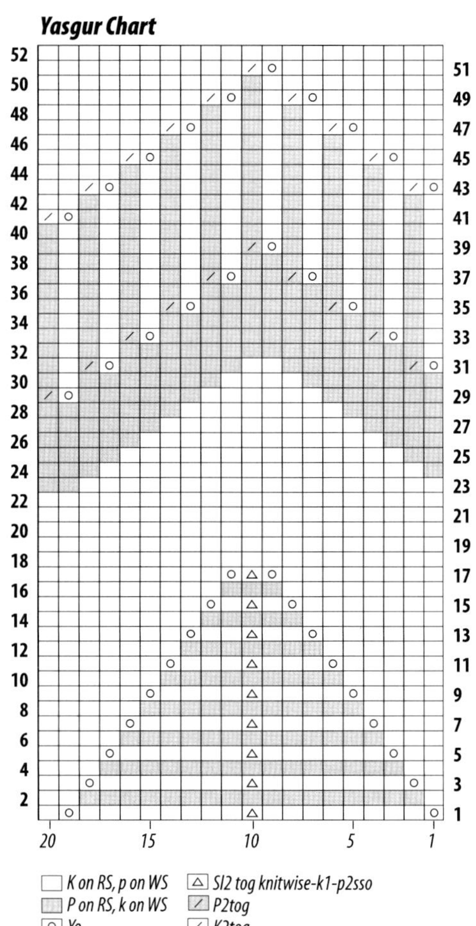

In these pieces I have used luxurious cashmere yarn and traditional styling to create designs which I hope will become cherished friends and remain in your wardrobe for many years. The offset cables accentuate the understated elegance of these two contemporary classics, which are certainly my idea of heaven.

# NIRVANA VEST AND CARDIGAN

**Sizes**
S (M, L).
Cardigan shown in size medium (Gray #116); vest shown in size small (Red #107).
Directions are for smallest size with larger sizes in parentheses. If there is only 1 set of numbers, it applies to all sizes.

**Finished measurements**
Chest (buttoned) 46 (50, 54)"
Length 27 (28, 29)"

**Yarn**
Jaeger 4-ply Cashmere
**Vest** 14 (16, 18) balls
**Cardigan** 21(24, 27) balls
(each 1oz/25g, 107yds/98m, 90% cashmere, 10% polyamide).

**Needles**
One pair each sizes 2 and 3 (2.75 and 3.25mm) needles, *or size to obtain gauge.*

**Extras**
Stitch markers and holders.
Cable needle (cn).
**Vest** Five ⅝" (15mm) buttons.
**Cardigan** Five ¾" (18mm) buttons.

**Gauge**
32 sts and 40 rows to 4"/10 cm in Xanadu chart pat using size 3 (3.25mm) needles.

**STITCHES**
**3/3 Right Cross (3/3RC)** Sl 3 sts to cable needle (cn) and hold in back, k3, then k3 from cn.
**3/3 Left Cross (3/3LC)** Sl 3 sts to cn and hold in front, k3, then k3 from cn.
**3/3 Seed Right Cross (3/3SRC)** Sl 3 sts to cn and hold in back, p1, k1, p1, then k3 from cn.
**3/3 Seed Left Cross (3/3SLC)** Sl 3 sts to cn and hold in front, k3, then k1, p1, k1 from cn.

**Seed st** (over any number of sts)
*Row 1* *K1, p1; rep from*. *Row 2* K the purl sts and p the knit sts. Rep row 2 for Seed st.

**Paradise buttonband pat** (for vest size S only)
*Rows 1, 3, 5* *K1, p1; rep from* to last st, k1.
*Rows 2, 4, 6* *P1, k1; rep from* to last st, p1.
*Row 7* K1, sl 4 sts to cable needle, hold to back, p1, k1, p1; then (k1, p1) twice from cable needle, k1.
*Rows 8* *P1, k1; rep from* to last st, p1.
Rep rows 1–8 rows for buttonband pat.

**Paradise buttonband pat** (for vest sizes M and L only)
*Rows 1, 3, 5, 7* *K1, p1, rep from* to last st, k1.
*Rows 2, 4, 6, 8* *P1, k1, rep from* to last st, p1.
*Row 9* K1, sl 5 sts to cable needle, hold to back, (p1, k1) twice; then p1, k1, p1, k1, p1 from cable needle, k1.
*Row 10* *P1, k1, rep from* to last st, p1.
Rep rows 1–10 for buttonband pat.

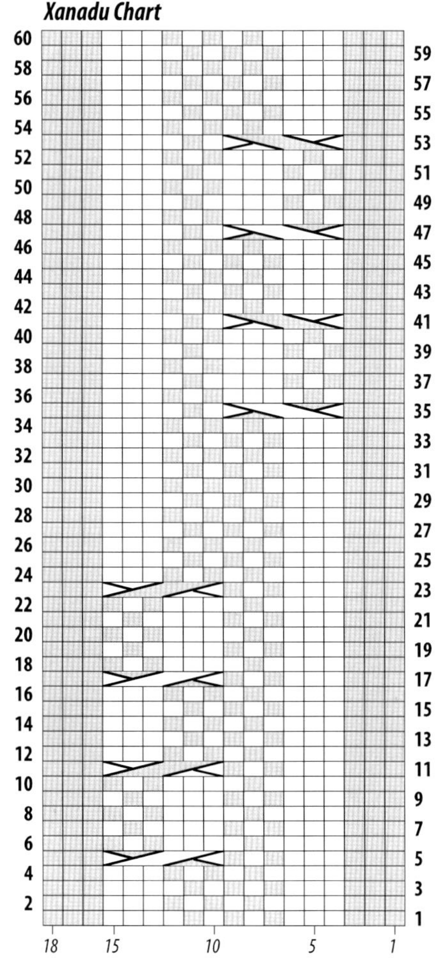


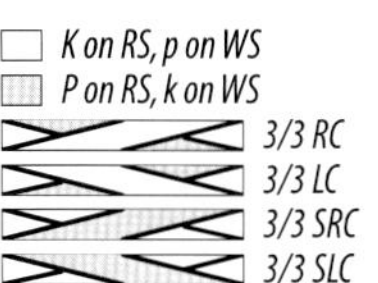


**BACK**
With smaller needles, cast on 186 (202, 218) sts. Work $1\frac{1}{4}$" in k2, p2 rib. Change to larger needles. *Beg Xanadu chart: Row 1* (RS) Reading chart from right to left, work sts 16–18 (17–18, 18), work 18-st rep 10 (11, 12) times, then work sts 1–3 (1–2, 1). *Row 2* Reading chart from left to right, work sts 3–1 (2–1, 1), work 18-st rep 10 (11, 12) times, then work sts 18–16 (18–17, 18). Cont chart pat as established until piece measures $16\frac{1}{4}$ ($17\frac{1}{4}$, $17\frac{3}{4}$)" from beg, end with a WS row.
**Cardigan: Shape armhole**
Bind off 7 (8, 8) sts at beg of next 2 rows. Dec 1 st each side of next row, then every other row 9 (9, 10) times more—152 (166, 180) sts. Work even until piece measures $26\frac{1}{2}$ ($27\frac{1}{2}$, $28\frac{1}{2}$)" from beg, end with a WS row.
**Cardigan: Shape shoulders and neck**
*Next row* (RS) Work 52 (58, 64) sts, turn and place rem sts on hold. Work each side of neck separately. *Rows 1 and 3* (WS) Dec 1 st, work to end. *Row 2* Bind off 16 (18, 20) sts, work to end. Row 4 Bind off rem sts.
With RS facing, join yarn and bind off center 48 (50, 52) sts, work to end. Work to correspond to first side, reversing shaping.
**Vest: Shape armhole**
Bind off 7 (8, 8) sts at beg of next 2 rows. Dec 1 st each side every row 14 (22, 20) times, then every other row 10 (6, 3) times more—124 (130, 136) sts. Work even until piece measures $26\frac{1}{2}$ ($27\frac{1}{2}$, $28\frac{1}{2}$)" from beg, end with a WS row.
**Vest: Shape shoulders and neck**
*Next row* (RS) Work 38 (40, 42) sts, turn and place rem sts on hold. Work each side of neck separately. *Rows 1 and 3* (WS) Dec 1 st, work to end. *Row 2* Bind off 12 (12, 13) sts, work to end. *Row 4* Bind off 12 (13, 13) sts, work to end. *Row 5* Work even. *Row 6* Bind off rem sts.
With RS facing, join yarn and bind off center 48 (50, 52) sts, work to end. Work to correspond to first side, reversing shaping.

**Pocket linings** (make 2)
With larger needles, cast on 38 sts and work 4 ($4\frac{1}{4}$, $4\frac{1}{4}$)" in St st. Place sts on hold.

**LEFT FRONT**
With smaller needles, cast on 92 (100, 108) sts. Beg with k2, work $1\frac{1}{4}$" in k2, p2 rib, inc 1 st at end of final WS row—93 (101, 109) sts. Change to larger needles. *Beg Xanadu chart: Row 1* (RS) Work sts 16–18 (17–18, 18), work 18-st rep 5 (5, 6) times, then work sts 0 (1–9, 0). *Row 2* Work sts 0 (9–1, 0), work 18-st rep 5 (5, 6) times, work sts 18–16 (18–17, 18). Work chart pat as established until piece measures $6\frac{1}{2}$ ($6\frac{3}{4}$, $6\frac{3}{4}$)" from beg, end with a WS row.
**Place pocket**
*Next row* (RS) Work 29 (28, 27) sts, place next 38 sts on hold, then with RS facing, work 38 sts of pocket lining, work rem 26 (35, 44) sts. Cont in pat until piece measures 16 ($16\frac{3}{4}$, $17\frac{1}{2}$)" from beg, end with a RS row.

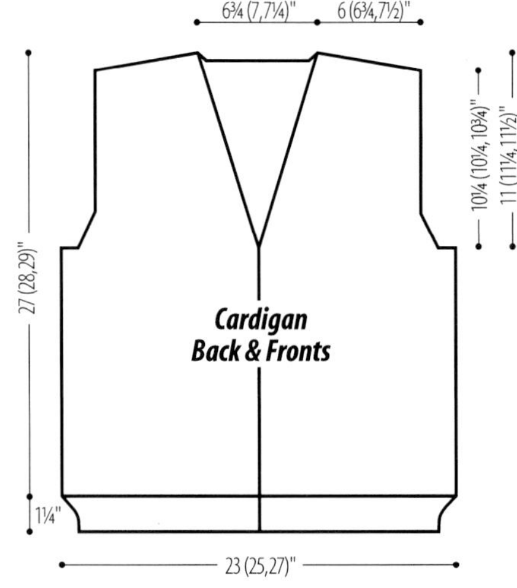


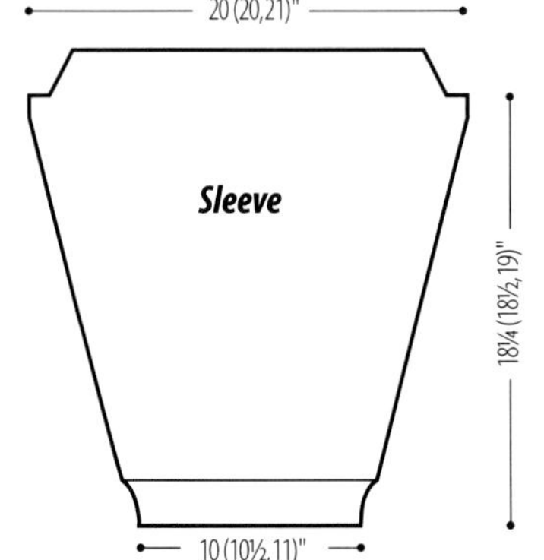

**Shape neck**
Dec 1 st at neck edge on next row, then every 3rd row 6 (6, 8) times more, then every 4th row 18 (19, 18) times, AT SAME TIME, when piece measures same as back to armhole and shoulder, shape armhole and shoulder at side edge as for cardigan or vest back.

**RIGHT FRONT**
With smaller needles, cast on 92 (100, 108) sts. Beg with p2, work 1¼" in k2, p2 rib, inc 1 st at beg of final WS row—93 (101, 109) sts. Change to larger needles. ***Beg Xanadu chart: Row 1*** (RS) Work sts 0 (10–18, 0), work 18-st rep 5 (5, 6) times, then work sts 1–3 (1–2, 1). Cont to work as for left front, reversing pocket placement and all shaping.

**SLEEVES** (cardigan only)
With smaller needles, cast on 80 (84, 88) sts. Beg with k2, work 1½" in k2, p2 rib, inc 8 sts evenly spaced across final WS row—88 (92, 96) sts. Change to larger needles. ***Beg Xanadu chart: Row 1*** (RS) Work sts 11–18 (18, 16–18), work 18-st rep 4 (5, 5) times, then work sts 1–8 (1, 1–3). ***Row 2*** Work sts 8–1 (1, 3–1), work 18-st rep 4 (5, 5) times, work sts 18–11 (18, 18–16). Work chart pat as established, AT SAME TIME, inc 1 st each side (working incs into chart pat) at beg of next RS row, then every 4th row 24 (11, 17) times more, then every 5th row 12 (23, 19) times—160 (160, 168) sts. Work even in pat until piece measures 18¼ (18½, 19)" from beg, end with a WS row.
**Shape cap**
Bind off 7 (8, 8) sts at beg of next 2 rows. Dec 1 st each side of next row, then every 2nd row 9 (9, 10) times more. Bind off rem sts.

**FINISHING**
Block pieces lightly. Sew shoulder seams.
**Vest: Front bands**
Place markers for 5 buttonholes on left front, the first ½" from bottom edge, the last ¾" below beg of neck shaping, and 3 others spaced evenly between. With smaller needles, cast on 9 (11, 11) sts. Work in Paradise buttonband pat, sewing band to garment as it is knit, beg at lower left front and end at lower right front, stretching slightly to fit. **Work vertical buttonholes at markers as foll: ***Next row*** (RS) Work 4 (5, 5) sts, turn, place rem sts on hold. Work 4 more rows in pat and place sts on hold. Beg with RS facing, work 5 rows on rem 5 (6, 6) sts. ***Next (joining) row*** (WS) Work across 9 (11, 11) sts.**
**Cardigan: Front bands**
Place markers for 5 buttonholes on left front, the first ½" from bottom edge, the last ¾" below beg of neck shaping, and 3 others spaced evenly between. With smaller needles, cast on 9 (11, 11) sts. Work in k1, p1 rib, sewing band to garment as it is knit, beg at lower left front and end at lower right front, stretching slightly to fit. Work vertical buttonholes at markers as for vest, from** to **.
**Armbands** (vest only)
With RS facing and smaller needles, pick up and k 186 (190, 206) sts evenly around armhole. Work 4 rows in k2, p2 rib. Bind off in rib.
**Pocket edgings**
With RS facing and smaller needles, work across 38 pocket sts on hold in k2, p2 rib. Work 4 rows more in rib. Bind off in rib. Sew edgings to fronts. Sew pocket linings to WS.
Set in sleeves. Sew side seams (including armbands for vest). Sew sleeve seams. Sew buttons on.

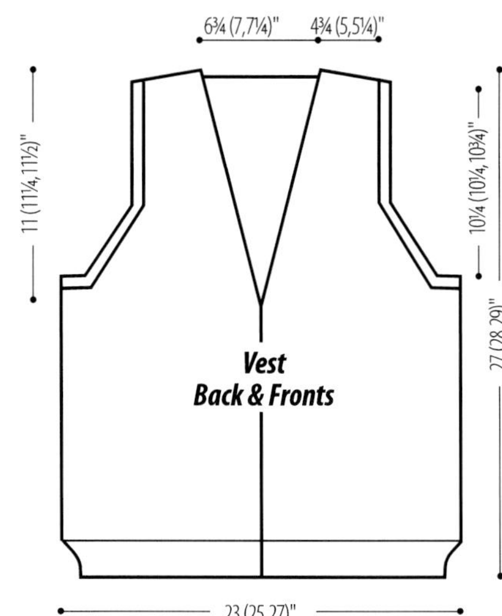

The early sixties saw a whole British generation inspired by the music, style, and attitudes of The Beatles. Styled after the fashion of their collarless suits, I made this piece reversible to reflect the Zen balance of opposites. The name comes from the Zen buddhist monastery at Tassajara for their wonderful bread book, on whose heavenly recipes my family was raised.

# TASSAJARA JACKET

**Sizes**

S (M, L).

Shown in sizes small (Colorway 1) and medium (Colorway 2).

Directions are for smallest size with larger sizes in parentheses. If there is only 1 set of numbers, it applies to all sizes.

**Finished measurements**

Chest (buttoned) 50 (54, 58)"

Length 27½ (27¾, 28)"

| | **Colorway 1** | **Colorway 2** |
|---|---|---|
| **A** | French Navy #607 | Chocolate #80 |
| **B** | Charcoal #625 | Cinnamon #691 |

**Yarn**

Rowan Designer DK

**A** 12 (13, 14) balls

**B** 11 (12, 13) balls

(each 1¾oz/50g, 126yds/115m, 100% wool)

**Needles**

One pair size 3 (3.25mm) needles; size 6 (4mm) circular needle, 24"/60cm long, *or size to obtain gauge.*

**Extras**

Stitch markers and holders.

Cable needle (cn).

Five ⅞"/22mm buttons.

**Gauge**

36 sts and 56 rows to 4"/10 cm in Sergeant Pepper pat using size 6 (4mm) needles.

NOTE Color A is the right side, but jacket is meant to be reversible, so care should be taken to keep all edges as neat and firm as possible.

**Sergeant Pepper pattern** (multiple of 2 sts)
***Row 1*** With A, *k1, sl 1 purlwise with yarn in front (wyif); rep from*. Do not turn work; sl sts to beg of needle.
***Row 2*** With B, *sl 1 purlwise with yarn in back (wyib), p1; rep from*. Turn work, making sure that yarns are crossed around each other to avoid leaving holes.
***Row 3*** With B *k1, sl 1 purlwise wyif; rep from*. Do not turn work; sl sts to beg of needle.
***Row 4*** With A *sl 1 purlwise wyib, p1; rep from*. Turn work, making sure that yarns are crossed around each other to avoid leaving holes.
Rep rows 1–4 for Sergeant pepper pat.

**BACK**
With size 6 needle and A, cast on 228 (246, 264) sts. Beg with row 1, work in Sergeant Pepper pat until piece measures 17 (16¾, 16½)" from beg, end with row 4.
**Shape armhole**
****Dec Row 1*** (RS) Sl 1 st to cable needle, hold to front, sl 1, then sl 1 st to cable needle and hold to front, sl st on right-hand needle back to left-hand needle, k2tog from cable needle, sl next 2 sts in pat, cont pat to end. ***Dec Row 2*** Sl 1, p2tog, cont pat to end. Work 2 rows even in pat. Rep from* 11 (13, 15) times more—180 (190, 200) sts. Work even until piece measures 27 (27¼, 27½)" from beg, end with row 4.
**Shape shoulder and neck**
Cont pat as foll: ***Row 1*** (RS) Work 64 (66, 70) sts; leave rem sts on hold. Work each side of neck separately. ***Row 2*** Work even on 64 (66, 70) sts. ***Rows 3–4*** Work dec rows 1–2. ***Row 1*** With A, k2tog across 20 (20, 22) sts and bind off at same time, then work pat row 1 to end. ***Row 2*** Work even. ***Rows 3–4*** Work dec rows 1–2. ***Row 1*** With A, bind off 20 (20, 22) sts as before. ***Rows 2–4*** Work even. Bind off rem sts.
***Reverse shaping and dec as foll: Row 1*** With RS facing, join yarn to rem sts and bind off center 52 (58, 60) sts as before, work to end. ***Row 2*** Work even on 64 (66, 70) sts. ***Rows 3–4*** Work dec rows 1–2. ***Rows 1–2*** Work even. ***Row 3*** Bind off 20 (20, 22) sts, work to last 4 sts, dec as before. ***Row 4*** Work to last 2 sts, p2tog. ***Rows 1–2*** Work 2 rows even. ***Row 3*** Bind off 20 (20, 22) sts, work to end. ***Rows 4, 1–2*** Work even. Bind off rem sts.

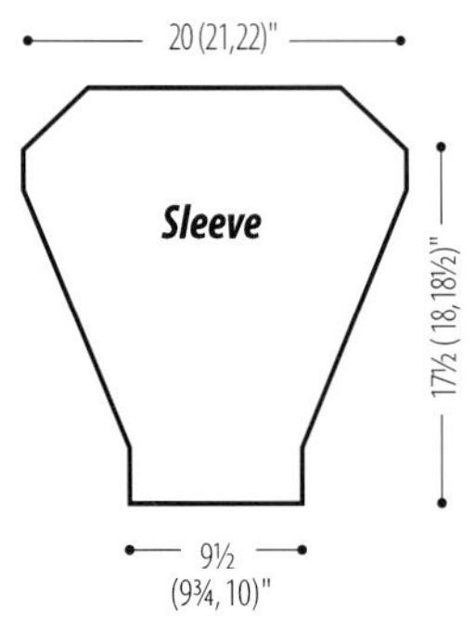


**RIGHT FRONT**
With size 6 needle and A, cast on 124 (132, 142) sts. Beg with row 1, work in Sergeant Pepper pat until piece measures 17 (16¾, 16½)" from beg, end with row 4.
Shape armhole
*Dec 1 st as for back at end of next 2 rows. Work 2 rows even. Rep from* 11 (13, 15) times more—100 (104, 110) sts. Cont in pat until piece measures 24½" from beg, end with row 4.
**Shape neck**
Bind off 22 (24, 24) sts at beg of next row. Work 3 rows even. *Dec 1 st at beg of next 2 rows. Dec 1 st at end of next 2 rows. Rep from* 3 (3, 4) times more. **Dec 1 st at beg of next 2 (2, 0) rows. Work 2 rows even. Rep from** 4 times more—60 (62, 66) sts. Work even until piece measures 27 (27¼, 27½)" from beg, end with a RS row.
**Shape shoulder**
*Bind off 20 (20, 22) sts at beg of next row, work to end. Work 3 rows even. Rep from* once. Bind off rem sts.

**LEFT FRONT**
Place 5 markers for buttons on right front, the first ¼" below neck shaping, the last 7" from lower edge and 3 others spaced evenly between. Work as for right front, reversing all shaping. Dec at beg of rows 1 and 2 for armhole. Beg neck shaping on row 3 and dec at beg of rows 3 and 4 and end of rows 1 and 2.
Work buttonholes on RS rows using color A opposite markers as foll: ***Next row*** Work to 12 sts before end, k1, *place next st on hold, k1, bind off previous k st; rep from* twice, work to end. ***Next row*** Work to last 12 sts (including bound-off sts), *p st on hold, bind off previous st; rep from* twice, work to end. Turn. ***Next row*** Work 7 sts, cast on 3 sts using thumb method, work to end. ***Next row*** Work 7 sts, *cast on 1 st, sl 1 of cast-on sts; rep from* twice, work to end. ***Next 2 rows*** Work even, working through the back lp of cast-on sts.

**SLEEVES**
With size 6 needle and A, cast on 84 (86, 92) sts. Beg with row 1, work in Sergeant Pepper pat until piece measures 2½" from beg, end with a WS row.

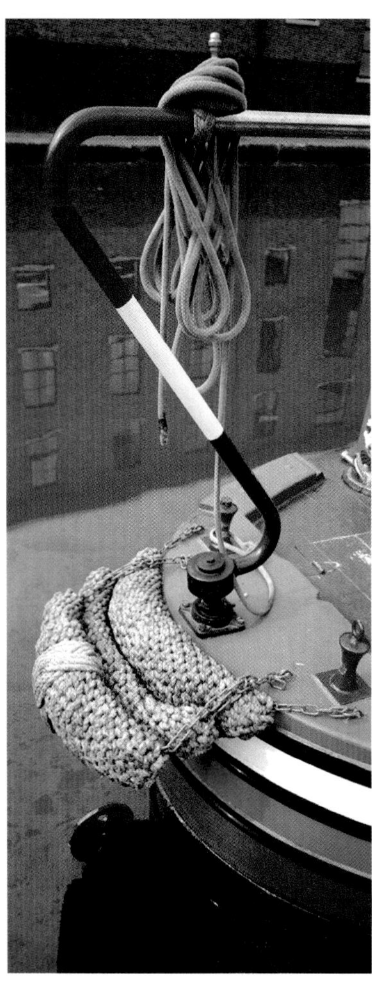

***For size S only: Inc row 1*** Inc twice into first st by working into it 3 times: once in first color, then in 2nd color, once more in first color, work to end. ***Inc row 2*** Work to last st, work 3 times into this st, keeping sequence correct. Work 8 rows even. Rep these 10 rows 5 times more. *Work the 2 inc rows, then work 6 rows even. Rep from* 17 times more—180 sts.
***For size M only: Inc row 1*** Work inc rows 1–2 as for size S. Work 6 rows even. Rep from* 25 times more—190 sts.
***For size L only: Inc row 1*** Work inc rows 1–2 as for size S. Work 6 rows even. Rep from* 26 times more—200 sts.
***For all sizes:*** Work even in pat until piece measures 17½ (18, 18½)" from beg, end with row 4.

**Shape cap**

*Dec at beg and end of next 2 rows. Work 2 rows even. Rep from* 11 (13, 15) times more. Bind off rem sts.

**LEFT FRONT POCKET**

With size 6 needle and A, cast on 34 (36, 36) sts. Beg with a p row, work 3¾ (4, 4)" in St st, end with a WS row. **Next row* (RS) Bind off 2 sts, k to end. ***Next row*** P to last 2 sts, p2tog. Rep from* 10 (11, 11) times more. Fasten off.

**RIGHT FRONT POCKET**

Work as for left pocket. Reverse shaping by starting shaping on WS row.

**FINISHING**

Block pieces. Sew shoulder seams using duplicate st in color A on RS and color B on WS (see drawing).

**Neckband**

With RS facing, smaller needles and A, beg at right front neck and pick up and k 30 (32, 34) sts to shoulder, 42 (44, 46) across back neck, 30 (32, 34) sts down left front neck—102 (106, 114) sts.
K 7 rows. Bind off all sts. Fold band and sew to WS.

**Pocket edgings**

With RS facing, smaller needles and A, pick up and k 36 (38, 38) sts along sloping edge of top of pocket. K 3 rows. Bind off.
Mark 3" up from lower edge of fronts on A side. Place lower edge of pockets on markers centered between side seam and center front. Sew into place.
Set in sleeves. Sew side and sleeve seams.
With A, sew the 2 layers of buttonholes tog neatly on very edge of buttonholes so that A is not visible on the WS. Sew buttons on.

**Duplicate st seam**

The portly frame of Bilbo Baggins, intrepid hero in Tolkien's *The Hobbit,* inspired this piece. I imagine he would have appreciated the accommodating style of the sweater, and I'm sure the myriad colors of the random-dyed yarn would have tickled his fancy. The rayon is machine-washable—always a bonus in children's sweaters.

# BILBO SWEATER

**Sizes**

S (M, L).

Shown in sizes small (Glacier #4021) and large (Aquarelle #4078).

Directions are for smallest size with larger sizes in parentheses. If there is only 1 set of numbers, it applies to all sizes.

**Finished measurements**

Chest 28 (29½, 31)"

Length 14 (14½, 15)"

**Yarn**

5 (6, 7) skeins Classic Elite Metro (each 1¾oz/50g, 110yds/100m, 100% rayon)

**Needles**

One pair each sizes 2 and 5 (2.75 and 3.75mm) needles, *or size to obtain gauge.*

Size 2 (2.75 mm) double-pointed needles (dpn).

**Extras**

Stitch markers and holders.

Two ½" (12mm) buttons.

**Gauge**

24 sts and 34 rows to 4"/10 cm in Gandalf pat using size 5 (3.75mm) needles.

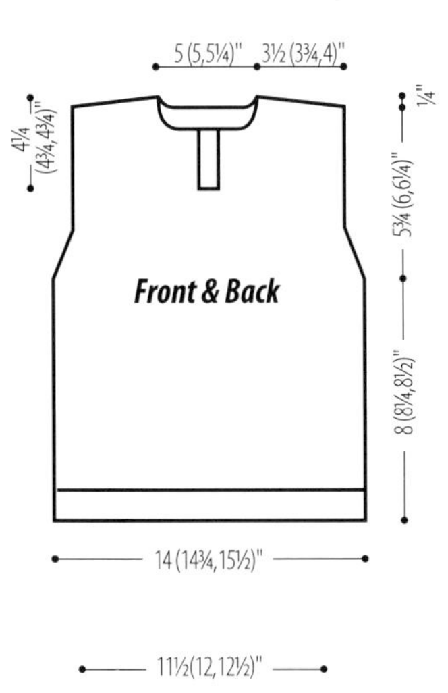


11½(12,12½)"

Sleeve

9¼ (10½, 10¾)"

**Gandalf Pattern**

*Row 1* *K1, p1; rep from*.

*Rows 2–10* K the purl sts and p the knit sts.

*Rows 11 and 13* Knit.

*Rows 12 and 14* Purl.

Rep rows 1–14 for Gandalf pat.

**BACK**

With smaller needles, cast on 84 (88, 94) sts. Work in 1½" in k2, p2 rib. Change to larger needles. Beg with row 1, work in Gandalf pat until piece measures 8 (8¼, 8½)" from beg, end with a WS row.

**Shape armhole**

***Next (dec) row*** (RS) K1, p1, ssk, cont pat to last 4 sts, k2tog, p1, k1. ***Next row*** (WS) P1, k1, p1, cont pat to last 3 sts, p1, k1, p1. Rep these two rows 5 (6, 7) times more—72 (74, 78) sts. Cont in pat, keeping 3 sts at each edge in k1, p1 rib as established until piece measures 13½ (14, 14½)" from beg, end with a WS row.

**Shape neck and shoulder**

Work 23 (24, 25) sts, turn and place rem sts on hold. Work each side of neck separately. ***Rows 1 and 3*** (WS) Dec 1 st at neck edge, work pat across. ***Row 2*** Bind off 10 (11, 11) sts, work to end. *Row 4* Bind off rem sts.

With RS facing, leave center 26 (26, 28) sts on hold, join yarn and work to end. Shape 2nd side as for first side.

**FRONT**

Work as for back until piece measures 9¾ (9¾, 10)" from beg, end with a WS row.

**Divide for placket**

*Next row* (RS) Work 33 (34, 36) sts, then work k1, p1, k1, p1, k1 on dpn, turn, place rem 34 (35, 37) sts on hold. Work each side of neck separately. Cont in pats as established, working 33 (34, 36) sts on larger needles and 5 sts of k1, p1 rib on dpn, AT SAME TIME, when piece measures 10½ (10¾, 11)" from beg, end with a RS row.

(NOTE The foll is for boys; work girls' buttonhole on opposite placket, reversing placement.)

**Work vertical buttonhole**: *Next row* (WS) Work 3 sts, turn, place rem sts on hold. Work 3 more rows in pat and place sts on hold. With WS facing, work 4 rows in pat on rem 35 (36, 38) sts. *Next row* (WS) Rejoin yarn and work across all sts. When piece measures 11¾ (12, 12½)" from beg, end with a WS row.

**Shape neck and shoulder**

*Next row* (RS) Work to last 10 (10, 11) sts, turn and place rem sts on hold. Cont in pat, dec 1 st at neck edge on next row, then every other row 6 times more, AT SAME TIME, when piece measures 13¾ (14¼, 14¾)" from beg, bind off at shoulder edge 10 (11, 11) sts once, 11 (11, 12) sts once.

**Second placket**

(NOTE This side has one more st than first side.)

With dpn and backward loop cast-on, cast on 5 sts, then with RS facing and larger needles, cont pat across 34 (35, 37) sts on hold. Work to correspond to first side, reversing shaping and pat placement (omitting buttonhole for boys and working buttonhole for girls). At shoulder edge, bind off 11(11, 12) once, then 11 (12, 12) sts.

**SLEEVES**

With smaller needles, cast on 36 (38, 40) sts. Work 2" in k2, p2 rib. Change to larger needles. Beg with row 1, work in Gandalf pat, AT SAME TIME, inc 1 st each side of next row, then every 3rd row 7 (0, 0) times, every 4th row 8 (16, 7) times, then every 5th row 0 (0, 9) times—68 (72, 74) sts. Work even until piece measures 9¼ (10½, 10¾)"from beg, end with a WS row

**Shape cap**

*Next (dec) row* (RS) K1, p1, ssk, work to last 4 sts, k2tog, p1, k1. ***Next row*** (WS) P1, k1, p1, work to last 3 sts, p1, k1, p1. Rep these two rows 5 (6, 7) times more. Bind off rem sts.

**FINISHING**

Block pieces lightly. Sew shoulder seams.

**Neckband**

With RS facing and smaller needles, beg at right neck edge and pick up and [k1, p1, k1, p1, k7 (7, 8)] from holder at right front, k13 (15, 17) along right neck edge, 2 from right back neck, 26 (26, 28) on hold at center back, 2 from left back neck, 13 (15, 17) along left neck edge, [k6 (6, 7) p1, k1, p1, k1] on hold at left front—77 (81, 89) sts. Beg with p1, work 1 row in k1, p1 rib.

**Buttonhole** (for boys; work buttonhole for girls on opposite side, reversing placement.)

*Next row* (RS) Work to last 5 sts, bind off 3 sts, p1, k1. Work 3 more rows in rib, casting on 3 sts over bound-off sts on next row. Bind off in rib.

Set in sleeves. Sew side and sleeve seams.

Sew buttons opposite buttonholes.

No tour of the sixties would be complete without mentioning the song *Mellow Yellow* by Donovan. It was one of the songs I learned when I first bought a guitar, and it immediately throws me back into my flower power period. So this piece is named after the song and knitted in the colors magenta or deep purple which, for me, epitomize the decade.

# SAFFRON TUNIC

**Sizes**
S (M, L) or
4–5 (6–7, 8–9) yrs.
Shown in sizes small (India #544) and large (Carnival #553 ).
Directions are for smallest size with larger sizes in parentheses.
If there is only 1 set of numbers, it applies to all sizes.

**Finished measurements**
Chest 32 (35, 37)"
Length 18 (19, 20)"

**Yarn**
8 (9, 10) balls Jaeger Pure Cotton (each 1¾oz/50g, 123yds/112m; 100% cotton)

**Needles**
One pair each sizes 2 and 3 (3 and 3.25mm) needles,
*or size to obtain gauge.*
Size 3 (3.25mm) circular needle 16"/40cm long.

**Extras**
Stitch markers and holders.

**Gauge**
28 sts and 32 rows to 4"/10cm in Crocus pat using size 3 (3.25mm) needles.

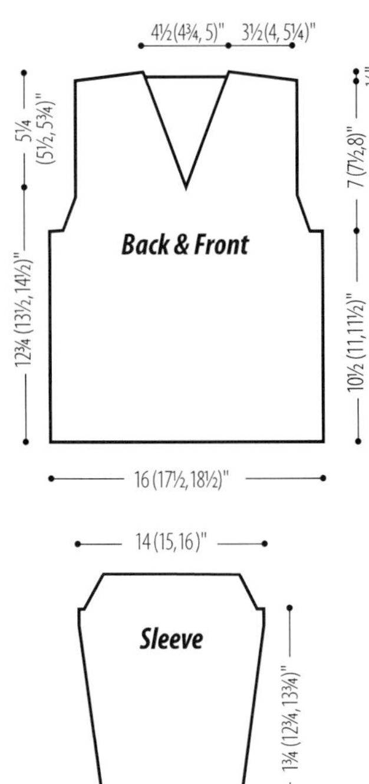


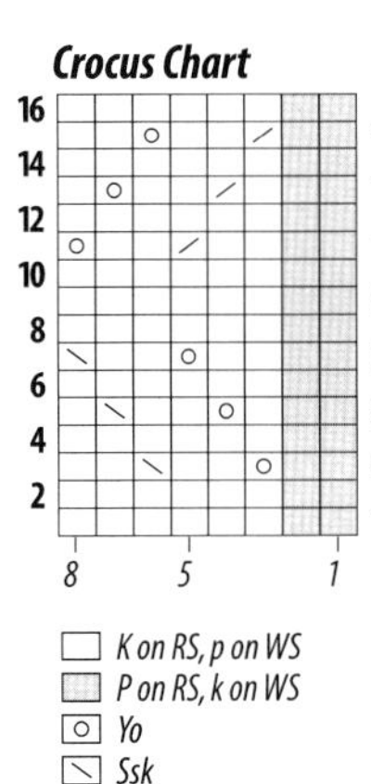


**Crocus pat** (multiple of 8 sts plus 2)
*Row 1* (RS) *P2, k6; rep from*, end p2.
*Row 2 and all WS rows* K2, *p6, k2; rep from*.
*Row 3* *P2, yo, k2, ssk, k2; rep from*, end p2.
*Row 5* *P2, k1, yo, k2, ssk, k1; rep from*, end p2.
*Row 7* *P2, k2, yo, k2, ssk; rep from*, end p2.
*Row 9* Rep row 1.
*Row 11* *P2, k2, k2tog, k2, yo; rep from*, end p2.
*Row 13* *P2, k1, k2tog, k2, yo, k1; rep from*, end p2.
*Row 15* *P2, k2tog, k2, yo, k2; rep from*, end p2.
*Row 16* K2, *p6, k2; rep from*.
Rep rows 1–16 for Crocus pat.

**BACK**
With larger needles, cast on 114 (122, 130) sts. K 2 rows. ***Beg Crocus Chart: Row 1*** (RS) Work 8-st rep across, work first 2 sts. ***Row 2*** Work sts 2–1, then work 8-st rep across. Work to top of chart as established, then rep rows 1–16 until piece measures 10½ (11, 11½)" from beg, end with a WS row.
**Shape armhole**
Cont pat, bind off 6 (6, 7) sts at beg of next 2 rows. Dec 1 st each side of next row, then every other row 8 times more—84 (92, 98) sts. Work even in pat until piece measures 17½ (18½, 19½)" from beg, end with a WS row.
**Shape shoulder and neck**
*Row 1* (RS) Work 27 (30, 32) sts; turn and leave rem 57 (62, 66) sts on hold. Work each side of neck separately. ***Rows 2 and 4*** Dec 1 st, cont pat to end. ***Rows 3 and 5*** Work 8 (9, 10) sts and place them on hold, work to end. Work 1 row even. Place rem sts on hold.
With RS facing, place center 30 (32, 34) sts on hold, join yarn to rem sts and work to end. Work to correspond to first side, reversing shaping.

**FRONT**
Work as for back until piece measures 12¾ (13½, 14¼)" from beg, end on chart row 8 or 16.
**Shape neck**
*Next row* (RS) Work 41 (45, 48) sts; turn and place rem 43 (47, 50) sts on hold. Work each side of neck separately. Work 1 row even. ***Next (dec) row*** Work to last 4 sts, k2tog, k2—40 (44, 47) sts. ***Next row*** Work even in pat. Rep last 2 rows 15 (16, 17) times more—25 (28, 30) sts. Work even until piece measures 17½ (18½, 19½)" from beg, end with a WS row.
**Shape shoulder**
**Next row* (RS) Work 8 (9, 10) sts at beg of next row and place them on hold, work to end. Work 1 row even. Rep from* once. Place rem sts on hold.
With RS facing, place center 2 sts on hold, join yarn to rem sts and work to end. Work to correspond to first side, reversing shaping as foll: At beg of row, k2, ssk, work to end.

**SLEEVES**
With smaller needles, cast on 42 (50, 50) sts. K 2 rows. ***Beg Crocus Chart: Row 1*** (RS) Work 8-st rep across, work first 2 sts. ***Row 2*** Work sts 2–1, then work 8-st rep across. Cont in chart pat until piece measures 2" from beg. Change to larger needles. Cont pat, AT SAME TIME, inc 1 st each side (working incs into chart pat) of next row, then every other row 7 (0, 0) times, then every 3rd row 21 (28, 31) times—98 (106, 112) sts. Work even until piece measures 11¾ (12¾, 13¾)" from beg, end with a WS row.
**Shape cap**
Bind off 6 (6, 7) sts at beg of next 2 rows. Dec 1 st each side of next row, then every other row 8 times more. Bind off rem sts.

**FINISHING**
Block pieces. Join shoulders using 3-needle bind-off.
**Neckband**
With RS facing and circular needle, beg at left shoulder seam and pick up and k 40 (42, 44) sts down left neck edge, place marker, 2 sts on hold at center front, place 2nd marker, 40 (42, 44) sts to shoulder seam, 2 sts down back neck, 30 (32, 34) sts across back neck and 2 sts up back neck—116 (122, 128) sts. Join and work 1 rnd as foll: *Yo, k2tog; rep from* to 2 sts before marker at center front, ssk, k2, k2tog, rep from* around. Bind off all sts (including yo's) and dec 1 st before and after markers at center front.
Set in sleeves. Sew side and sleeve seams.

The heady perfume of patchouli immediately evokes memories of the beads and bell-bottoms of the psychedelic sixties in London. Mellow pastels color the triangles, which are knitted in an easy short-row technique, creating a pillow on which to reminisce.

# PATCHOULI PILLOW

**Sizes**

S (L).

Shown in sizes small (Aqua/Mint/Ice) and large (Apricot/Lemon/Mushroom).

Directions are for smaller size with larger size in parentheses. If there is only 1 set of numbers, it applies to both sizes.

**Finished measurements**

Width 12 (16)"

Length 12 (16)"

| | Colorway 1 | Colorway 2 |
|---|---|---|
| A | Aqua #123 | Apricot #4 |
| B | Mint #416 | Lemon #30 |
| C | Ice #47 | Mushroom #84 |

**Yarn**

Rowan Lightweight DK

**A** 2 (3) skeins

**B** 3 (3) skeins

**C** 3 (4) skeins

(each ⅞oz/25g, 74yds/67m, 100% wool)

**Needles**

One pair each sizes 3 and 5 (3.25 and 3.75mm) needles, *or size to obtain gauge.*

Size G/6 (4.5mm) crochet hook.

**Gauge**

24 sts and 32 rows to 4"/10 cm in St st using size 5 (3.75mm) needles.

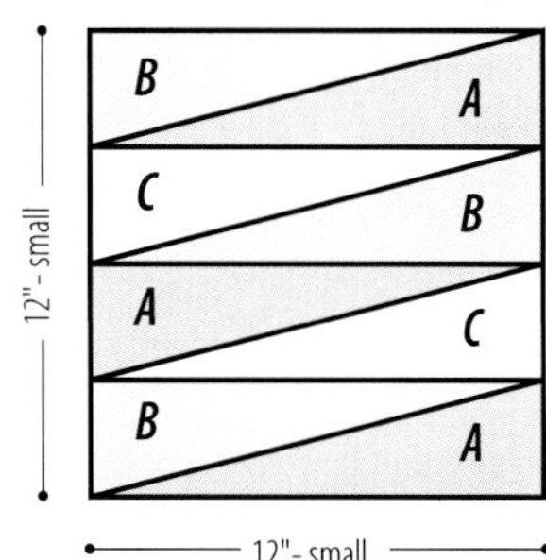


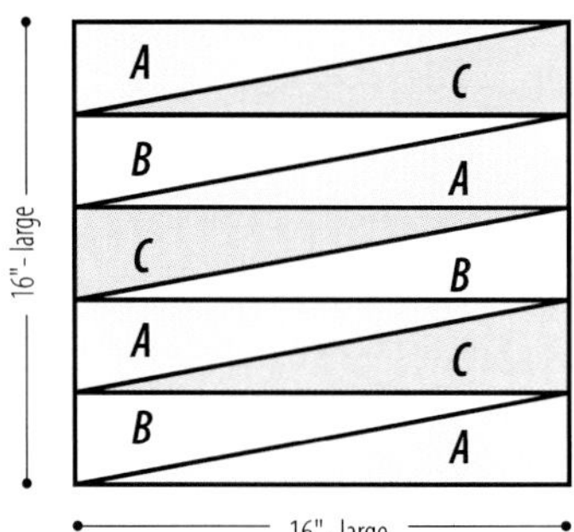


| | Colorway 1 | Colorway 2 |
|---|---|---|
| A | Aqua #123 | Apricot #4 |
| B | Mint #416 | Lemon #30 |
| C | Ice #47 | Mushroom #84 |

**Frangipani pat** (Work in St st throughout)
***Row 1*** Work to last 6 (7) sts, wrap next st and return to LH needle, turn. ***Row 2*** Work back across row. Rep these two rows 11 (12) times until 6 (7) sts remain.

**FRONT**
(NOTE This piece will be 100 (135) rows long before foldline.)
With larger needles and A, cast on 78 (98) sts. ****Beg Frangipani pat*** (RS) Work Short row pat sequence, end with a WS row. Change to B and work across all sts, concealing the wrapped sts by knitting them tog with their wraps. ***Next row*** (WS) Cont Short row pat sequence, end with a RS row. Change to C and work across all sts, concealing the wrapped sts by purling them tog with their wraps. Rep pat from* and cont to work color sequence per schematic. Work final row across all sts in B (A).

**Hem**
***Next row***: (RS) Purl 1 row to form foldline. Change to smaller needles. Beg with a purl row, work in St st until piece measures 3½" from foldline. Bind off firmly.

**BACK**
Work 100 (135) rows as for back. Bind off in B (A).

**FINISHING**
Turn 3½" St st hem of front to WS and sew in place along side seams only. With WS tog, crochet hook and C, work 1 row of single crochet (sc) across foldline of front, then join front to back on rem 3 sides with sc. Work 2nd row of sc around pillow, leaving top open. Fasten off. Insert pillow form, tucking pillow end under hem.

**Short row wrap, knit side**

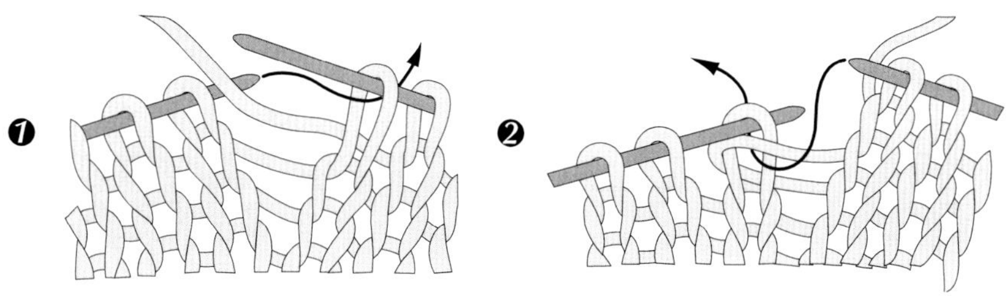

**Short rows wrap**

❶ With yarn in back, slip next stitch as if to purl. Bring yarn to front of work and slip stitch back to left needle as shown. Turn work.

❷ When you come to the wrap on a right-side row, make it less visible by working the wrap together with the stitch it wraps.

**Purl side**

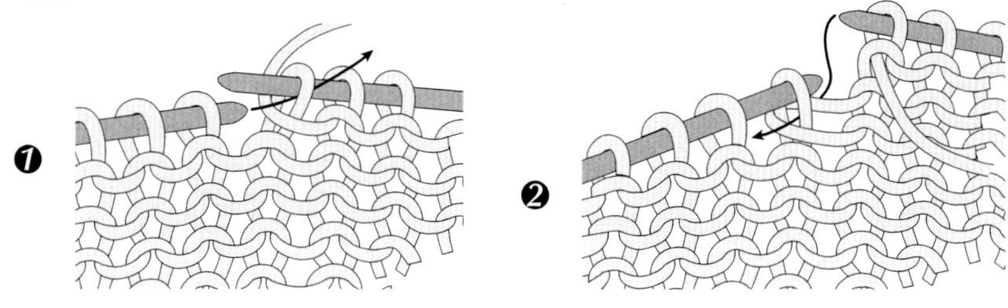

❶ With yarn in front, slip next stitch as if to purl. Bring yarn to back of work and slip stitch back to left needle as shown.
Turn work.

❷ When you come to the wrap on the following purl row, make it less visible by inserting right needle under wrap as shown, placing the wrap on the left needle, and purling it together with the stitch it wraps.

In the stripes and squares within squares of this piece, I wanted to capture the mood of the graphic black-and-white canvases of the British Op Art painter, Bridget Riley. The strip knitting technique creates a playful project which is portable as well as versatile. Whether knitted in contrasting, tone on tone or myriad stripes, this is a project which will let your creative spirit soar.

# ZEBRA THROW

**Sizes**
One size,
shown in Colorways 1 and 2.

**Finished measurements**
(without fringe)
Width 44"
Length 80"

| | Colorway 1 | Colorway 2 |
|---|---|---|
| A | Black #951 | Sage #939 |
| B | Cream #931 | Sage #939 |

**Yarn**
13 balls of A, 18 balls of B
Jaeger ExtraFine Merino
(each 1¾oz/50g, 137yds/125m,
100% wool)

**Needles**
One pair each sizes 6 and 7
(4 and 4.5mm) needles,
*or size to obtain gauge.*
Two size 5 (3.75mm) circulars,
each 36"/90cm long
(for joining strips).
Size K/10½ (7mm) crochet hook.

**Gauge**
20 sts and 28 rows to 4"/10 cm in St st using size 7 (4.5mm) needles.

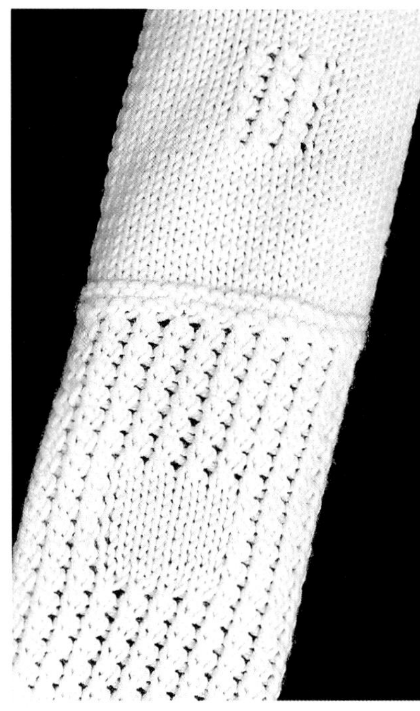

## STITCHES

**Freefall pat** (over an odd number of sts)
***Row 1*** (RS) *P1, sl 1 purlwise with yarn in back; rep from*, end p1.
***Row 2*** *K1, p1; rep from*, end k1.
Rep rows 1–2 for Freefall pat.

## THROW

(NOTE The throw is worked in 11 strips.)

**Pulsar Strip 1** (make 3)
With larger needles and B, cast on 26 sts. ***Beg Pulsar Chart:*** *Work rows 1–3. Change to smaller needles and work rows 4–40. Change to larger needles and work rows 41–80. Rep from* 6 times more. Piece should measure 80" from beg. Work rows 1–3, then bind off all sts.

**Pulsar Strip 2** (make 2)
With larger needles and B, cast on 26 sts. ***Beg Pulsar Chart:*** *Work rows 41–80, then work rows 1–3. Change to smaller needles and work rows 4–40. Change to larger needles. Rep from* 6 times more, then work rows 41–43. Bind off all sts.

**Freefall Strip** (make 6)
With smaller needles and A, cast on 17 sts. Beg with row 1, work in Freefall pat until piece measures same as Pulsar strips. Bind off all sts.

**Freefall Pat**

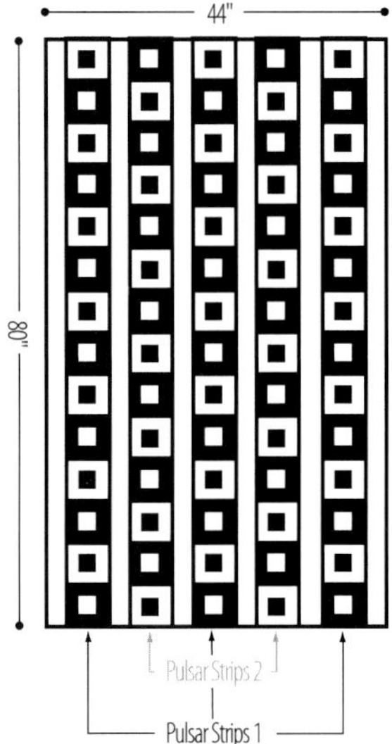


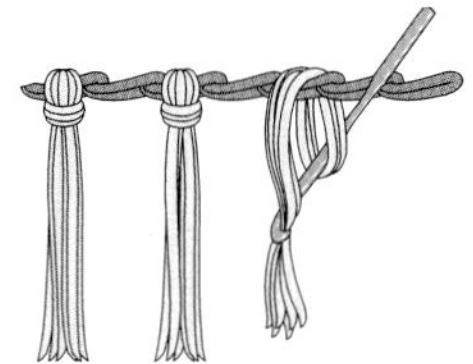

## FINISHING

***Join strips*** (see schematic for placement) On long right edge of Freefall strip, place markers to correspond to positions of rectangles (each 40 rows) on Pulsar strip. With RS facing, circular needle, and A, beg at lower edge of Freefall strip, pick up and k 34 sts to first marker, 34 sts between each pair of markers, then 34 sts to top—476 sts. Purl 1 row. With RS facing, 2nd circular needle, and B, starting at top edge of Pulsar strip 1, pick up and k 476 sts to correspond to Freefall strip. Purl 1 row. Place needles parallel with RS's of strips tog. With A and a 3rd needle, bind off each of the 476 sts of Freefall strip tog with sts of Pulsar strip 1. In same way, join rem strips.

***Fringed edging*** Cut 16" long strands of yarn. Fold 6 strands of yarn held tog in half. With crochet hook, pull the 6 folded strands through throw edge, then draw ends through and tighten. In same way, attach fringe along the 2 shorter edges of throw as foll: 3 fringes in A along edges of each Freefall strip, 7 fringes in B along edges of each Pulsar strip—53 fringes each side. Trim fringes evenly across.

***Pulsar Chart***

26 sts

- ☐ *K on RS, p on WS*
- ▒ *P on RS, k on WS*
- ⊙ *Yo*
- ⧅ *Ssk*

# INTO THE MILLENNIUM

A true work of design must move people, convey feelings, bring back memories, surprise, transgress . . . it must make us feel, intensely, that we are living our one single life . . . in sum, it has to be poetic.

Alberto Alessi 1998

My imagination is constantly fired by precious visual fragments which I've stored away for future use. The unforgettable ceiling of the Basilica of St Francis, in Assisi, painted by Giotto, the kaleidoscopic dancing rainbows of a single glass crystal, the harlequin patterns of a Venetian carnival mask, or a timeworn marbled pebble from the shores of Connemara—all are in my personal scrapbook of memories, waiting to resurface when their time comes.

Whether I'm at work designing knitwear, or in the kitchen or garden, my approach is similar. I try to create dishes which are a feast for the eyes as well as the taste buds, by using color combinations I've relished. Texture is important in food also, and since I'm a vegetarian, I love to experiment with foods like tofu and seitan to achieve the chewiness which is more often associated with meat. In the garden it is wonderful to have a whole landscape on which to experiment with color, form, and texture. I love surprises, and it is the promiscuous poppy, self-seeded in a sea of bluebells, accentuating both colors, that specially delights me.

Since I am fascinated by art in the landscape, the Yorkshire Sculpture Park was a wonderful location for this section of the book. The unexpected is around every corner there, bringing new ways of seeing the sculptures depending on the season, weather, time of day, or mood of the viewer. It is so exciting to be able to juxtapose the sculptured stitches of a sweater with a three-dimensional piece of art. The gnarled roots of a massive upended tree, the solid mass of weather-worn granite, the transient glinting of sleek aluminum curves—we were spoiled for choice in the enviable task of finding sculptures to complement each sweater.

The last decade of the century does not have a decorative art movement in the way that the twenties had Art Deco. Today's style is eclectic and postmodern in its inspiration and direction, abundant with ethnic, traditional, classical, and contemporary references. From beach or forest, attic or scrap yard, found objects play an important part in today's interiors, making the creative process of decorative art more generally accessible. Computer graphics have added another dimension, and I often wonder what Belle Époque artists would have made of it all.

In this section many of the designs follow through ideas I've collected over the past twenty years. I have always loved traditional textiles from all corners of the world and constantly use ethnic symbolism in my work; for instance, the fish, a potent image in many cultures, protects against the evil eye and brings good luck. The pared-down simplicity of many traditional patterns offers rich pickings for the designer. I have tried to develop simple ideas in this section, without sacrificing style and originality, as I feel that today's knitter doesn't necessarily have the time or expertise to invest in complicated pieces.

The word millennium has often meant a golden age of peace and happiness. With this in mind, many of the names I have chosen express my hopes for the future. I hope that, as we enter the age of Aquarius, you will enjoy the adventure of knitting my designs, and that, like the juniper tree, they will become long-lived and trusted old friends. As we navigate the unknown of the third millennium, I look forward to a renaissance of the spirit of Gaia and a healthy planet for us all.

In this sexy camisole I wish to capture the Aquarian mood of freedom and permissiveness. Easy-to-wear and easy-to-knit, it will look great worn with shorts, jeans, or dressed up for the evening with a slinky straight skirt.

# AQUARIUS CAMISOLE

**Sizes**
S (M, L).
Shown in sizes small (Frosting #540) and medium (White #600).
Directions are for smallest size with larger sizes in parentheses.
If there is only 1 set of numbers, it applies to all sizes.

**Finished measurements**
Bust 36 (38, 40)"
Length 17 (17, 18)"

**Yarn**
4 (4, 5) balls Jaeger Pure Cotton (each 1¾oz/50g, 123yds/112m, 100% cotton)

**Needles**
One pair each sizes 2 and 3 needles (3 and 3.25mm),
*or size to obtain gauge.*
Size 2 (3mm) double-pointed needles (dpn).

**Extras**
Stitch markers and holders.

**Gauge**
23 sts and 34 rows to 4"/10 cm in St st using size 3 (3.25mm) needles.

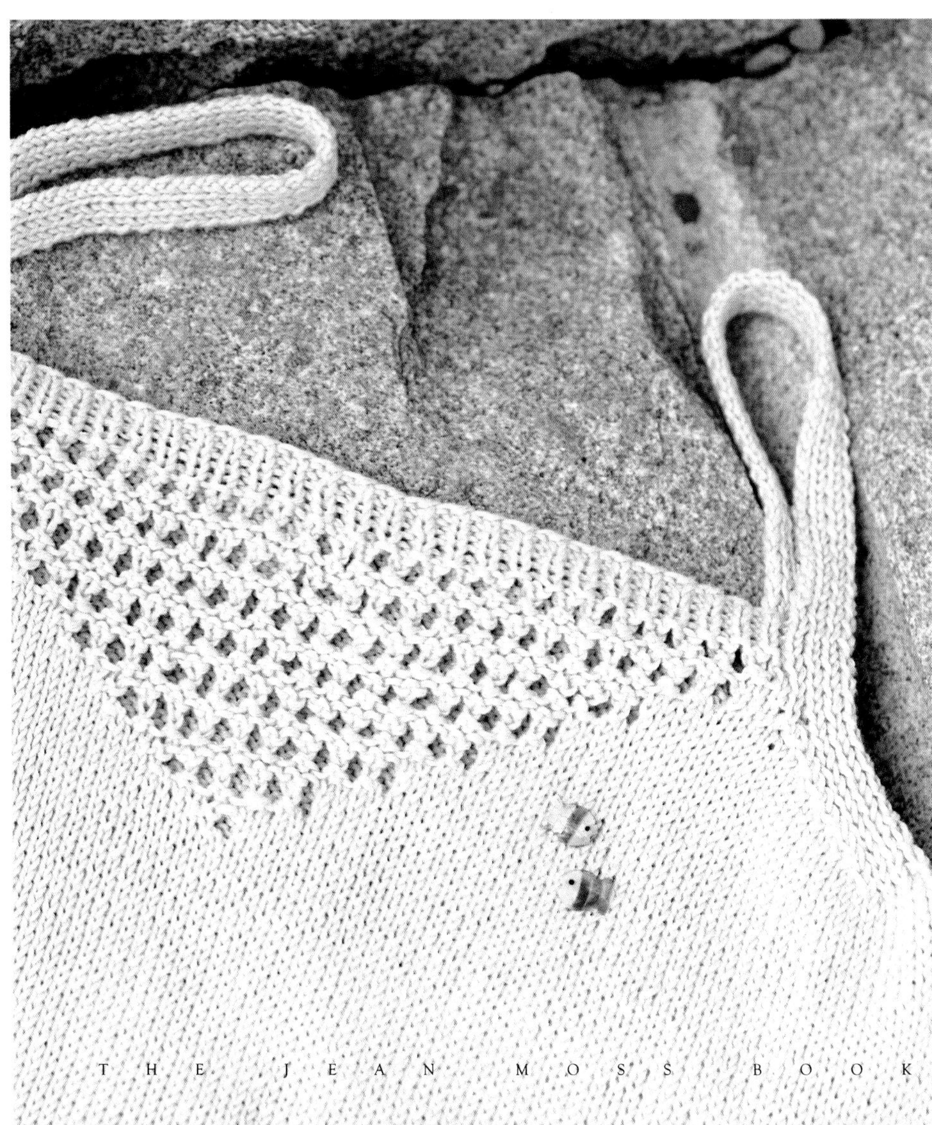

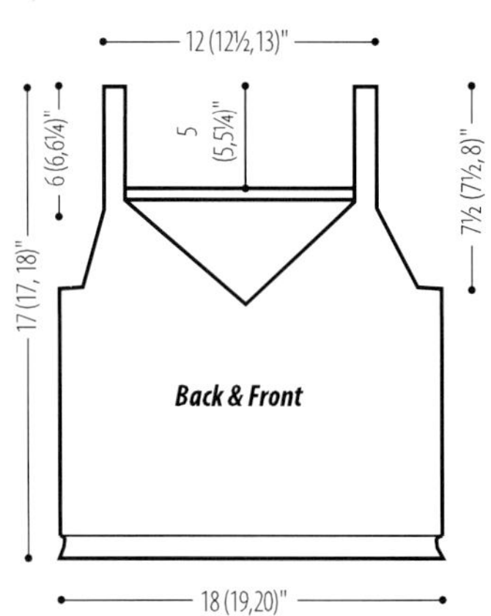


**K1, p1 graft**

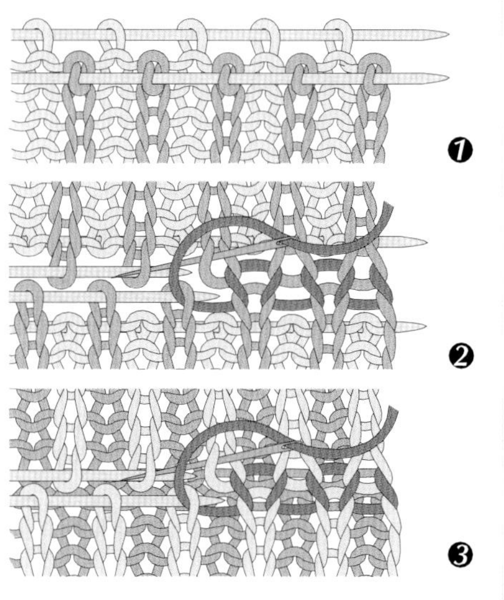


- K on RS, p on WS
- P on RS, k on WS
- Yo
- See between [ ] on Row 1
- K2tog
- No stitch

## STITCHES

**Eau-de-vie stitch** (multiple of 2 sts)

***Row 1*** *Yo, [sl 2 sts knitwise, one at a time, with yarn in front, then sl the 2nd st on right-hand needle over the first st and off the needle, k the rem st by inserting left-hand needle into the back of it and knitting it]; rep from*.

***Rows 2, 3, and 4*** Knit.

Rep rows 1–4 for Eau-de-vie st.

## BACK

With smaller needles, cast on 106 (112, 118) sts. Work ¾" in k1, p1 rib. Change to larger needles. Work in St st (k on RS, p on WS) until piece measures 9½ (9½, 10)" from beg, end with a WS row.

### Shape armhole

Bind off 6 (7, 8) sts at beg of next 2 rows. ***Dec row 1*** (RS) [K1, p1] 3 times, ssk, work to last 8 sts, k2tog, [p1, k1] 3 times—92 (96,100) sts. ***Dec row 2*** [P1, k1] 3 times, p2tog, work to last 8 sts, p2tog through the back loop (tbl), [k1, p1] 3 times. Rep last 2 rows 3 (3, 4) times more—78 (82, 82) sts. Change to smaller needles and mark 2 center sts. ***Next row*** [K1, p1] 3 times, ssk, *p1, k1; rep from* to center marked sts, p2tog, rib to last 9 sts, p1, k2tog, [p1, k1] 3 times. ***Next row*** [P1, k1] 3 times, p2tog, cont rib to last 9 sts, k1, p2tog tbl, [k1, p1] 3 times. Rep last 2 rows once more, omitting the dec'd center st—69 (73, 73) sts. ***Next row*** Work first 7 sts and place them on hold, bind off center 55 (59, 59) sts in rib, work last 7 sts then place them on hold.

## FRONT

Work as for back until piece measures 8 (8, 8¾)" from beg, end with a WS row.

***Beg Eau-de-vie Chart: Row 1*** Work 25 (26, 29) sts, place marker, work 56 (60, 60) sts of chart, place 2nd marker, work 25 (26, 29) sts. Working sts before and after markers in St st, work through chart rows 34 (36, 36). AT SAME TIME, when piece measures same as back to armhole, shape armhole as for back, keeping the 7 sts of k1, p1 rib correct at each side. After final chart row, cont as foll: ***Next row*** [K1, p1] 3 times, k1, bind off the center 55 (59, 59) sts in rib, [k1, p1] 3 times, k1.

Working each strap separately, cont in rib until strap measures 11 (11, 11½)". Place sts on hold. With WS facing, join yarn to rem strap and work as for first strap. Place sts on hold.

## FINISHING

Block pieces lightly. Sew side seams.

### Join straps

***Work K1, p1 graft:*** ❶ Divide the sts on hold from front and back onto 2 dpn, the k sts on one dpn, the p sts on 2nd dpn. ❷ Using diagram as guide and with RS tog, graft knit sts tog. *3* Turn work and graft rem sts tog. Rep for 2nd strap.

**Eau-de-vie Chart**

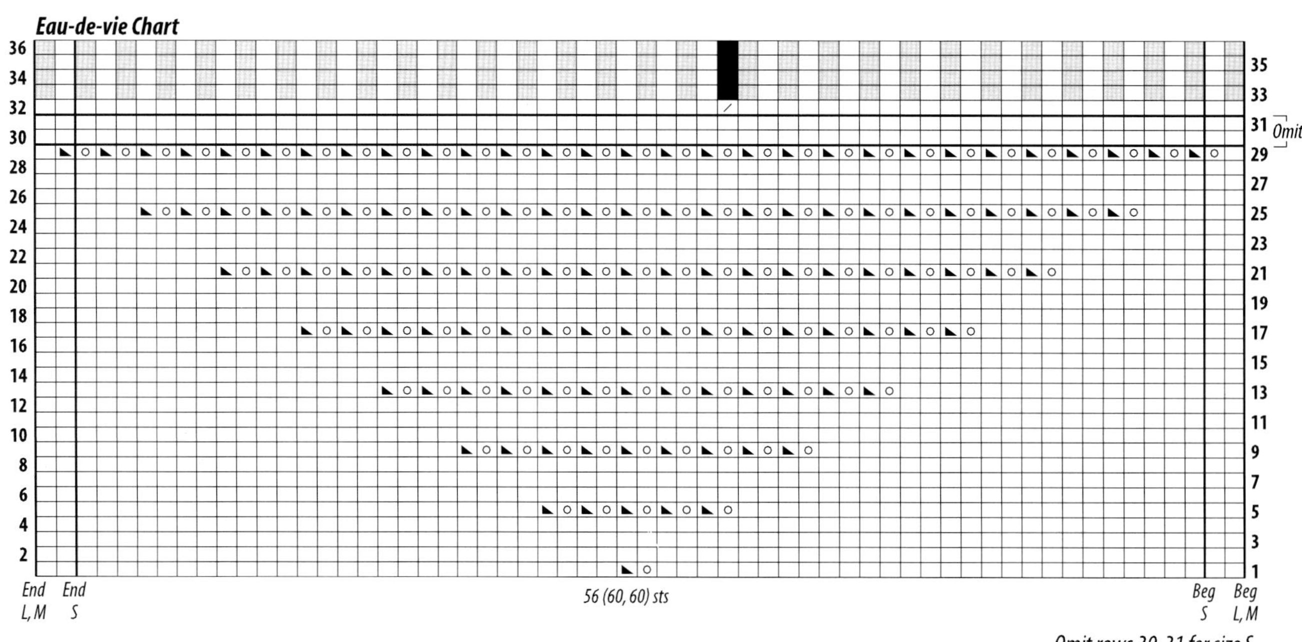


*Omit rows 30-31 for size S.*

The juniper tree lives for up to 2000 years
and the tree of life is one of the most ancient symbols
of longevity known to mankind.
This sweater expresses my hopes
for the long and healthy life of our planet
in the next millennium.

# JUNIPER SWEATER

**Sizes**

S (M, L).
Shown in sizes small (Malachite #556) and medium (Kiora #549).
Directions are for smallest size with larger sizes in parentheses.
If there is only 1 set of numbers, it applies to all sizes.

**Finished measurements**

Bust 40 (43, 46)"
Length 27 (27½, 28)"

**Yarn**

13 (14, 15) balls Jaeger Pure Cotton (each 1¾oz/50g, 123yds/112m, 100% cotton)

**Needles**

One pair each sizes 2 and 3 (2.75 and 3.25 mm) needles, *or size to obtain gauge.*
Size 2 (2.75mm) circular needle, 16"/40cm long.

**Extras**

Stitch markers and holders.

**Gauge**

27 sts and 32 rows to 4"/10 cm in Sempervivum pat using size 3 (3.25mm) needles.

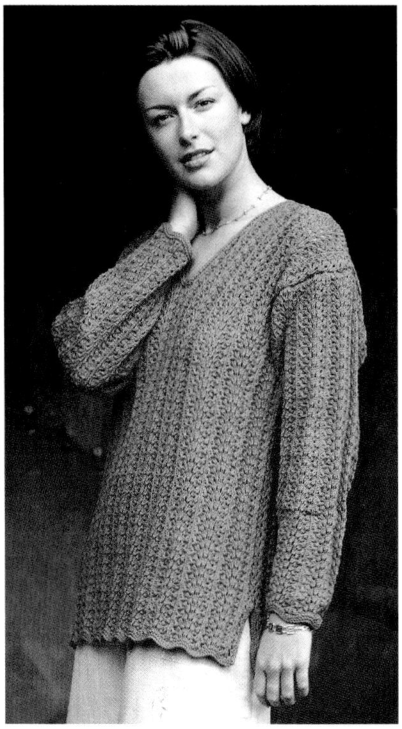

**Sempervivum Stitch** (multiple of 14 sts plus 1)
(NOTE When shaping, work pat on edge sts of Row 3 as foll: When there are 5 sts, beg row (k1, yo) twice, k3togtbl; end row k3tog, (yo, k1) twice. When there are 6 sts: beg row k2, yo, k1, yo, k3togtbl; end row k3tog, yo, k1, yo, k2. When there are 7 sts: beg row (k1, yo) 3 times, k4tog tbl; end row k4tog, (yo, k1) 3 times.
*Row 1* (RS) *K1 through the back loop (tbl), k13; rep from* to last st, k1 tbl.
*Rows 2 and 4* P1 tbl, *p13, p1tbl; rep from*.
*Row 3* *K1 tbl, k4tog, (yo, k1) 5 times, yo, k4tog tbl; rep from* to last st, k1 tbl.
Rep rows 1–4 for Sempervivum pat.

**BACK**
With smaller needles, cast on 141 (149, 157) sts. K 4 rows. Change to larger needles. ***Beg Sempervivum Chart: Row 1*** (RS) ***For sizes S and L*** K0(1); ***for size M*** Work chart sts 1–4; ***for all sizes*** work 14-st rep; ***end sizes S and L*** k1 (2); ***end size M*** work chart sts 19–23. ***Row 2, For sizes S, L*** P1 (2); ***for size M*** Work chart sts 23–19; ***for all sizes*** work 14-st rep; ***end sizes S and L*** p0(1); ***end size M*** work chart sts 4–1. Cont in pat as established, placing markers each side at 4¾ (4¾, 5)" from beg. When piece measures 18 (18, 18½)" from beg, end with a WS row.
**Shape armhole**
Cont pat, dec 1 st each side on next row, then every other row 12 (10, 10) times more—115 (127, 135) sts. Work even until piece measures 26½ (27, 27½)" from beg, end with a WS row.
**Shape neck**
Work 41 (46, 49) sts, turn and place rem sts on hold. Work each side of neck separately. ***Rows 1 and 3*** (WS) Dec 1 st, cont pat to end. ***Rows 2 and 4*** Work even in pat. Bind off rem sts firmly. With RS facing, leave center 33 (35, 37) sts on hold, join yarn and work 2nd side to correspond to first side.

**FRONT**
Work as for back until piece measures 19 (19¼, 19½)" from beg, end with a WS row.
**Shape neckline**
Work 57 (63, 67) sts, place next (center) st on hold, join a 2nd ball of yarn and work to end. Working both sides at same time, dec 1 st at each neck edge on next row, then every 3rd row 17 (18, 19) times more—39 (44, 47) sts rem each side. Cont in pat until piece measures 27 (27½, 28)" from beg, end with a WS row. Bind off rem sts.

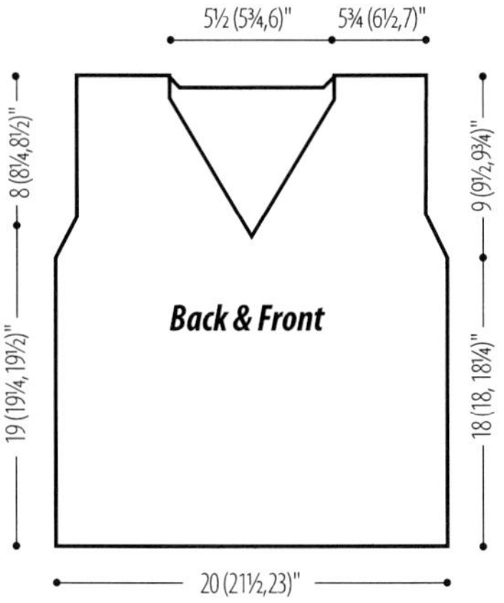


**SLEEVES**
With smaller needles, cast on 61 sts. K 4 rows. Change to larger needles. ***Beg Sempervivum chart: Row 1*** (RS) K2, work 14-st rep 4 times, work st 19, k2. Cont in pat as established, AT SAME TIME, inc 1 st each side (working incs into 14-st Sempervivum pat) every 3rd row 8 (16, 12) times, then every 4th row 22 (18, 22) times—121 (129, 129) sts. Work even until piece measures 15½ (16½, 17)" from beg, end with a WS row.
**Shape cap**
Dec 1 st each side of next row, then every other row 12 (10, 10) times more. Bind off rem sts.

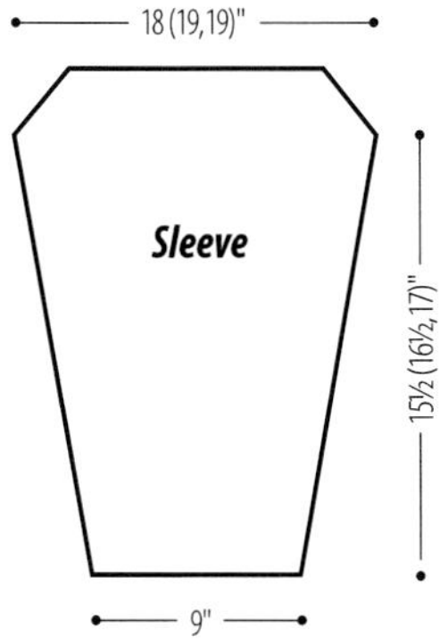


**FINISHING**
Block pieces lightly. Sew shoulder seams.
**Neckband**
With RS facing and circular needle, beg at left shoulder and pick up and k 57 (59, 61) sts along left front, 1 st on hold at center front, 57 (59, 61) sts along right front, 2 sts along right back neck, 33 (35, 37) sts on hold at center back, and 2 sts along left back neck—152 (158, 164) sts. Place marker, join and p 1 rnd, then k 2 rnds, binding off on last rnd.
Set in sleeves. Sew side seams above markers. Sew sleeve seams.
**Slit edgings**
With RS facing and smaller needles, beg at lower edge and pick up and k 32 (32, 34) sts to top of slit, then 32 (32, 34) sts down other side—64 (64, 68) sts. K 2 rows, binding off on 2nd row.

**Sempervivum Chart**

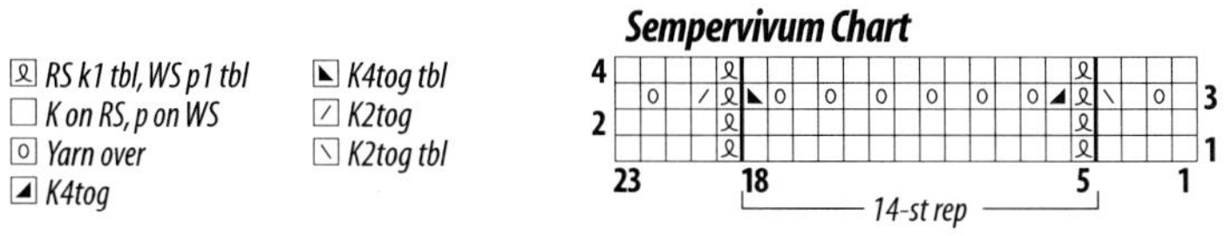

Named after the Greek goddess of the earth
who rewards those who protect her
and punishes those who harm her,
this piece aims for a harmony and balance
which will reflect the ecological message of its inspiration.
Knitted in extra-fine merino wool,
this is definitely a jacket for all earth mothers!

**Sizes**
S (M, L).
Shown in sizes small (Oatmeal #936) and medium (Blueberry #946).
Directions are for smallest size with larger sizes in parentheses.
If there is only 1 set of numbers, it applies to all sizes.

**Finished measurements**
Bust (buttoned) 38 (41, 44)"
Length 20 (20½ 21)"

**Yarn**
11 (12,13) balls Jaeger Extra Fine Merino
(each 1¾oz/50g, 137yds/125m, 100% wool)

**Needles**
One pair each sizes 3 and 6 (3.25 and 4mm) needles,
*or size to obtain gauge.*

**Extras**
Stitch markers and holders.
Six ⅝"/15mm buttons.

**Gauge**
22 sts and 32 rows to 4"/10 cm in Lovelock pat using size 6 (4mm) needles.

# GAIA JACKET

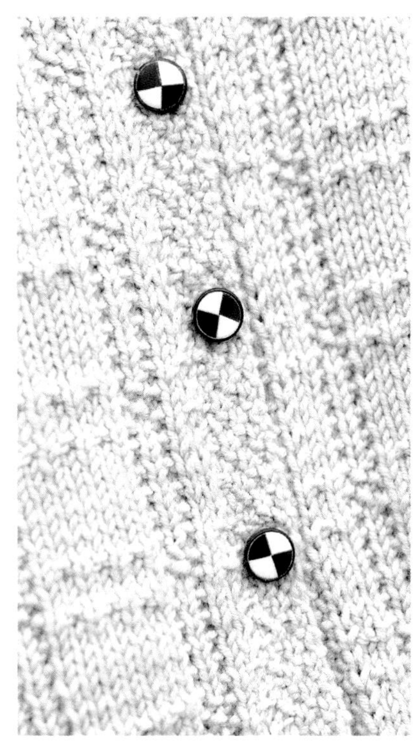

**STITCHES**
**Irish moss st** (multiple of 2 sts)
*Row 1* (RS) *K1, p1; rep from*.
*Row 2* *P1, k1; rep from*.
*Row 3* *P1, k1; rep from*.
*Row 4* *K1, p1; rep from*.
Rep rows 1–4 for Irish Moss st.

**BACK**
With smaller needles, cast on 102 (112, 120) sts. K 4 rows. Beg with row 1, work in Irish moss stitch until piece measures 3¾" from beg, end with a WS row. Change to larger needles. ***Beg Lovelock Chart: Row 1*** (RS) Work st 10 (10, 0), work 10-st rep 10 (11, 12) times, work st 1 (1, 0). Cont in chart pat as established until piece measures 11" from beg, end with a WS row.
**Shape armhole**
Bind off 4 (4, 5) sts at beg of next 2 rows. Dec 1 st each side of next row, then every other row 4 (5, 5) times more—84 (92, 98) sts. Work even until piece measures 19½ (20, 20½)" from beg, end with a WS row.
**Shape neck and shoulder**
Work 29 (32, 34) sts, turn and leave rem 55 (60, 64) sts on hold. Work each side of neck separately. ***Rows 1 and 3*** (WS) Dec 1 st (neck edge), work to end. ***Row 2*** Bind off 9 (10, 10) sts, work to end. ***Row 4*** Bind off 9 (10, 11) sts, work to end. Work 1 row even. Bind off rem sts. With RS facing, leave center 26 (28, 30) sts on hold and work in pat across rem 29 (32, 34) sts. Work to correspond to first side, reversing shaping.

**POCKET LININGS** (make two)
With larger needles, cast on 20 sts. Beg with a p row, work 3½" in St st. Place sts on hold.

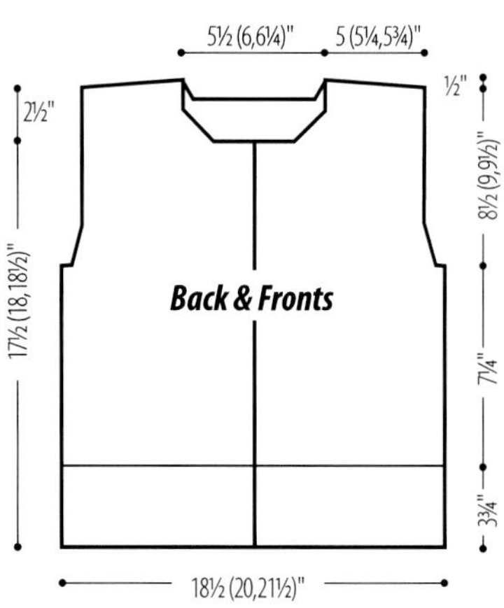


**LEFT FRONT**
With smaller needles, cast on 56 (61, 65) sts. K 4 rows. Beg with row 1, work in Irish moss st until piece measures 3¾" from beg, end with a RS row.
**Place pocket**
*Next row* (WS) Work 5 sts and place these sts on hold, work across 15 (18, 20) sts, bind off next 20 sts in pat, work to end. Change to larger needles. ***Beg Lovelock Chart row 1: Place pocket*** (RS) K 16 (18, 20) sts, with RS facing k across 20 sts of pocket lining, k to end. ***Next row*** (WS) Work chart sts 0 (5–1, 0), work 10-st rep 5 (5, 6) times, work chart sts 10 (10, 0). ***Next row*** (RS) Work chart sts 10 (10, 0), work the 10-st rep 5 (5, 6) times, work chart sts 0 (1–5, 0). Work to top of chart, then rep rows 1–14 until piece measures 11" from beg, end with a WS row.
**Shape armhole**
Bind off 4 (4, 5) sts at beg of next row. Work 1 row even. Dec 1 st at beg of next row, then every other row 4 (5, 5) times more—42 (46, 49) sts. Work even until piece measures 17½ (18, 18½)" from beg, end with a RS row.
**Shape neck**
Bind off 7 (7, 8) sts at beg of next row. Dec 1 st at neck edge on next row, then every row 3 (4, 4) times more, then every other row 4 times. Work even until piece measures 19½ (20, 20½)" from beg, end with a WS row.
**Shape shoulder**
At shoulder edge, bind off 9 (10, 10) sts once, 9 (10, 11) sts once. Bind off rem sts.

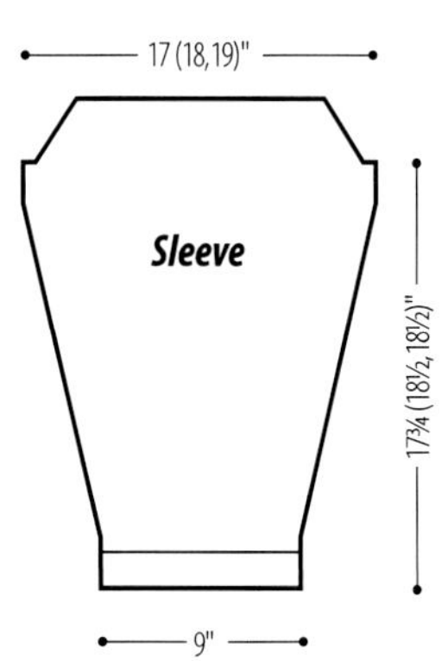


**RIGHT FRONT**
Work as for left front, reversing all shaping and pocket placement. AT SAME TIME, when piece measures 3½" from beg, end with a WS row. ***Work first buttonhole: Next row*** Work 2 sts, bind off 2 sts, work to end. On next row, cast on 2 sts over bound-off sts of previous row. On foll row, work cast-on sts through the back lp. Center chart pat as foll: ***Row 1*** (RS) Work chart sts 0 (6–10, 0), work 10-st rep 5 (5, 6) times, work chart st 1 (1, 0).

**SLEEVES**
With smaller needles, cast on 50 sts. K 4 rows. Beg with row 1, work in Irish moss st until piece measures 1¼" from beg, end with a WS row. Change to larger needles. Beg with row 1, work in

chart pat, AT THE SAME TIME, inc 1 st each side (working incs into chart pat) every 4th row 0 (0, 9) times, every 5th row 12 (18, 18) times, then every 6th row 10 (6, 0) times—94 (98, 104) sts. Work even until piece measures 17¾ (18½, 18½)" from beg, end with a WS row.

**Shape cap**

Bind off 4 (4, 5) sts at beg of next 2 rows. Dec 1 st each side of next row, then every other row 4 (5, 5) times more. Bind off rem sts.

## FINISHING

Block pieces. Sew shoulder seams.

**Buttonband**

Sl 5 sts on hold at left front to smaller needle. With RS facing, join yarn and cont in Irish moss st until band, slightly stretched, fits along left front. Sew band in place as it is knit. Bind off all sts. Place 6 markers on band, the first opposite buttonhole on right front, the last ¼" down from top of band and 4 others spaced evenly between.

**Buttonhole band**

Work as for buttonband, joining yarn with WS facing. Work buttonholes on RS rows opposite markers as foll: Work 2 sts, bind off 2 sts, work final st. On next row, cast on 2 sts over bound-off sts of previous row. On foll rows, work cast-on sts through the back lp.

**Collar**

With RS facing and smaller needles, beg 2 sts in from right front neck edge, pick up and k 24 (25, 26) sts to shoulder seam, 2 sts down back neck, 26 (28, 30) sts from back neck, 2 sts up along back neck and 25 (26, 27) sts along left neck edge, end 2 sts in from center front edge—79 (83, 87) sts. ***Next row*** (WS) *K1, p1; rep from* to last st, k1. ***Next row*** *P1, k1; rep from* to last st, p1. Rep last 2 rows once more. Cont as foll: ***Row 1*** (WS) [K1, p1] twice, inc 1 st in next st, k to last 5 sts, inc 1 st in next st, [p1, k1] twice. ***Row 2*** [P1, k1] twice, k to last 3 sts, p1, k1, p1. Rep rows 1–2 for 2¼", end with row 2. ***Next row*** (K1, p1) twice, k to last 4 sts, (p1, k1) twice. ***Next row*** (P1, k1) twice, k to last 3 sts, p1, k1, p1. Bind off loosely. Set in sleeves. Sew side and sleeve seams. Sew pocket linings to WS. Sew buttons on, taking care that the pattern is in line across the jacket.

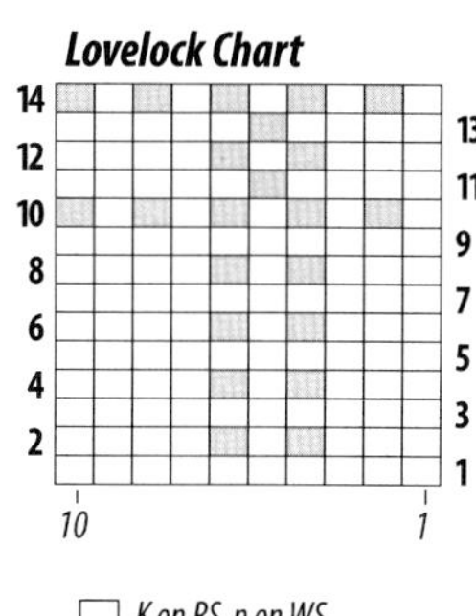

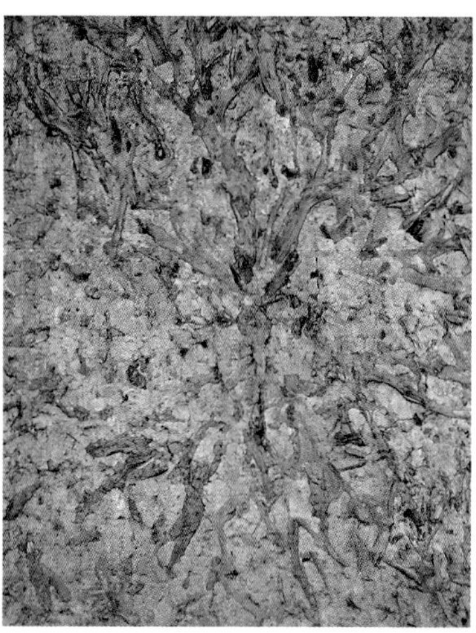

The Renaissance was a turning point in Western civilization, heralding the flowering of a new vitality and spirit and celebrating the diversity of human creativity and curiosity. I have used this allover lacy pattern as it suggests to me constant renewal and rebirth for the new millennium. The svelte lines of the piece would look great on any latter-day renaissance madonna.

# RENAISSANCE COAT

**Sizes**

S (M, L).
Shown in sizes medium (Rust #663) and sleeveless small (Aubergine #659).
Directions are for smallest size with larger sizes in parentheses. If there is only 1 set of numbers, it applies to all sizes.

**Finished measurements**

Chest (buttoned) 43 (45½, 48)"
Length 48" (with sleeves)
44" (sleeveless in photo)
Pat is written for 48" length for both styles.

**Yarn**

Rowan Designer DK
21 (22, 24) balls (with sleeves)
15 (16, 17) balls (sleeveless)
(each 1¾oz/50g, 126 yds/115m, 100% wool)

**Needles**

One pair each sizes 3 and 6 (3.25 and 4mm) needles, *or size to obtain gauge.*

**Extras**

Stitch markers and holders.
Eight ½" (12mm) buttons.

**Gauge**

24 sts and 34 rows to 4"/10 cm in Leonardo Chart pat using size 6 (4mm) needles.

NOTE Directions for Back and Fronts are for long-sleeved and sleeveless versions.

**BACK**

With larger needles, cast on 129 (137, 145) sts. K 6 rows. ***Beg Leonardo Chart: Row 1*** (RS) Work 8-st rep 16 (17, 18) times, end k1. Work to top of chart then rep rows 1–8 until piece measures 39 (38¾, 38½)" from beg, end with a WS row.

**Shape armhole**

Bind off 6 (7, 7) sts at beg of next 2 rows. Dec 1 st each side every row 6 (10, 16) times, then every other row 10 (8, 5) times—85 (87, 89) sts. Work even until piece measures 47½" from beg, end with a WS row.

**Shape neck and shoulders**

Work 29 sts, join a 2nd ball of yarn and bind off center 27 (29, 31) sts, work to end. Working both sides at same time, dec 1 st at each neck edge twice, AT SAME TIME, bind off from each shoulder edge 13 sts once, then 14 sts once.

**LEFT FRONT**

With larger needles, cast on 65 (73, 73) sts. K 6 rows. ***Beg Renaissance Chart: Row 1*** (RS) Work 8-st rep 8 (9, 9) times, end k1. Cont in pat as established until piece measures 36½ (36¼, 36)" from beg, end with a RS row.

**Shape neck**

Dec 1 st at neck edge on next row, then every 4th row 0 (9, 0) times more, every 5th row 4 (11, 12) times, then every 6th row 11 (0, 5) times, AT SAME TIME, when piece measures same as back to armhole, shape armhole at side edge as for back. When piece measures 47½" from beg, shape shoulder as for back.

**RIGHT FRONT**

Work as for left front, reversing shaping.

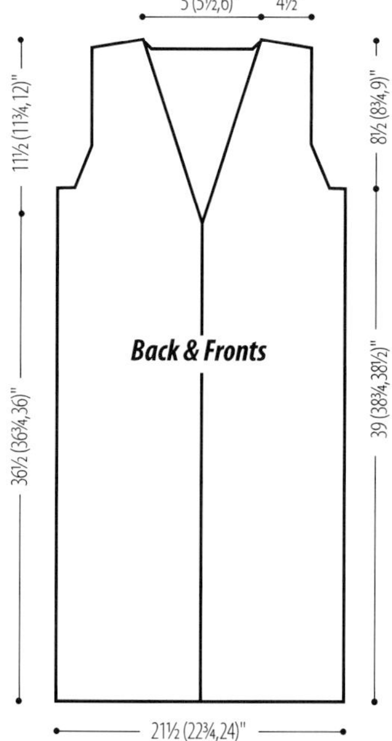


**SLEEVES**

With smaller needles, cast on 49 (52, 52) sts. K 6 rows, inc 0 (5, 5) sts evenly across final row—49 (57, 57) sts. Change to larger needles. ***Beg Leonardo Chart: Row 1*** (RS) Work 8-st rep 6 (7, 7) times, end k1. Cont in pat as established, AT SAME TIME, inc 1 st each side every 6th row 13 (0, 0) times, every 7th row 6 (12, 16) times, then every 8th row 0 (5, 2) times—87 (91, 93) sts. Work even until piece measures 16½ (16¾, 17)" from beg, end with a WS row.

**Shape cap**

Bind off 6 (7, 7) sts at beg of next 2 rows. Dec 1 st each side every row 4 times, then every other row 20 (21, 22) times—27 sts. Bind off 3 sts at beg of next 2 rows, then 5 sts beg of next 2 rows. Bind off rem sts.

***Leonardo Chart***

8-st rep

***Key***

K on RS, p on WS
Yo
K2tog
Ssk
S2kp2

**Leonardo pat** (multiple of 8 sts plus 1)
***S2kp2*** Sl2 sts tog knitwise, k1, p2sso.
***Row 1*** (RS) *K2, yo, ssk, k1, k2tog, yo, k1; rep from* to last st, k1.
***Rows 2, 4, and 6*** Purl.
***Row 3*** *K1, yo, ssk, yo, s2kp2, yo, k2tog, yo; rep from* to last st, k1.
***Rows 5 and 7*** *K1, yo, s2kp2, yo, k1, yo, s2kp2, yo; rep from* to last st, k1.
***Row 8*** Purl.
Rep rows 1–8 for Leonardo pat.

**FINISHING**

Block pieces lightly. Sew shoulder seams.

**Armbands** (for sleeveless version)

With RS facing and smaller needles, pick up and k 120 (126, 132) sts evenly around armhole. K 3 rows. Bind off.

**Front bands**

With smaller needles, cast on 5 sts and work as foll: ***Row 1*** Knit. ***Row 2*** K2, yo, k2tog, k1. Rep rows 1–2, sewing band to right front, stretching slightly to fit, until band fits around back neck to lower left front. Bind off.

Set in sleeves, distributing any fullness evenly across top of shoulder. Sew side and sleeve seams.

Mark position of 8 buttons on left band, the first 25" from lower edge, the last ¼" down from beg of neck shaping, and 6 others spaced evenly between. Sew buttons at markers.

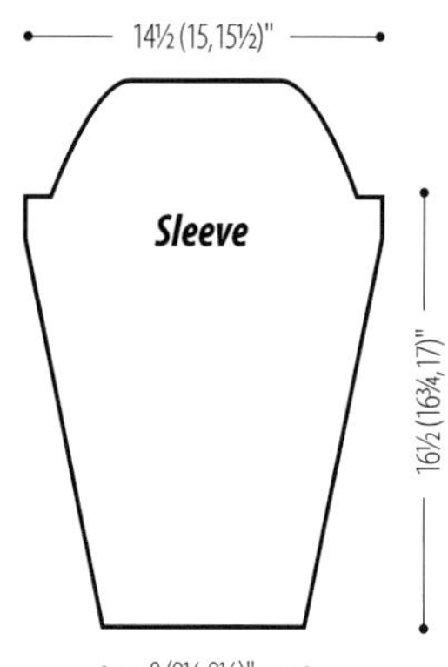

This sweater was designed by my son, Felix, after I asked him what sort of sweaters teenagers like to wear. This classy combination of bold horizontal stripes and vertical stitch pattern creates a versatile sweater of timeless style, which can be happily worn by people of all generations.

# FELIX SWEATER

**Sizes**

S (M, L).

Shown in sizes small (Colorway 1) and medium (Colorway 2).

Directions are for smallest size with larger sizes in parentheses. If there is only 1 set of numbers, it applies to all sizes.

**Finished measurements**

Chest 46 (50, 54)"

Length 26 (27, 28)"

| | **Colorway 1** | **Colorway 2** |
|---|---|---|
| MC | Linen #568 | Capri #542 |
| A | Indigo #607 | Black #606 |
| B | Auburn #546 | Umber #55 |

**Yarn**

Jaeger Pure Cotton

| | |
|---|---|
| MC | 11 (12, 13) balls |
| A | 2 (2, 3) balls |
| B | 3 (3, 4) balls |

(each 1¾oz/50g, 123 yds/112m, 100% cotton)

**Needles**

One pair each sizes 2 and 3 (2.75 and 3.25mm) needles, *or size to obtain gauge.*

Circular needle size 2 (2.75mm), 24"/60cm long.

**Extras**

Stitch markers and holders.

**Gauge**

25 sts and 34 rows to 4"/10 cm in Elysium pat using size 3 (3.25mm) needles.

**Elysium pattern** (multiple of 8 sts)
***Row 1*** (RS) Knit.
***Row 2*** *P4, k1, p3; rep from*.
Rep rows 1–2 for Elysium pat.

## BACK

With smaller needles and A, cast on 145 (157, 169) sts. Work 1½" in k1, p1 rib. Change to larger needles and MC. ***Beg Elysium pat: Row 1*** (RS) Knit. ***Row 2*** P0 (2, 0), work 8-st rep of Elysium pat 18 (19, 21) times, p1 (3, 1). Cont in pats as established, working first 0 (2, 0) sts and last 1 (3, 1) sts in St st until piece measures 12¾ (13¼, 13¾)" from beg, end with a WS row. With A, work 6 rows more in pat. With B, cont pat until piece measures 16 (16¾, 17½)" from beg, end with a WS row.

### Shape armhole

Bind off 7 sts at beg of next 2 rows—131 (143, 155) sts. Work even until armhole measures 5 (5, 5¼)", end with a WS row. With MC, cont pat until piece measures 25½ (26½, 27½)" from beg, end with a WS row.

### Shape neck and shoulder

Work 47 (52, 57) sts, place rem sts on hold. Work each side separately as foll: ***Rows 1, 3, and 5*** (WS) Work pat across. ***Row 2*** Bind off 15 (16, 18) sts, work pat to last 3 sts, k2tog, k1. ***Row 4*** Bind off 15 (17, 18) sts, work pat to last 3 sts, k2tog, k1. ***Row 6*** Bind off rem sts. With RS facing, leave center 37 (39, 41) sts on hold, join yarn and work to end. Complete as for first side, reversing shaping.

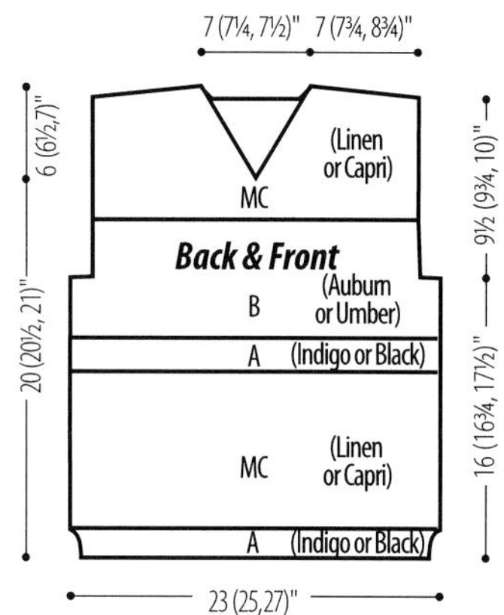


| | Colorway 1 | Colorway 2 |
|---|---|---|
| MC | Linen #5682 | Capri #542A |
| A | Indigo #607 | Black #606 |
| B | Auburn #546 | Umber #551 |

## FRONT

Work as for back until piece measures 20 (20½, 21)" from beg, end with a WS row.

### Shape neck

Work 65 (71, 77) sts, place next (center) st on hold, join a 2nd ball of yarn and work to end. Working both sides at same time, dec 1 st at each neck edge on next row, then every other row 16 (15, 14) times more, then every 3rd row 3 (5, 7) times—45 (50, 55) sts rem each side. Work even in pat and when piece measures same as back to shoulder, shape shoulder as for back.

## SLEEVES

With smaller needles and A, cast on 60 (62, 66) sts. Work 2 rows in k1, p1 rib. Change to B and cont in rib until piece measures 1½" from beg. Change to larger needles and MC. ***Beg Elysium pat: Row 1*** Knit. ***Row 2*** P2 (3, 1), work 8-st rep 7 (7, 8) times, p2 (3, 1). Shape piece and work color pat as foll: Inc 1 st each side every 4th row 5 (2, 0) times, every 5th row 23 (27, 23) times, then every 6th row 0 (0, 6) times, AT SAME TIME, work with B until piece measures 12½ (13½, 14½)" from beg, end with a WS row. With A, work 6 rows in pat. With MC, cont pat to end, working even on 118 (122, 126) sts until piece measures 19 (20, 21)" from beg. Bind off all sts.

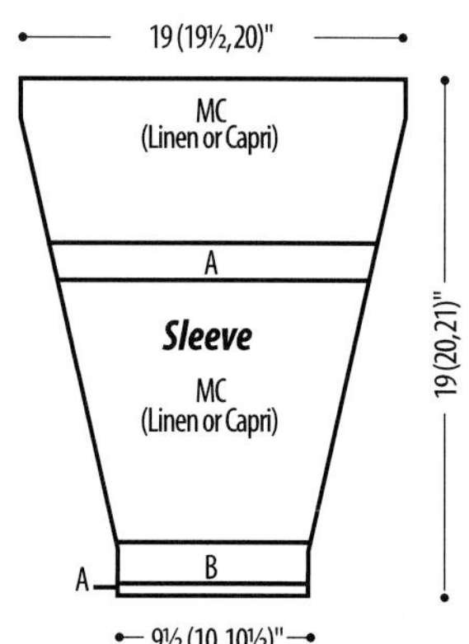


## FINISHING

Block pieces lightly. Sew shoulder seams.

### Neckband

With RS facing, circular needle and B, beg at left front shoulder and pick up and k 43 (47, 51) sts along left neck, place marker (pm), 1 st on hold, pm, 43 (47, 51) sts to shoulder, 2 sts from back neck, 37 (39, 41) sts on hold and 2 sts to shoulder—128 (138, 148) sts. Place 3rd marker, join and work in rnds of k1, p1 rib as foll: ***Rnd 1*** *K1, p1; rep from* to 3 sts before marker, k1, p2tog, k1 (center st), p2tog through the back loop (tbl), **k1, p1; rep from**. ***Rnd 2*** *K1, p1; rep from* to 2 sts before marker; k2tog, k1, k2tog tbl, **p1, k1; rep from**, end p1. Rep rnds 1–2 twice more, then rnd 1 once. With A, work rnd 2 once. Bind off in rib.
Set in sleeves. Sew side and sleeve seams.

The traditional fisher gansey, with its ropes, cables, knots, and ladders has been a longtime favorite. I have always been intrigued by the glorious textures simply created by the use of knit and purl stitches and a cable needle. In this piece botany wool gives great stitch definition while being beautifully soft to handle, creating a sweater in which to navigate your way into the 21st century.

# MARINER SWEATER

**Sizes**
S (M, L).
Shown in sizes small (Camouflage #562) and medium (Conker #555).
Directions are for smallest size with larger sizes in parentheses. If there is only 1 set of numbers, it applies to all sizes.

**Finished measurements**
Chest 50 (54, 58)"
Length 28 (28, 29)"

**Yarn**
NOTE Use 2 strands of yarn held tog throughout.
22 (24, 26) balls Rowan True 4-ply Botany (each 1¾oz/50g, 186yds/170m, 100% wool)

**Needles**
One pair each sizes 5 and 7 (3.75 and 4.5mm) needles, *or size to obtain gauge.*
Size 5 (3.75mm) circular needle, 16"/40cm long.

**Extras**
Stitch markers and holders.
Cable needle (cn).

**Gauge**
25 sts and 32 rows to 4"/10 cm in Voyager Chart using size 7 (4.5mm) needles.

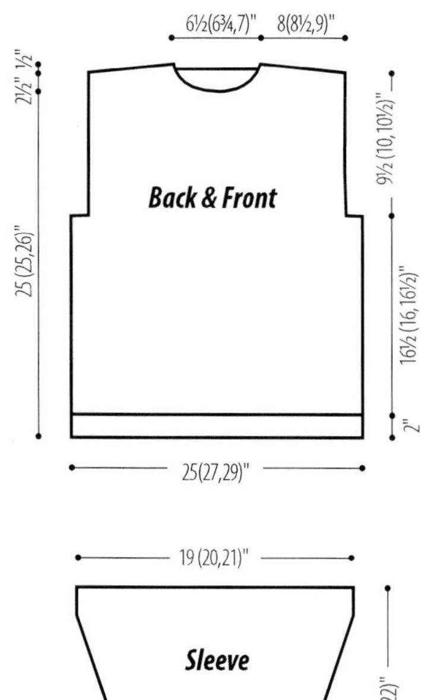


### STITCHES

**2/2 Left Cross (2/2LC)** Sl 2 sts to cable needle (cn) and hold in front, k2, then k2 from cn.
**3/3 Right Cross (3/3RC)** Sl 3 sts to cn and hold in back, k3, then p1, k1, p1 from cn.
**3/3 Left Cross (3/3LC)** Sl 3 sts to cn and hold in front, k1, p1, k1, then k3 from cn.
**3/3 Seed Right Cross (3/3SRC)** Sl 3 sts to cn and hold in back, p1, k1, p1, then k3 from cn.
**3/3 Seed Left Cross (3/3SLC)** Sl 3 sts to cn and hold in front, k3, then k1, p1, k1 from cn.

**Seed st**
***Row 1*** *K1, p1; rep from*. ***Row 2*** K the purl sts and p the knit sts. Rep row 2 for Seed st.

### BACK

With smaller needles and 2 strands of yarn held tog, cast on 158 (170, 182) sts. Beg with a k row, work 8 rows in St st. Beg with row 1, work 12 rows in Seed st. Change to larger needles. *Beg Voyager Chart: Row 1* (RS) K5 (11, 1), place marker (pm), reading chart from right to left, work 32-st rep of chart 4 (4, 5) times, then work sts 1–20, end k5 (11, 1). ***Row 2*** K5 (11, 1) sts, reading chart from left to right, work chart sts 20–1, work 32-st rep 4 (4, 5) times, end k5 (11, 1). Cont in pats as established, working sts before and after markers in garter st (k every row), until piece measures 18 (17½, 18)" from beg of Seed st (above rolled St st edge), end with a WS row.

**Shape armhole**
Bind off 10 (10, 11) sts at beg of next 2 rows—138 (150, 160) sts. Cont in pat until piece measures 27½ (27½, 28½)" from beg of Seed st, end with a WS row.

**Shape neck and shoulder**
Work 51 (56, 60) sts, turn and place rem 87 (94, 100) sts on hold. Work each side separately as foll: ***Rows 1 and 3*** (WS) Dec 1 st at beg of row, work to end. ***Rows 2 and 4*** Work 16 (18, 19) sts and place them on hold, work to end. ***Row 5*** Work even. Place rem 17 (18, 20) sts on hold. With RS facing, leave center 36 (38, 40) sts on hold, join yarn and work 2nd side of neck and shoulder shaping to correspond to first side.

### FRONT

Work as for back until piece measures 25 (25, 26)" from beg of Seed st, end with a WS row.

**Shape neck**
Work 60 (66, 70) sts, place rem 78 (84, 90) sts on hold. Work each side separately as foll: Dec 1 st at neck edge every row 6 (8, 8) times, then every other row 5 (4, 4) times, AT SAME TIME, when piece measures same as back to shoulder, shape shoulder as for back. Leaving center 18 (18, 20) sts on holder, shape 2nd side of neck and shoulder to correspond to first side.

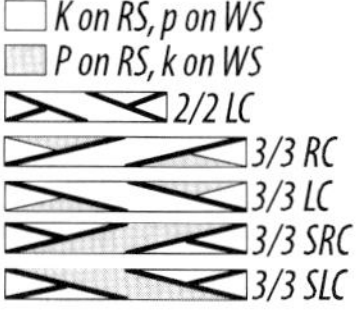


### SLEEVES

With smaller needles and 2 strands of yarn held tog, cast on 62 sts. Work 8 rows in St st and 12 rows in Seed st as for back. Change to larger needles. ***Beg Voyager Chart: Row 1*** (RS) Work sts 7–12, sts 2–32, sts 1–19, end by working sts 9–14. Cont in pat as established, inc 1 st each side (working incs into sts 2–12 of chart pat) every 3rd row 0 (0, 4) times, every 4th row 12 (28, 31) times, then every 5th row 16 (4, 0) times, —118 (126, 132) sts. Work even until piece measures 21 (21½, 22)" from beg of Seed st. Bind off all sts.

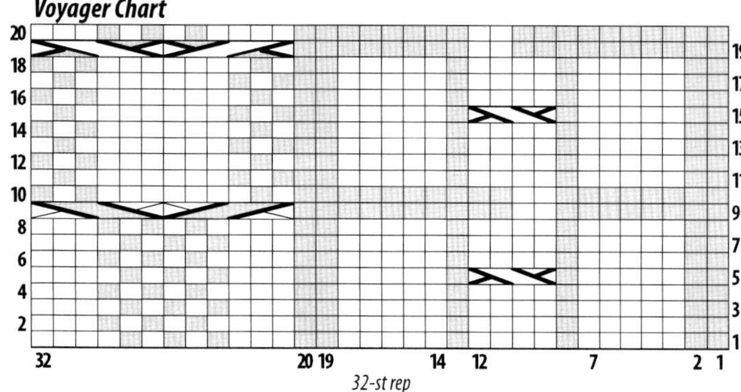


### FINISHING

Block pieces lightly. Join shoulders using 3 needle bind-off.

**Neckband**
With RS facing and circular needle, beg at left shoulder and pick up and k as foll: 23 (24, 26) sts along left neck, 18 (18, 20) sts on hold, 23 (24, 26) sts to shoulder, 2 sts along right back neck, 36 (38, 40) sts on hold and 2 sts to shoulder—104 (108, 116) sts. Place marker, join and work 2½" in rnds of k2, p2 rib. Bind off in rib.
Set in sleeves. Sew side and sleeve seams.

In Roman mythology, Cupid was the son of Venus, goddess of love. Sometimes he appears as a mischievous boy who indiscriminately wounds both gods and humans with his arrows, thereby causing them to fall deeply in love. In this piece, I have used the traditional folk art pattern of sculptured hearts to encourage Cupid to shoot his global arrows wisely to bring us a peaceful planet in the new millennium.

# CUPID WAISTCOAT

**Sizes**

S (M, L)
or 2–3 (4–5, 6–7) yrs.
Shown in sizes small (Scarlet #44) and large (Celadon #89).
Directions are for smallest size with larger sizes in parentheses.
If there is only 1 set of numbers, it applies to all sizes.

**Finished measurements**

Chest (buttoned) 26½ (29, 32½)"
Length 14½ (16, 18¾)"

**Yarn**

8 (10, 11) balls
Rowan Lightweight DK
(each 1oz/25g, 73yds/67m, 100% wool)

**Needles**

One pair each sizes 2 and 5 (3 and 3.75mm) needles, *or size to obtain gauge.*

**Extras**

Stitch markers and holders.
Five ½"/12mm buttons.

**Gauge**

30 sts and 34 rows to 4"/10 cm in Amourette Chart pat using size 5 (3.75mm) needles.

10 (10½, 11¼)"

6¼ (6¾, 7½)"

6 (6¼, 6½)"

14½ (16, 18¾)"

Back & Fronts

13¾ (14½, 16¼)"

**Eros Rib** (multiple of 4 sts plus 1)

***Row 1*** (WS) *K1, p3; rep from* to last st, end k1.

***Row 2*** *P1, sl 1, k2tog, psso; rep from* to last st, end p1.

***Row 3*** *K1, (p1, k1, p1) into front of next st; rep from* to last st, end k1.

***Row 4*** *P1, k3; rep from* to last st, end p1.

Rep rows 1–4 for Eros rib pat.

***Amourette Chart***

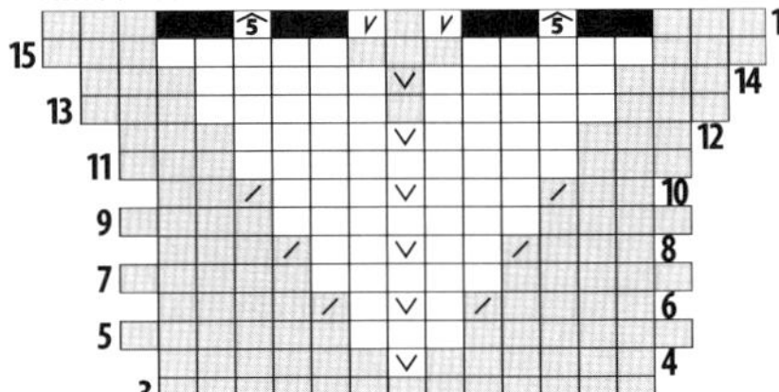


*K on RS, p on WS*

*P on RS, k on WS*

*No stitch*

*Central double inc: [K1b, k1] in st, insert left-hand needle behind vertical strand that runs down between these 2 sts and k1b.*

*P2tog*

*P1-yo-p1 in st*

*P in front and back of st*

*5-to-1 dec: Sl 3,* pass 2nd st on right-hand needle over first (center) st, sl center st back to left-hand needle and pass 2nd st over it,* sl center st back to right-hand needle and rep from* to *; p center st.*

## BACK

With smaller needles, cast on 101 (109, 125) sts. Beg with row 1, work 12 rows in Eros rib. Change to larger needles. ***Beg Amourette Chart: Row 1*** (WS) Cont Eros rib over 4 (8, 16) sts, place marker (pm) reading chart from left to right, *work 13-st rep, p3; rep from* 4 times more, work 13-st rep, cont Eros rib to end. ***Row 2*** Work Eros rib to marker, *reading chart from right to left, work 13-st rep, cont Eros rib over 3 sts; rep from* 4 times more, work 13-st rep, cont Eros rib to end. Cont in pats as established until piece measures 8½ (9¾, 12¼)" from beg, end with a WS row.

**Shape armholes**

Bind off 6 (6, 7) sts at beg of next 2 rows. Dec 1 st each side of next 5 (9, 14) rows, then every other row 6 (4, 4) times—67 (71, 75) sts. Work even until piece measures 14 (15½, 18¼)" from beg, end with a WS row.

**Shape neck and shoulders**

***Row 1*** (RS) Work 19 (20, 22) sts; turn and leave rem 48 (51, 53) sts on hold. Work each side of neck separately. ***Rows 2 and 4*** Dec 1 st, cont pat to end. ***Row 3*** Work 8 (9, 10) sts and place them on hold, work to end. ***Row 5*** Work rem sts and place them on hold.

With RS facing, join yarn to rem sts and bind off center 29 (31, 31) sts, work to end. Work to correspond to first side, reversing shaping.

**Pocket Linings** (make 2)

With larger needles, cast on 20 sts. Beg with a p row, work 2" in St st. Place all sts on hold.

## RIGHT FRONT

With smaller needles, cast on 49 (53, 61) sts. Beg with row 1, work 12 rows in Eros rib. Change to larger needles. ***Beg Amourette Chart: Row 1*** (WS) Work Eros rib over 4 (8, 16) sts, pm, *work 13-st rep, p3; rep from* once, work 13-st rep. ***Row 2*** *Work 13-st rep, cont Eros rib over 3 sts; rep from* once, work 13-st rep, work Eros rib to end. Cont in pats as established until piece measures 4½" from cast on edge, end with a WS row. ***Place pocket: Next row*** (RS) Work 14 sts, place next 20 sts on holder, then cont pat across 20 sts of first pocket lining, work rem sts. Work even until piece measures 8¼ (9¼, 11¼)" from beg, end with a WS row.

**Shape neck**

Dec 1 st at beg of next row (neck edge), then every 3rd row 14 (15, 9) times more, then every 4th row 0 (0, 6) times, AT SAME TIME, when piece measures 8½ (9¾, 12¼)" from beg, end with a RS row.

**Shape armhole**

Bind off 6 (6, 7) sts at beg of next row. Work 1 row even. Dec 1 at at beg of next 5 (9, 14) rows, then every other row 6 (4, 4) times—17 (18, 20) sts. Work even until piece measures 14 (15½, 18¼)" from beg, end with a RS row.

**Shape shoulders**

Work 8 (9, 10) sts and place them on hold, work to end. Work 1 row even. Place rem sts on hold.

## LEFT FRONT

Work as for right front, reversing all shaping and pocket placement. Place chart pat as foll: ***Row 1*** (WS) Work 13-st rep, *p3, work 13-st rep; rep from* once, pm, cont Eros rib to end. ***Row 2*** Work Eros rib to marker, *work 13-st rep, cont Eros rib over 3 sts; rep from* once, work 13-st rep.

## FINISHING

Block pieces. Join shoulder seams using 3-needle bind-off.

**Armbands**

With RS facing and smaller needles, beg at underarm and pick up and k 109 (117, 121) sts evenly around each armhole. Work rows 1–4 of Eros rib. Bind off in rib.

**Neckband**

Place 5 markers for buttonholes on right front (for girls) or left front (for boys) as foll: The first ½" from lower edge, the 5th at beg of neck shaping and 3 others spaced evenly between. With smaller needles, cast on 7 sts. ***Row 1*** (WS) P1, k1, p3, k1, p1. ***Row 2*** K1, p1, sl 1-k2tog-psso, p1, k1. ***Row 3*** P1, k1, (p1, k1, p1) into front of next st, k1, p1. ***Row 4*** K1, p1, k3, p1, k1. Rep rows 1–4, sewing to vest with RS facing, stretching slightly to fit and leaving spaces of 1/3" each time you come to a marker for buttonhole. When band fits around front edges and back neck to other side, end with row 4. Bind off. Neaten buttonholes. Sew buttons, taking care that the pattern is in line.

**Pocket edgings**

Sl 20 pocket sts onto smaller needles. With RS facing, p 1 row for foldline. Beg with a p row, work 4 rows in St st. Bind off firmly. Fold edging and sew to WS.

Sew side seams, including armholes.

The fish is a potent symbol of wealth and abundance and is said to deflect the evil eye in many traditions. As I feel our children need as much protection as we can give them, I have covered this piece in little fishes. A cozy quick-knit in aran wool to keep your little tiddler toasty warm.

# TIDDLER JACKET

**Sizes**

S (M, L).

Shown in sizes small (Colorway 1) and large (Colorway 2). Directions are for smallest size with larger sizes in parentheses. If there is only 1 set of numbers, it applies to all sizes.

**Finished measurements**

Chest (buttoned) 30 (33, 37)"

Length 14½ (16, 19)"

| | **Colorway 1** | **Colorway 2** |
|---|---|---|
| MC | Pesto #768 | Berry #684 |
| CC | Spark #767 | Turq #308 |

**Yarn**

Rowan Magpie Tweed:

3 (4, 5) skeins MC

1 skein CC

(each 3½oz/100g, 186yds/170m, 100% wool)

**Needles**

One pair each sizes 6 and 8 (4 and 5mm) needles, *or size to obtain gauge.*

Size 6 (4mm) circular needle, 24"/60cm long.

**Extras**

Stitch markers and holders.

Four ¾" (18mm) buttons.

**Gauge**

17 sts and 26 rows to 4"/10 cm in Small Fry Chart pat using size 8 (5mm) needles.

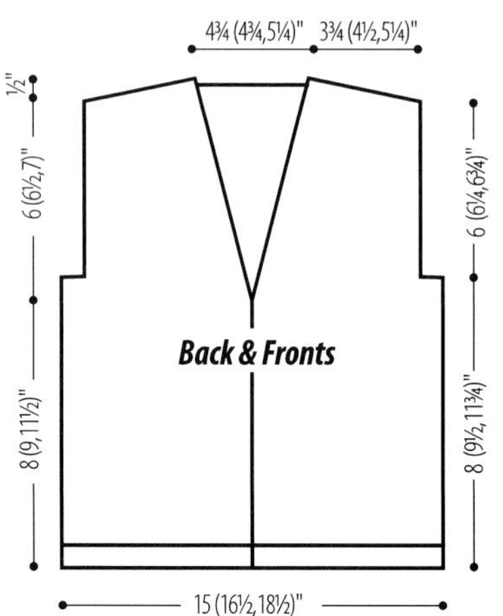


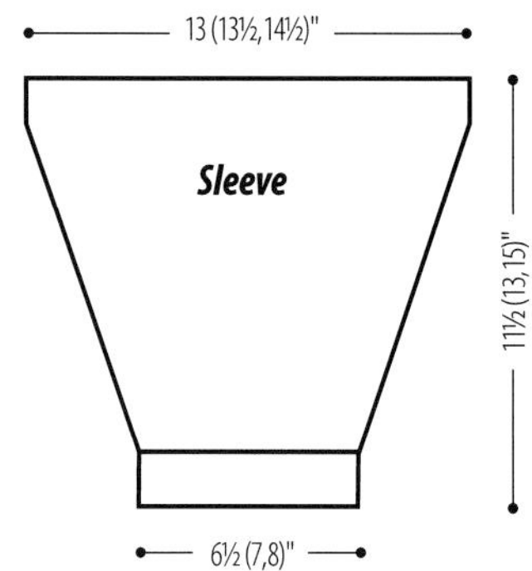


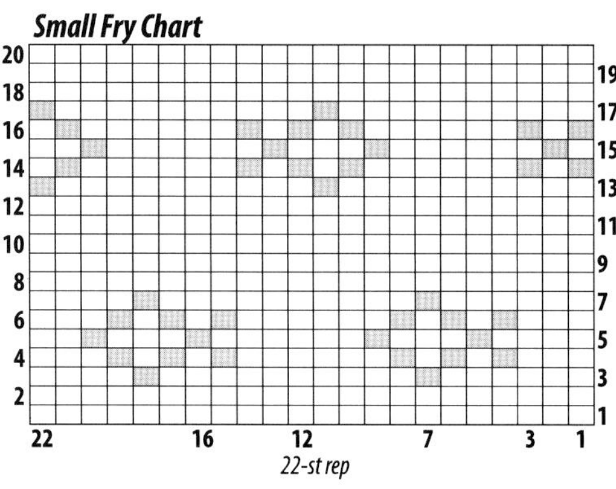


☐ *K on RS, p on WS*
▩ *P on RS, k on WS*

**BACK**

With smaller needles and CC, cast on 64 (72, 80) sts. K 6 (6, 8) rows. Change to larger needles and MC. ***Beg Small Fry Chart: Row 1*** (RS) Reading chart from right to left, work sts 13–22 (20–22, 16–22), work 22-st rep 2 (3, 3) times, work sts 1–10 (1–3, 1–7). ***Row 2*** Reading chart from left to right, work sts 10–1 (3–1, 7–1) work 22-st rep 2 (3, 3) times, work sts 22–13 (22–20, 22–16). Cont in pat as established until piece measures 8 (9½, 11¾)" from beg, end with a WS row.

**Shape armhole**

Bind off 6 (7, 7) sts at beg of next 2 rows—52 (58, 66) sts. Work even in pat until piece measures 14 (15½, 18½)" from beg, end with a WS row.

**Shape neck and shoulder**

Work 18 (21, 24) sts, turn and place rem 34 (37, 42) sts on hold. Work each side of neck separately. ***Row 1*** (WS) Dec 1 st, work to end. ***Rows 2 and 4*** Work even. ***Row 3*** Dec 1 st, work to last 8 (9, 11) sts and place them on hold. Place rem sts on hold. Leaving center 16 (16, 18) sts on hold, work other side of neck and shoulder to correspond to first side.

**LEFT FRONT**

With smaller needles and CC, cast on 32 (36, 40) sts. K 6 (6, 8) rows. Change to larger needles and MC. ***Beg Small Fry chart: Row 1*** (RS) Work sts 13–22 (20–22, 16–22), work 22-st rep once, work sts 0 (1–11, 1–11). Cont in pat as established until piece measures 8 (9, 11½)" from beg, end with a WS row.

**Shape neck and armhole**

Dec 1 st at end of this RS row (neck edge), then every 4th row 9 (9, 10) times more, AT SAME TIME, when piece measures same as back to armhole, shape armhole as for back. Work even and when piece measures same as back to shoulder, shape shoulder as for back, placing sts on hold.

**RIGHT FRONT**

Work as for left front, reversing all shaping. Place chart as foll: ***Row 1*** (RS) Work sts 0 (12–22, 12–22), work 22-st rep once, work sts 1–10 (1–3, 1–7).

**SLEEVES**

With smaller needles and CC, cast on 28 (30, 34) sts. K 6 rows. Change to larger needles and MC. ***Beg Small Fry chart: Row 1*** (RS) Work sts 20–22 (18–22, 17–22), work 22-st rep once, work sts 1–3 (1–5, 1–6). ***Row 2*** Work sts 3–1 (5–1, 6–1), work 22-st rep once, work sts 22–20 (22–18, 22–17). Cont in chart pat as established, AT SAME TIME, inc 1 st each side (working incs into chart pat) every 4th row 8 (0, 0) times, every 5th row 6 (14, 6) times, then every 6th row 0 (0, 8) times—56 (58, 62) sts. Work even until piece measures 11½ (13, 15)" from beg. Bind off all sts.

**FINISHING**

Block pieces lightly. Join shoulders using 3 needle bind-off.

**Pockets** (Make 2)

With larger needles and CC, cast on 14 (16, 20) sts. Beg with a k row, work 4 rows in St st. ***Beg Small Fry chart: Row 1*** (RS) K1 (2, 4), work sts 1–12 of chart pat (1 fish), k1 (2, 4). Work first and last 1 (2, 4) sts in St st and work through chart row 7. Work 5 (5, 7) rows more in St st over all sts. Change to smaller needles. K 5 (5, 7) rows, binding off on last row.

**Collar and buttonbands** (worked in one piece)

Place markers for 4 buttonholes on right (for girls) or on left (for boys) front, the first ½" from lower edge, the last ½" below beg of neck shaping, and 2 others spaced evenly between. With RS facing, smaller needles and CC, beg at lower edge of right front and pick up and k 34 (38, 48) sts to beg of V-neck shaping, 33 (35, 38) sts to shoulder—67 (73, 86) sts. Place all sts on hold. In same way, beg at left shoulder seam and pick up as for right front along left front. Place sts on 2nd holder. With RS facing, circular needle and CC, pick up and k 16 (16, 18) sts on hold at back neck. Work back and forth in garter st (k every row) as foll: Turn and k16 (16, 18), then k2 from right front holder. Turn and k18 (18, 20), then k2 from left front holder. In same way, cont to k 2 sts from holders at end of each row 28 (24, 20) times more, then 1 st every row 6 (18, 32) times—82 (86, 94) sts. All sts between beg of neck shaping and shoulder are now incorporated into collar. ***Next row*** Beg at lower left front, k rem sts on hold and collar sts, working buttonholes at markers as foll: bind off 2 sts; on next row, cast on 2 sts over bound-off sts. K 2 (4, 4) rows more. Bind off in knit.

Set in sleeves. Sew side and sleeve seams. Center pockets and sew to fronts with bottom of pocket 1¾ (1¾, 2)" from lower edge. Sew buttons on.

The Greenwich Meridian, an imaginary line of longitude
connecting the poles of the earth,
inspired the sculptured straight lines of this piece.
Knitted in a lightweight silk tweed yarn, this throw
is just the thing in which to snuggle up
with a glass of champagne,
while Big Ben chimes in the new millennium.

# MERIDIAN THROW AND SCARF

**Sizes**

One size, shown in Rosy (#701) and Frost (#704).

**Finished measurements**

**Throw** Approx 48" x 80" (without fringe)

**Scarf** Approx 12" x 80" (without fringe)

**Yarn**

**Throw** 26 balls Rowan Silken Tweed

**Scarf** 7 balls Rowan Silken Tweed

(each 1¾ oz/50g, 120 yds/110m; 55% wool, 37.5% silk, 7.5% cotton)

**Needles**

Size 6 (4mm) circular needle, 29"/72cm long, *or size to obtain gauge.*

Size G/6 (4.5mm) crochet hook.

**Gauge**

18 sts and 14 rows to 4"/10 cm in Meantime pat using size 6 (4mm) circular needle.

**❶ K1, wrapping yarn twice around needle**

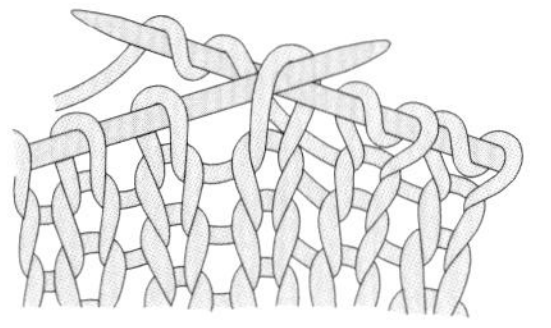

**❷ Knitting 2nd wrap tog with 1st wrap**

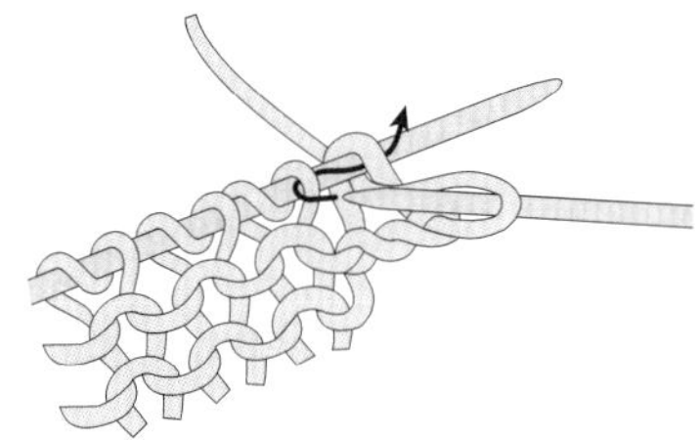

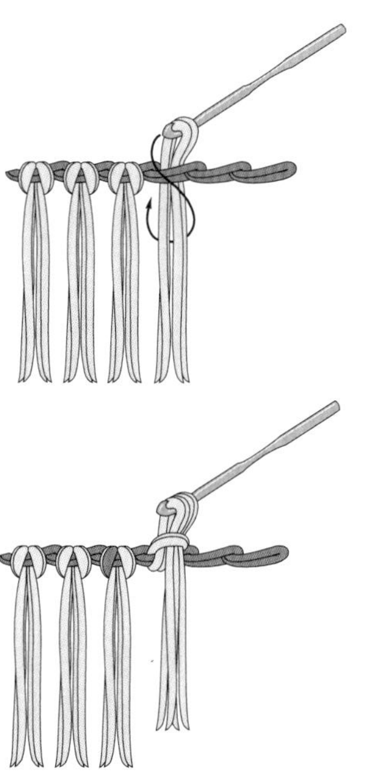

## STITCH

### Meantime pattern

***Foundation row*** K1, *k1 wrapping yarn twice around needle (see ❶); rep from*.

***Row 1*** K the first wrap (or loop) of first st, leaving 2nd wrap on needle; *k this 2nd wrap tog with first wrap of next st (see ❷), wrapping yarn twice around needle and leaving 2nd wrap of next st on needle; rep from* across.

Rep row 1 for Meantime pat.

## THROW AND SCARF

With circular needle, cast on 360 sts. Work foundation row. Work Row 1 of Meantime pat until piece measures 48" from beg. For reversible scarf, stop after 10" or 12". ***Next row*** Rep row 1, wrapping once around each needle. ***Next row*** Knit and bind off very loosely at same time.

## FINISHING

***Fringed edging*** Cut 18" long strands of yarn. Fold 6 strands of yarn held tog in half. With crochet hook, pull the 6 folded strands through blanket edge, then draw ends through and tighten. In same way, attach fringe at end of every ridge along shorter sides of piece. Trim fringe evenly across.

In Roman mythology Neptune was the god of the sea,
but the inspiration for this piece came from
his original role as god of springs and streams.
In the watery idyll of this pillow,
the sculptured fishes and flowing rivers
are given voluptuous definition by the lustrous cotton,
creating a place to indulge your dreams.

# NEPTUNE PILLOW

**Sizes**

S (L).
Shown in sizes
small (Banoffie #548)
and large (Umber #551).
Directions are for smaller size with
larger size in parentheses.
If there is only 1 set of numbers,
it applies to both sizes.

**Finished measurements**

Width 16½ (18½)"
Length 17 (18½)"

**Yarn**

5 (7) balls Jaeger Pure Cotton
(each 1¾oz/50g, 123yds/112m,
100% cotton)

**Needles**

One pair each sizes 2 and 3
(2.75 and 3.25 mm) needles,
*or size to obtain gauge.*

**Gauge**

23 sts and 26 rows to 4"/10 cm
in Poseidon Chart pat using size
3 (3.25mm) needles.

**❶ K1, wrapping yarn twice around needle**

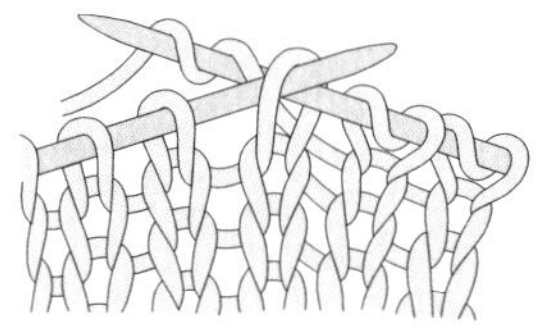

**❷ Knitting 2nd wrap tog with 1st wrap**

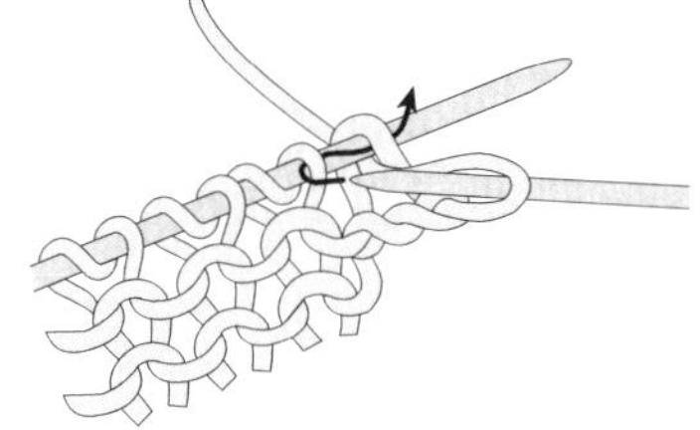

**STITCH**

**Oceanus pattern**

***Foundation row*** K1, *k1 wrapping yarn twice around needle (see ❶); rep from*.
***Pat row*** K the first wrap (or loop) of first st, leaving 2nd wrap on needle; *k this 2nd wrap tog with first wrap of next st (see ❷), wrapping yarn around needle twice and leaving 2nd wrap of next st on needle; rep from* across row, end by k 2nd wrap with last st on needle.
***Finishing row*** Work row 1, wrapping once around needle.

**FRONT and BACK**

With larger needles, cast on 95 (108) sts. In Oceanus pat, *work Foundation row, then work Pat row 6 (8) times. Work Finishing row. Beg with a k row, work 4 rows in St st. ***Beg Poseidon Chart 1: Row 1*** (RS) [K4, work 9 sts of chart] 7 (8) times, end k4. ***Row 2*** P4, [work 9 sts of chart, p4] 7 (8) times. Work pats as est to top of chart. P 1 row—a total of 20 (22) rows have been worked. Rep from* 5 times more, substituting Poseidon Chart 2 for Poseidon Chart 1 on first and 3rd rep. End last rep with 2nd St st row after Oceanus pat—110 (122) rows.

**For back**

*Next row* (RS) Bind off all sts firmly.

**For front**

**Work hem** Change to smaller needles and purl 1 row for foldline. ***Next row*** (WS) Beg with a purl row, work 3" in St st. Bind off all sts firmly.

**FINISHING**

Fold 3" hem at foldline and sew to WS along side seams only. Sew around three sides of pillow, leaving top end open. Insert pillow form, tucking end under hem, and sew 4th sides together.

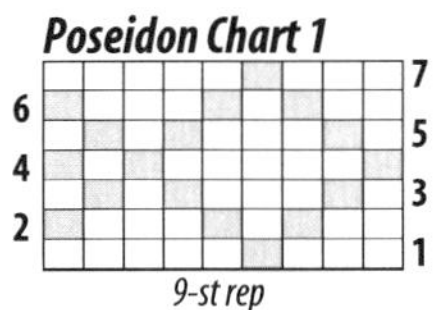


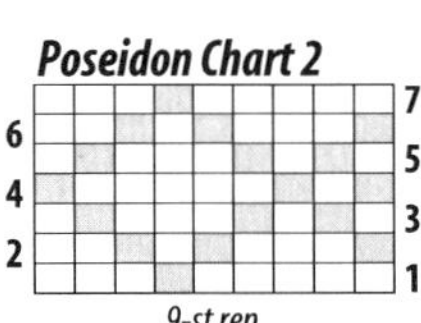


☐ *K on RS, p on WS*
▩ *P on RS, k on WS*

## Backward loop cast-on

**Uses** To cast on a few stitches for a buttonhole or the start of a sleeve.
Form required number of backward loops on needle

**Backward loop cast-on**

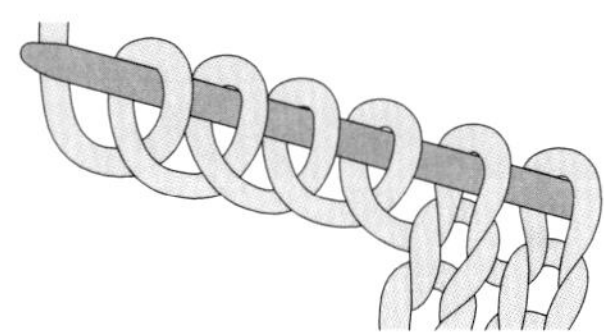

## Cable cast-on

**Uses** A cast-on that is useful when adding stitches within the work.

1 Make a slipknot on left needle.
2 Working into this knot's loop, knit a stitch and place it on left needle.
3 Insert right needle between the last two stitches. From this postion, knit a stitch and place it on left needle. Repeat step 3 for each additional stitch.

**Cable cast-on**



## Make 1

(Single increase, M1.)

1 With right needle from back of work, pick up strand between last st knitted and next st. Place on left needle and knit through back (or purl through back for M1 purlwise.)
2 This increase can be used as the left increase in a paired increase (M1L).
3 For the right-paired increase, with left needle from back of work, pick up strand between last stitch knitted and next stitch. Knit twisted.
4 This is a right M1 (M1R).

**Make 1**

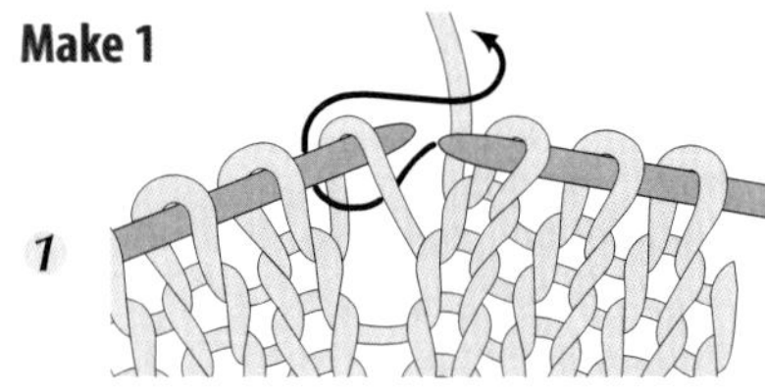


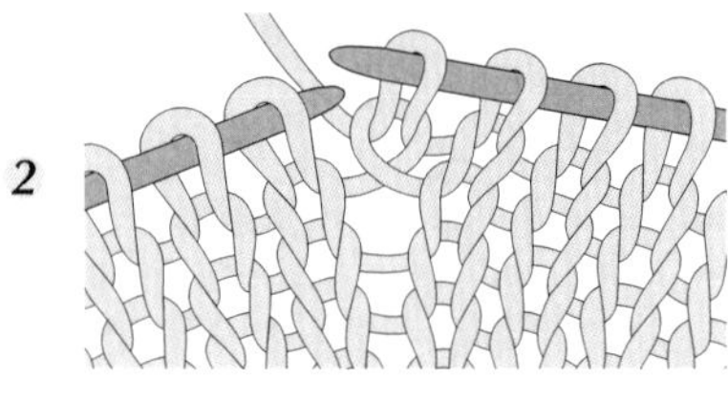


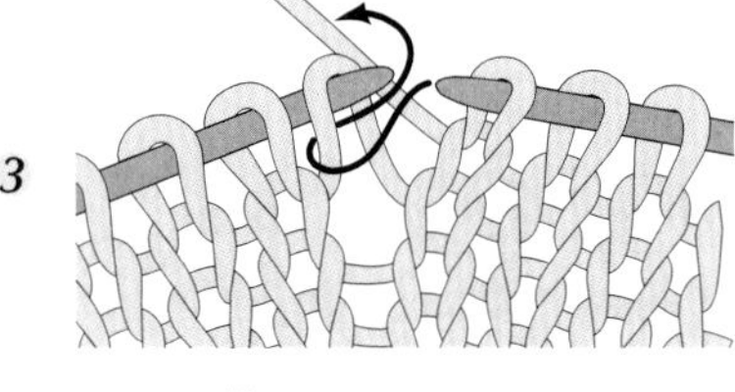


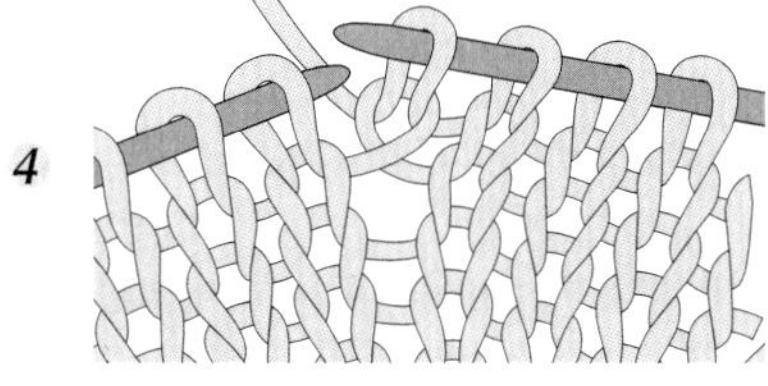


## Lifted increase

For a right increase, knit into next st on left needle in row below 1, knit into next st 2. For a left increase, knit into

last st on right needle in 2nd row below 3.

**Lifted increase**

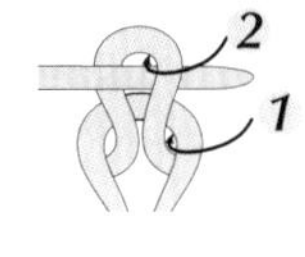


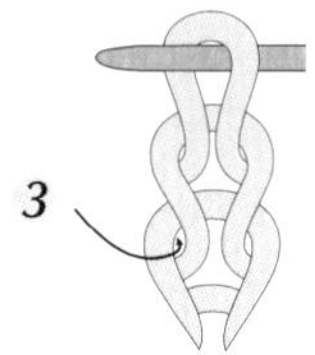


## Ssk

**Uses** Ssk is a left-slanting single decrease.

1 Slip 2 sts separately to right needle as if to knit.
2 Knit these 2 sts together by slipping left needle into them from left to right: 2 sts become 1; the right st is on top.

**Ssk**

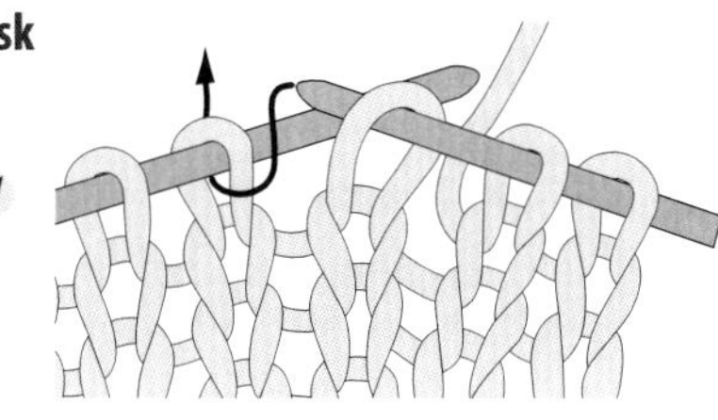


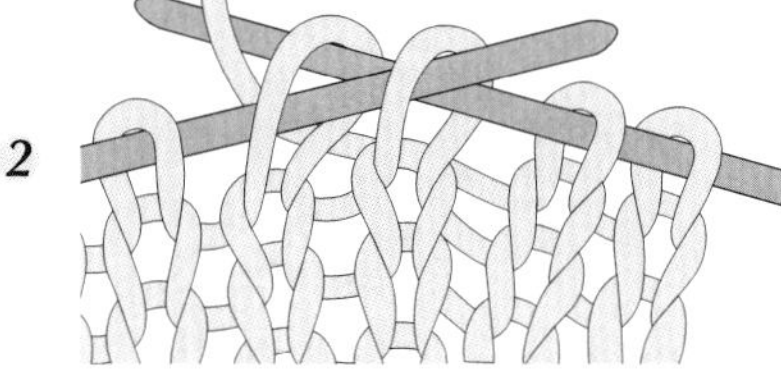


## Sl 2-k1-p2sso

**Uses** A centered double decrease.

1 Slip 2 sts together to right needle as if to knit.
2 Knit next st.
3 Pass 2 slipped sts over knit st and off right needle.
4 Completed: 3 sts become 1; the center st is on top.

**Sl 2-k1-p2sso**

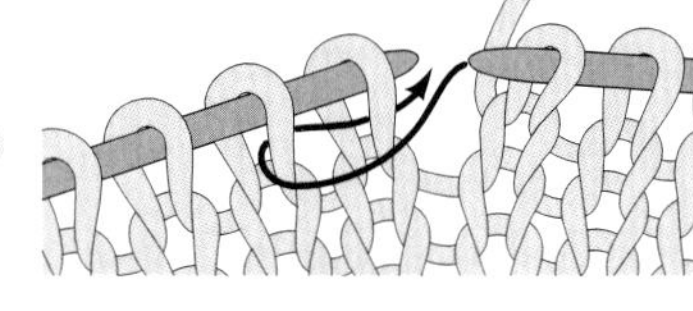


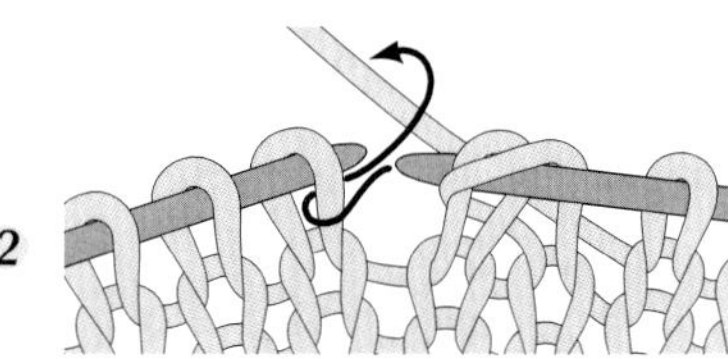


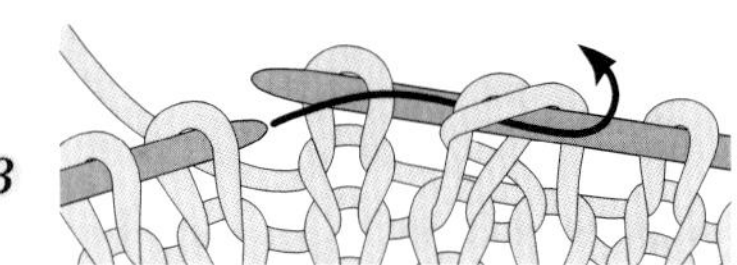


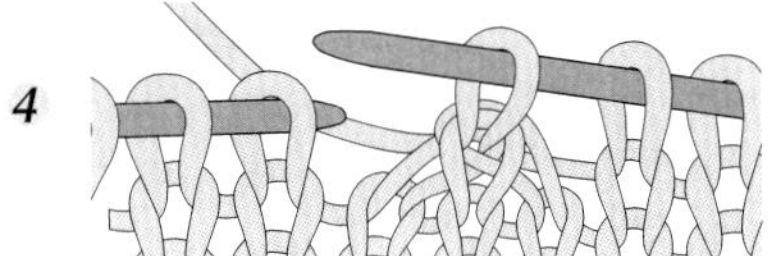


## 3-needle bind-off

**Uses** Instead of binding off stitches and sewing.
Place right sides together, back stitches on one needle and front stitches on another. *K2tog (1 from front needle and 1 from back needle). Rep from* once. Bind first stitch off over 2nd stitch. Continue to k2tog (1 front stitch and 1 back stitch) and bind off across.

**3-needle bind-off**

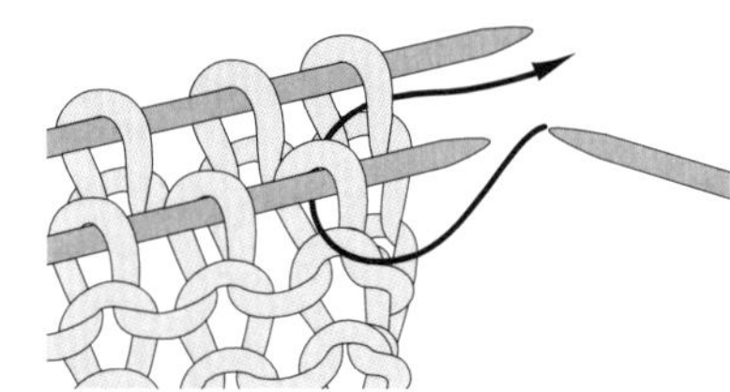

Tassels

1 2

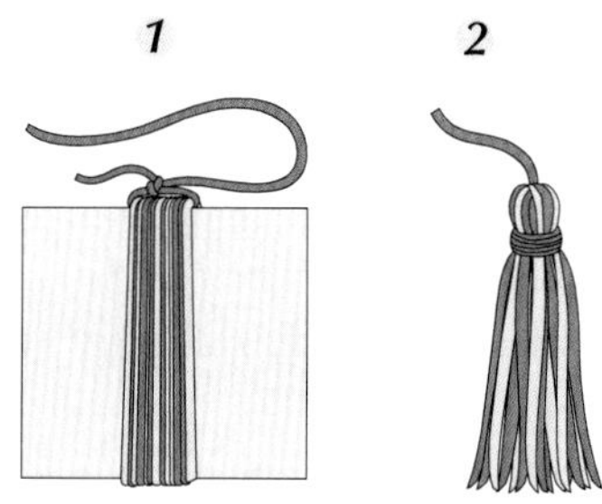

3-st I-cord

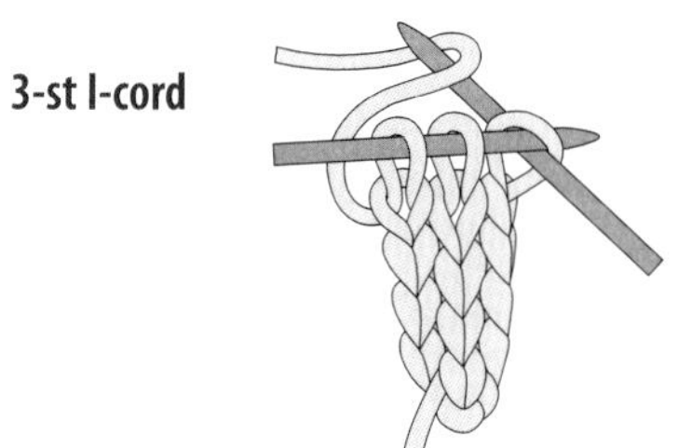

Stockinette graft

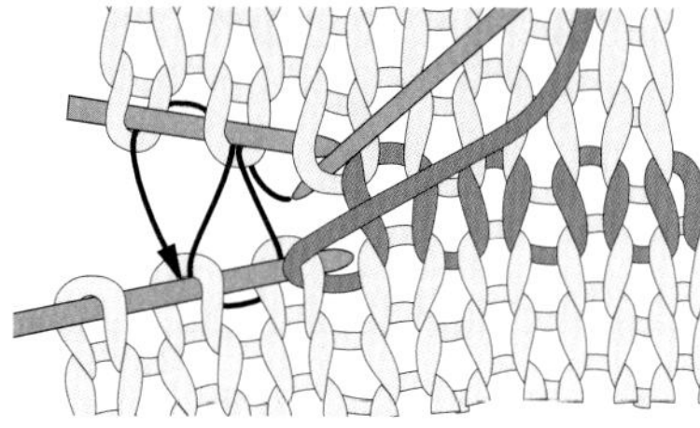

Mattress stitch

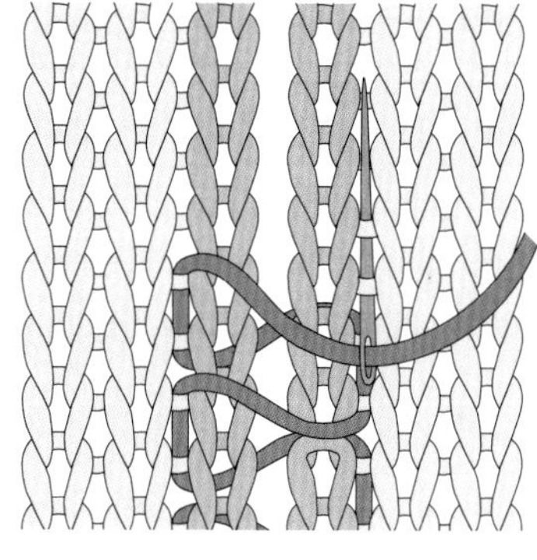

Single crochet

1

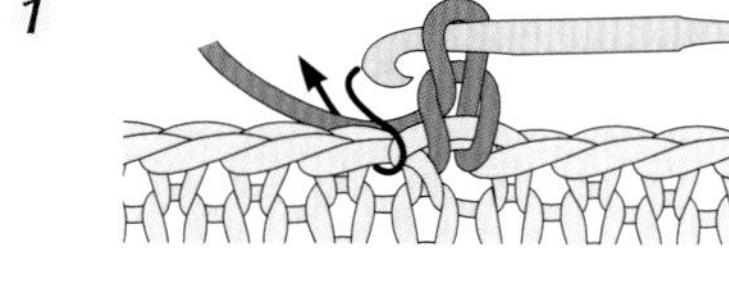

2

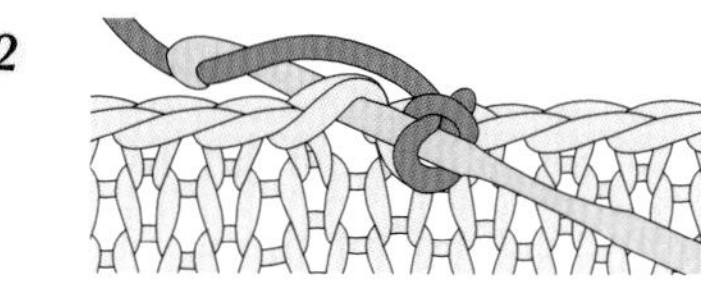

3

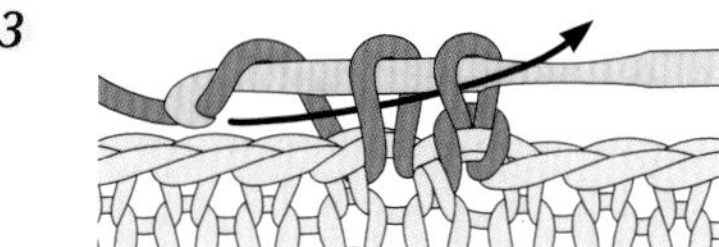

## Tassels

1. Wrap yarn around a piece of cardboard that is the desired length of the tassel. Thread a strand of yarn under the wraps and tie it at the top of the cardboard, leaving a long end.
2. Cut the wraps at the bottom of the cardboard. Wrap the long end of yarn around the upper edge and thread the yarn into the top, as shown. Trim the strands.

## 3-st I-cord

I-cord is a tiny tube of stockinette stitch, made with 2 double-pointed needles.

**1** Cast on 3 sts.

**2** *Knit 3. Do not turn work. Slide stitches to right end of needle. Rep from.*

## Stockinette graft

**1** Arrange stitches on two needles.

**2** Thread a blunt needle with matching yarn (approximately 1" per stitch).

**3** Working from right to left, with right sides facing you, begin with steps 3a and 3b:

**3a** Front needle: yarn through 1st stitch as if to purl, leave stitch on needle.

**3b** Back needle: yarn through 1st stitch as if to knit, leave on.

**4** Work 4a and 4b across:

**4a** Front needle: through 1st stitch as if to knit, slip off needle: through next st as if to purl, leave on needle.

**4b** Back needle: through 1st stitch as if to purl, slip off needle: through next st as if to knit, leave on needle.

**5** Adjust tension to match rest of knitting.

## Mattress stitch

**1** Thread blunt needle with yarn.

**2** Working between selvage stitch and next stitch (in diagram, selvage stitch is darker), pick up 2 bars.

**3** Cross to matching place in opposite piece, and pick up 2 bars.

**4** Return to first piece, go down into the hole you came out of, and pick up 2 bars.

**5** Return to opposite piece, go down into the hole you came out of, and pick up 2 bars.

**6** Repeat steps 4 and 5 across, pulling thread taut as you go.

## Single crochet (sc; U.K. double crochet)

Work slip stitch to begin.

1. Insert hook into next stitch.
2. Yarn over and through stitch; 2 loops on hook.
3. Yarn over and through both loops on hook; single crochet completed. Repeat Steps 1–3.

## Stitch charts

Each square on a chart represents one stitch. Each row of squares represents a row or round of stitches. A chart can begin with a right-side or a wrong-side row. Right-side rows are numbered to the right of the chart; for example, rows 2, 4, 6 and 8 are right-side rows. Right-side rows are read from right to left. Wrong-side rows are numbered to the left of the chart; for example, rows 1, 3, 5 and 7 are wrong-side rows. Wrong-side rows are read from left to right. Heavy lines separate a specific stitch repeat (a 6-st rep in our example).

With these general rules in mind, follow the specific instructions given in each pattern for how to work the charted stitches for that pattern.

## Abbreviations

**approx** approximate(ly)
**beg** begin(ning)(s)
**CC** contrasting color
**cn** cable needle
**cm** centimeter(s)
**cont** continu(e)(ed)(es)(ing)
**dec** decreas(e)(ed)(es)(ing)
**dpn** double-pointed needle(s)
**foll** follow(s)(ing)
**g** gram(s)
**"** inch(es)
**'** foot (feet)
**inc** increas(e)(ed)(es)(ing)
**k** knit(ting)(s)(ted)
**lb** pound(s)
**m** meter(s)
**mm** millimeter(s)
**MC** main color
**oz** ounce(s)
**p** purl(ed)(ing)(s)
**pat(s)** pattern(s)
**pm** place marker
**psso** pass slipped stitch(es) over
**rem** remain(s)(ing)
**rep** repeat(s)
**rev** reverse(d)
**RS** right side(s)
**rnd** round(s)
**sc** single crochet (U.K. double crochet)
**sl** slip(ped)(ping)
**ssk** slip, slip, knit 2tog
**st(s)** stitch(es)
**St st** stockinette stitch
**tog** together
**WS** wrong side(s)
**wyib** with yarn in back
**wyif** with yarn in front
**yd(s)** yard(s)
**yo** yarn over (U.K. yarn forward)

## Stitch charts

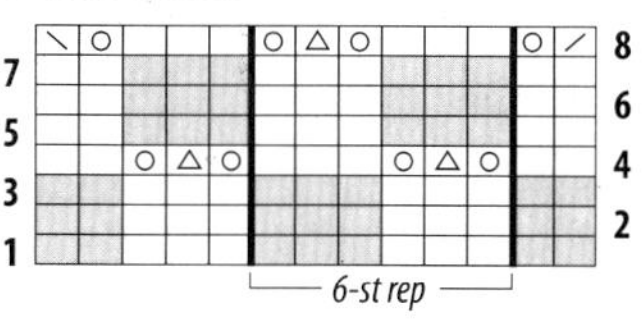


*K on RS, p on WS*
*P on RS, K on WS*
*Yo*
*K2tog*
*Ssk*
*Sl 1wyif-k2tog-psso*

## DESIGN RESOURCES

**ALESSI, Alberto,** Italian designer and manufacturer of kitchenware and tableware. Designs commissioned from Philippe Starck and Aldo Rossi among others. Major showrooms in Milan and New York. Alberto Alessi, *The Dream Factory: Alessi since 1921,* Konemann 1998.

**ASTAIRE, Fred,** 1899–1987, American dancer, singer, and actor, who starred in numerous Hollywood musicals like *The Gay Divorcée* (1934), *Top Hat* (1935) and *Swing Time* (1936).

**BAGGINS, Bilbo,** hero of J.R.R. Tolkien's *The Hobbit* (1937) and its sequel *Lord of the Rings* (1954-55).

**BEARDSLEY, Aubrey Vincent,** 1872–98, English poster designer and illustrator of books such as *Morte d'Arthur,* Oscar Wilde's *Salome, The Yellow Book* magazine, and his own *Under the Hill.*

**CHANEL, Coco,** 1883–1971, French fashion designer and founder of Maison Chanel.

**CHRYSLER, Walter Percy,** 1875–1940, American automobile manufacturer.

**CLIFF, Clarice,** 1899–1972, British ceramic designer, best known for her Bizarre range produced at Newport Pottery, Stoke-on-Trent.

**COLETTE, Sidonie Gabrielle,** 1873–1954, French writer. *Cheri* (1920), *La Chatte* (1933) and *The Stories of Colette* (1958). Herbert Lottman, *Colette: A Life,* Secker & Warburg 1991.

**DIAGHILEV, Sergei,** 1872–1929, Russian impresario of exhibitions, theatre, dance and music, founder of the *Ballets Russes,* who worked with, among many others, such luminaries as Cocteau, Picasso, Stravinsky, and Nijinsky.

**DUNCAN, Isadora,** 1878–1927, American dancer and choreographer. *My Life* (1926) is her autobiography.

**ERTÉ, Romain de Tirtoff,** 1892–1990, Russian illustrator and theater designer working in Paris. Covers for *Harper's Bazaar* (1916-26) and sets for Folies Bergère and Ziegfeld Follies in the 20s.

**FITZGERALD, Francis Scott Key,** 1896–1940, American novelist whose works include *The Great Gatsby* (1925), *Tender is the Night* (1934), and short stories *Tales of the Jazz Age* (1922).

**FORTUNY, Mariano,** 1871–1949, Spanish-born textile and dress designer. His fifteenth century Venetian home and studio is now the Fortuny Museum.

**GAIA** Hypothesis was advanced by James Lovelock in *Gaia: A New Look at Life on Earth,* Oxford University Press 1979, and argued that all living things on the planet should be considered as part of a single being.

**GARBO, Greta,** 1905–1990, Swedish-born American film actress whose many films include *Queen Christina* (1933), *Anna Karenina* (1935), *Camille* (1937), and *Ninotchka* (1939).

**GAUDI, Antoni,** 1859–1926, Spanish architect. Buildings can be seen in Barcelona, particularly the Sagrada Familia Cathedral, Casa Batllo, and Park Güell.

**GREENAWAY, Kate,** 1846–1901, English artist and illustrator of children's books, such as *Mother Goose, Under the Windows,* and *Little Ann.*

**KLIMT, Gustav,** 1862–1918, Austrian painter and designer, founder of the avant-garde Vienna Secession. Major works include *The Kiss* and *Expectation* in Österreichische Galerie, Vienna.

**LALIQUE, René,** 1860–1945, French designer of jewelry and glass. Works to be seen in Musée des Arts Decoratifs, Paris, and many other European and US galleries.

**LE CORBUSIER,** 1887–1965, Swiss-born Modernist French architect, town planner, and furniture designer.

**MORRIS, William,** 1834–96, British writer, designer, craftsman, visionary, and socialist. The William Morris Room at the Victoria and Albert Museum, London. Also William Morris Gallery, Walthamstow, London.

**POIRET, Paul,** 1879–1944, French couturier and theater designer, instrumental in the creation of Le Syndicat de Défense de la Grande Couture Francaise in 1914.

**QUANT, Mary,** 1934 – , British Pop Art fashion designer responsible for the mini-skirt, skinny-rib sweaters, and hipster trousers.

**RILEY, Bridget,** 1931–, English painter, leading Op Artist. Many works in The Tate Gallery, London.

**TASSAJARA BREAD BOOK,** Edward Espe Brown, Shambala 1970. Tassajara Zen Mountain Center, Tassajara Springs, Carmel Valley, CA 93924.

**TIFFANY, Louis Comfort,** 1848–1933, American glass designer and interior decorator, inventor of favrile glass. Workshop in Corona, Long Island. Metropolitan Museum of Art, New York.

**TOULOUSE-LAUTREC, Henri de,** 1864–1901, French painter and poster designer.
*Posters of the Belle Époque,* Jack Rennert, New York, 1990. Musée Toulouse-Lautrec, Albi.

**VALENTINO, Rudolph,** 1895–1926, Italian- born American silent-film actor, who starred in *The Four Horsemen of the Apocalypse* (1921), *The Sheik* (1921), and *The Young Rajah* (1922).

**VASARELY, Viktor,** 1908–1997, Hungarian-born French painter and designer. Gallery in Gordes, Vaucluse, Provence, which was once his home. Also in Tate Gallery, London.

## YARN SOURCES

The yarns in *Sculptured Knits* are available at fine yarn stores everywhere.
Or, write to these companies for a local supplier:

**CLASSIC ELITE YARNS**, 300 Jackson Street, Bldg. 5, Lowell MA 01852, USA
S. R. Kertzer, Ltd., 105A Winges Road, Woodbridge, ON L4L 6C2, Canada

**COLINETTE YARNS**, Unique Kolours, 1428 Oak Lane, Downingtown, PA 19335, USA
Diamond Yarn, 9697 St. Laurent, Montreal, PQ H3L 2N1, Canada
Colinette Yarns, Ltd., Units 2–5, Banwy Workshops, Llanfair Caereinion, Powys SY21 0SG, UK

**JAEGER, Knitting Fever, Inc.**, 35 Debevoise Ave, Roosevelt, NY 11574, USA
Diamond Yarn, 9697 St. Laurent, Montreal, PQ H3L 2N1, Canada
Jaeger Handknits, Green Lane Mill, Holmfirth, West Yorks HD7 1RW, UK

**ROWAN, Westminster Fibers**, 5 Northern Blvd., Amherst, NH 03031, USA
Diamond Yarn, 9697 St. Laurent, Montreal, PQ H3L 2N1, Canada
Rowan Yarns, Green Lane Mill, Holmfirth, West Yorks HD71RW, UK

Jean Moss yarns and knit kits for all the designs are available from the author.
Write for a price list:
Jean Moss, 17 Clifton Dale, York, YO30 6LJ, UK
phone: 01904-646-282
web site: www.moss.dircon.co.uk

England in the spring is carpeted with daffodils. They bloom in endless green fields, dotting churchyards, college quads, tidy fenced-in yards, and the banks of moats surrounding the medieval walls of York.

There, almost touched by the shadows of the spires of York Minster (the largest Gothic Cathedral north of the Alps), through Bootham Bar, one of York's medieval gates, down Bootham, past the Churchill Hotel lives Jean Moss.

She used to live down a dirt road, through four gates, and across four fields, in a small, isolated farmhouse. "We had this huge menagerie of animals," Jean says, "thirteen goats, a donkey, three ponies, bees, ducks, geese, chickens, dogs, cats, you name it, we had it.

"My husband was a teacher and worked 90 miles away. I was tied down and soon felt absolutely ground down with always milking the goats, making the bread, caring for the kids, and all the animals every day. There had to be a better way of making a living from home." We're so lucky she chose knitting.

And so, there we were, heading toward Manchester, the location for our first shoot for *Sculptured Knits*. We almost didn't make it. Can you imagine reserving a minivan and instead being handed the keys to an eleven-seat bus; driving it on the 'wrong' side of the narrow, winding lanes of the English countryside—while sitting on the passenger side; using a left-hand stick; all after a trans-Atlantic flight?

Moby, as we nick-named our white monster tour bus, proved more responsive to the steady hands of Alvis Upitis, the Twin Cities international photographer. Alvis had kindly offered to document the shoot with his brand-new Hasselblad panoramic camera, and his breath-taking vistas grace the pages of this book. Alvis, long my mentor and teacher, this time served as my assistant. Imagine Salieri in the presence of Mozart and you get the picture.

Also calling Moby home were XRX Web Editor Amy Detjen, who staked out the middle of the bus with her bags of lace knitting, and Book Editor Elaine Rowley who knitted by the sliding door—to more easily dash out to delis and roadside stores for sustenance.

*(Clockwise from right) The Jean Moss Book of Sculptured Knits comes to life—hair and makeup session; the Yorkshire Moors; York Minster; Philip, Felix, and Amy hard at work; Beningbrough Hall; a well-dressed local surveys the valley; Moby; Millie and Digger making their photo debut; Yorkshire Sculpture Park; playing peek-a-boo by the canal; daffodils; Jean and crew in Manchester; Punch-and-Judy show; York timbered house.*

# COLOPHON

We began shooting in Manchester, where Jean, partner Philip Mercer, and son Felix, who made their modeling debuts, awaited us. England's second city, with its canals and brick-and-iron architecture, became the backdrop for Pop Art. "I want street scenes," Jean said, "a hard, urban landscape. Manchester's Castlefield is a wonderful location."

Soon we were stopping traffic in York. We shot Art Deco outside Harkers and the Churchill Hotel, the home of our *Knitter's* team. Jean said, "It's really nice to have pictures of the place where we live in the book."

Jean wanted the book's title, *Sculptured Knits,* reflected in the photographs, and we shot Into the Millennium at the Yorkshire Sculpture Park.

For Belle Époque, Jean envisaged an English country house setting. The thought of shooting at Castle Howard, of Brideshead Revisited fame, almost made me giddy. But at Beningbrough Hall, near York, a smaller, more intimate country estate, we were able to capture the timeless essence of the English countryside.

Easter Sunday was a day of rest. We visited Castle Howard, and then set off for the Yorkshire Moors, where deep valleys cut by glaciers into the green, rolling hills are bordered by dry-stone walls and overcast skies.

Now this incredibly beautiful landscape borders *Sculptured Knits.*

—Alexis Yiórgos Xenakis
Sioux Falls, SD

## AUTHOR'S ACKNOWLEDGEMENTS

This book is the result of the combined effort of many people.
My love and thanks go to:

Annabelle Hill, Rachel Light, Lesley Grant and Becky Bloxwich
for their efficient help on the shoots.
Kate Lofthouse for her advice and ideas,
and for generously letting me free-range in her wonderful wardrobe.
Sheelagh Killeen, costume designer extraordinaire,
for her helpful suggestions.
Lynda Murphy and Mark Hallett for access to their library,
and their brilliant four-legged models, Digger and Millie.
Gill Barker for assistance with makeup.
Rowan Moss and Rachel Light for the use of their Castlefields flat.
Ann Banks, Beryl Anderson, Denise Andrews, Hilary Andrews, Susan Armitage, Mrs Brigham,
Pat Carwithen, Mrs Cobbledick,
Mary Coe, Joan Crawford, Glennis Garnett, Ann Hart,
Mrs Madgwick, Yvonne Morrison, Jenny Poole, Moira Porter,
Margaret Race, Mrs Tracey, Gwen Veale, Jean Wilson
for making my vision a reality through their knitting.
Staff at Laura Ashley, Monsoon, East, Austin Reed and Stonegate Antiques Centre in York for
their clothes, accessories and patience.
Drusilla White for her marvellous shop, Duttons for Buttons in York.
Alexis for his splendid photography, and Alvis and Amy
for their work on the shoots–
I can never look at a scrim again and not think of Amy!
Elaine, for her enthusiasm, support and belief in the project.
David and Benjamin Xenakis
for sorting me out with the computer software.
The great bunch of people at XRX, especially Bob and Lynda,
for being good people to work with throughout the inevitable
trials and tribulations of book production.
Philip Mercer, for being there.
He has worked tirelessly behind the scenes, doing
everything which was asked and more.
To paraphrase Marx, a model in the morning,
a craftsman in the afternoon, a critic in the evening,
and a diplomat after dinner.

Together I think we got it right.

PUBLISHER'S ACKNOWLEDGEMENTS

The publisher would like to thank the following
for kindly providing clothes, jewelry, and accessories for photography:

Monsoon, 19 Davygate, York YO1 2QR (orange dress p5 and 6, embroidered denim skirt p31, blue beaded dress p38, cream blouse p47, cream linen suit pp56 & 57, white embroidered dress p67, white shirt (just seen) p73, batik skirt p73, skirt p85, crocheted sweater p93, green skirt p109, gray silk trousers p121, linen dress pp124 &125, pink check dress p127)
Accessorize, 11 Davygate, York YO1 2QR (bracelet p27, hat p31, scarf p43 and p44, hair grip p47, aqua feather boa (just seen) p51, beaded bag p79, necklace pp84 & 85, hat and necklace pp88 & 90, hessian bag, bracelet p89, hair grips, necklace, bag p93, earrings p120, fish pendant p123, copper necklace and bracelet pp124 &125)
East, 13 Davygate, York YO1 2QR (blue blouse and velvet skirt, p17, chiffon dress pp43 & 44, scarf p85, trousers and scarf p89, bracelet and earrings p95)
Austin Reed, 26 Davygate, York Y01 8RJ (denim shirt and green chinos p23, tie p47, navy cravat, navy jeans pp59 & 60, black umbrella, silver/lapis cufflinks p59, chambray denim shirt p63, white shirt pp98 & 99, white tee shirt, gray shirt, chinos p100, shirts and chinos pp102 & 103)
Laura Ashley, 7 Davygate, York YO1 2QR (black velvet trousers p13, linen trousers p47, pumps p57, crocheted hat p73, taupe knit dress p131)
Signatures, 49 Fossgate, York YO1 9TF (fountain pen, p46)
Valerie Waggott (compact, p55), Fee Butler (silver marcasite chrysophase earrings, pp56 & 57), Harpers (pocket watch, p147), Dianne Winship (jet necklace, p42), and Trisha Joyce (Clarice Cliff crocus cup and saucer, p51) at Stonegate Antiques Centre, 41 Stonegate, York YO30 1DD
James and Susan Boldry of Northern Vintage & Classic Cars, Westfield House, Stockton on Forest, York YO32 9UU

The publisher and author would also like to thank the following for kindly
allowing their premises to be used for photography:

The National Trust, Beningbrough Hall, York
Harkers Café Bar, St Helens Square, York.
Churchill Hotel, Bootham, York
Barça, Catalan Square, Castlefields, Manchester.
Denise and Kelly Cavanagh for use of their narrowboat Kelagh
Geoffrey Fitch for his narrowboat Yiasas
Yorkshire Sculpture Park, Bretton Hall, West Bretton, Wakefield WF4 4LG.
Particular thanks to the following sculptors whose works appear in the photos: Federico Assler, Michael Dan Archer, Brian Fell, Phillip King, Joanna Mowbray, Joanna Przybyla, Jørgen Haugen Sørensen, Don Rankin, Michael Lyons

Models
Mitchell Yeoman Boldry, Robert Coulson-Smith, Louise Driscoll, Keeley Freeman, Amelia and Charles Hancock, Rebecca Harley, Leanne Hope, Nick Hopper, Douglas Krier, Kristy Lee, Jack Lunam-Cowan, Felix Moss, Philip Mercer, Lynda Murphy and her Jack Russells, Millie and Digger, Claire O'Regan, James and Annabel Reeder, Owen Sheperdson, Harriet, Georgina, and Danielle Sherwood, Rosie Williams, Vicky Wiltshire

Locations

| | |
|---|---|
| Belle Époque | Beningbrough Hall, York |
| Art Deco | The City of York |
| Pop Art | Catalan Square, Castlefields, Manchester |
| Into the Millennium | Yorkshire Sculpture Park, Wakefield |

## XRX WANTS TO KNOW

We can't publish all the knitting books in the world—only the finest.

We are knitting enthusiasts and book lovers. Our mission is simple:
to produce quality books that showcase the beauty of the knitting and give our readers inspiration, confidence, and skill-building instructions.

Publishing begins as a partnership between author and publisher. XRX Books attracts the best authors and designers in the knitting universe because we share their passion for excellence. But books also require a shared vision: photographer Alexis Xenakis and his team bring the garments and fabrics to glorious life. This is where our journey begins.

Cutting-edge computer technology allows us to focus on editing and designing our publications. XRX Books Editor Elaine Rowley can exchange files from South Dakota with our knitting editor in New York or our authors, wherever they happen to live, within a matter of minutes. Our digital consultant, David Xenakis, and his team insure accuracy of color and texture in our images. Graphic Artist Bob Natz, believing that design is not good unless it functions well, produces beautiful, easy-to-read pages.

Now those pages are in your hands and your journey begins.

Tell us what you think:


- by mail
  XRX Books
  PO Box 1525
  Sioux Falls, South Dakota
  57101-1525
- by phone
  605-338-2450
- by fax
  605-338-2994
- by e-mail
  erowley@xrx-inc.com
- on knittinguniverse.com
  You may visit our XRX Books site
  on the World Wide Web:www. knittinguniverse.com
- On our Knitter's OnLine forums:
  Join the conversation and post your reactions and comments in our book discussion bulletin boards:
  www.knittinguniverse.com/script/webx.dll?xchange


We look forward to hearing from you. New journeys are under way.

| | |
|---|---|
| Typography | Headlines: Futura medium outline<br>Subhead copy: Futura medium<br>Body copy: Optima book 9/10.5<br>End pages: Futura book 10/13<br>Technical column: Bulmer MT regular |
| Panorama Photos | Alvis Upitis |

the photography crew at dawn in Manchester, England

| | |
|---|---|
| Prepress Scanning | Howtek ScanMaster 4500 drum scanner<br>XRX, Inc. prepress department:<br>Daren Morgan, Lynda Selle,<br>David Xenakis, John Glenski,<br>Andrew Holman |
| Color Separations | Adobe Photoshop™ 5<br>XRX, Inc. prepress department:<br>Daren Morgan, Lynda Selle,<br>David Xenakis |
| Illustrations | Adobe Illustrator™ 8<br>XRX, Inc. prepress department:<br>Jay Reeve, Lynda Selle, Kellie Meissner |
| Composing | QuarkXPress™ 4<br>XRX, Inc. prepress department:<br>Lynda Selle |
| Color Proofing | Epson Stylus 5000<br>CMYK simulation by Daren Morgan<br>and David Xenakis |
| Film | Graphic Speed, Sioux Falls, SD |

other publications from **XRX** BOOKS

Sally Melville Styles

Magnificent Mittens

Ethnic Socks and Stockings

The Great American Afghan

Socks Socks Socks!

Kids Kids Kids!

The Best of Knitters
Shawl and Scarves

Knitter's Magazine

 BOOKS